Vampire God

Vampire God

The Allure of the Undead in Western Culture

MARY Y. HALLAB

Cover design by Kevin Prufer

Cover image: bd3489-001/Tim Flach/courtesy of Getty Images

Published by
State University of New York Press, Albany

Printed in the United States of America

For information, contact State University of New York Press, Albany, NY
www.sunypress.edu

Production by Eileen Meehan
Marketing by Michael Campochiaro

Library of Congress Cataloging-in-Publication Data

Hallab, Mary Y., 1940–
Vampire god : the allure of the undead in Western culture / Mary Y. Hallab.
p. cm.
Includes bibliographical references and index.
ISBN 978-1-4384-2859-8 (hardcover : alk. paper)
ISBN 978-1-4384-2860-4 (pbk. : alk. paper)
1. Vampires in literature. 2. Vampire films. 3. Vampires on television. 4. Folk literature—History and criticism. 5. Fantasy fiction—History and criticism. I. Title.

PN56.V3H36 2009
809.3'9375—dc22 2009005250

10 9 8 7 6 5 4 3 2 1

Contents

Acknowledgments

This book couldn't have been completed without the valuable help of Kevin Prufer and Martha Collins. Thanks also to Sheryl Craig, Celia Kingsbury, Charles Martin, Don Melichar, and the good people at the University of Central Missouri's Interlibrary Loan office.

This book is dedicated to Kevin Prufer.

Introduction

Why is the vampire so popular? Why has the vampire been so often seemingly dead and so often revived in literature and drama? Tony Thorne in his study *Children of the Night: Of Vampires and Vampirism* (1999) is astonished to realize that, today, a survey of world cultural history reveals "the constant presence of a Vampire or vampire-like monster in our narratives—both grand and humble—and our popular culture." He concludes that the creature survives by its "uncanny" ability to mutate into "whatever our society shuns, but secretly demands" (4). In our society, the vampire, much like its Eastern European and Greek folkloric antecedents, usually manifests itself as a dead human who rises from the grave and behaves as though he is living, more or less. My question is: what hidden void is modern Western society trying to fill with this fantasy? What is it trying to tell itself? What does it "secretly demand"?

In *Reading the Vampire* (1994), discussing Bram Stoker's *Dracula* (1897), Ken Gelder says that "a veritable 'academic industry' has built itself around this novel" (65). He provides an extensive, though not exhaustive, review of differing critical interpretations of vampire literature from relatively early ethnographic studies of vampire folklore—like John Lawson's comparison of Greek folklore and ancient Greek religion (1909)—to his own postmodern approach to recent vampire films. These lead him to conclude, like Thorne, that the vampire will not die for the reason that it is so "highly adaptable" that it can appeal to fundamental urges like desire and fear and respond to cultural and societal issues (141). And, we might add, because of its unique bipolarity—both human and supernatural, alive and dead—the vampire leads us to a larger consideration of the nature of the individual and his search for significance in a vast and terrifying universe.

Both folkloric and literary, ancient and modern vampires are various and difficult to sum up with a single set of characteristics. Folklore vampires are often mixed up in various ways with other supernatural beings, such as nereiads, morae, witches, werewolves, and ghosts, so that observers are forced to make arbitrary choices as to what they will or will not classify as a *vampire*. We face the same problem today: for example, is Keats's "Belle

Dame sans Merci" a vampire or a demon lover? Are the creatures in *Night of the Living Dead* (1968) zombies or vampires? I have chosen to include as vampires only those figures—folkloric, mythical, or literary—who are dead *humans* who are still capable of behaving as though they are alive. I will not consider creatures like various incubi and succubae or lamias or mindless, lurching zombies simply because they can take human form. Nor will I consider living humans who drink blood or avoid sunlight, no matter what they call themselves.

My discussion of folklore vampires will stick to those of Eastern Europe and the Mediterranean because they are the ones that have provided the "germ" for vampire literature and the modern mania for vampires in Western Europe and the Americas. Recognizing, too, that even modern literary vampires may vary in form and function from culture to culture, I will limit my focus primarily to those in England and America, with the aim of discovering what the vampire *does* for those who engage with it. What are vampires good for? What do the critics think? What do I think?

The Function of Vampires

Criticism of Bram Stoker's *Dracula* explains its popularity through many theories going in various directions—psychological, Marxist, social, feminist, queer, Gothic, historical, and archetypal, to mention a few. Dracula is said to represent the tyranny of the patriarchy, the power of the corrupt aristocracy or of the nouveau bourgeois capitalists; he represents decadent foreigners, Slavs or Jews; he is a homosexual, a social outcast, even a mother; and he is dangerously erotic. Summaries of these and other interesting approaches to vampires occur in Ken Gelder's *Reading the Vampire* cited earlier and in Milly Williamson's *The Lure of the Vampire* (2005).[1] Many of these are convincing interpretations justifiable in the context of a complex, ambiguous, and multileveled work. Dracula, at least, fulfills more than one modern need.

A rather unfortunate approach, I believe, derives from those theories that interpret the works in terms of some sort of latent or repressed content that the writer was supposedly unaware of—and that appeals to the reader's unconscious desires or fears. Many of these are psychoanalytic: the unconsciously sexual vampire appeals to our unconscious sexual urges or anxieties. There is indeed a good deal of sexuality in much vampire literature, often quite overt (although not necessarily explicit), beginning as early as Heinrich August Ossenfelder's short poem "The Vampire" (1748) in which the vampire promises to "come creeping" to the young lady's chamber and kiss her "life's blood" away. One does not need psychology to find sexuality in a similar scene in James Malcolm Rymer's[2] *Varney the Vampyre or The Feast of Blood* (1847), or in modern movie vampires like Anne Rice's *Vampire Lestat* (1985). However, although the repressed sexuality explanation may fit many vampires, from Dracula to Buffy's Angel, it hardly explains the popularity of vampire toys, vampire jokes, vampire ballets, operas, breakfast cereals, cartoons, including good vampires, bad vampires, child, adult, male, female, geriatric vampires, vampires from space, from next door, dog and bunny vampires, psychological and psychic vampires, ugly, beautiful, happy, sad vampires, vampire punks, detectives, cab drivers, travel agents, artists and art collectors, even clergymen and obstreperous adolescents. Not *all* vampires are sexy.

But all vampires are living dead—and therefore supernatural and mythical. Because vampires survive across the impassable boundary, even the puniest of them have an aura of mystery and transcendence that, coming from the land of the dead, takes us beyond the mundane. When vampires *are* sexy, they are so because they are powerful, dangerous, and forbidden, and not the reverse, although their erotic attractiveness may be a lure into danger. True, in early stories like the anonymous "The Mysterious Stranger" (1860), the message seems to be to young ladies: Beware of infatuation with attractive strangers. This is the same moral we find in many modern serial killer movies. But, as with the serial killer, the danger itself is not forbidden or quirky sex, but death. If the killer enticed children with shiny toys, we would not say that the story was about shiny toys. Although there may be (intentional or not) a comment on the dangers of sexuality, as in ballads of the demon lover, the erotic vampire seducer may say more about the attractiveness of danger and death than about sex.

Possibly, vampires like Dracula allowed nineteenth-century writers and readers to explore (supposedly) forbidden topics while pretending to be frightened, but modern audiences certainly have no such need. Even on television commercials, we see tampons waved about and enthusiastic touting of products to cure male impotency. We see talk shows in which the guests tell about their lives as prostitutes, their incestuous abuse as children, and their strange plastic surgeries. We have nearly inescapable internet porn. What do we need vampires for? Yet they survive and even flourish, suggesting that they must offer something besides sex or even danger that is uniquely their own.

To take another example, even though Stoker's Dracula may be a foreigner in England, not all literary vampires incite a fear of foreigners or other outsiders.[3] Not all vampires *are* foreigners. John Polidori's Lord Ruthven in his story "The Vampyre" (1819) is only a Scotsman; the English Varney the Vampyre and the Styrian Carmilla are not foreign within the context of their stories. For exotic nefariousness or even seductiveness, poor Varney, for example, seems so inadequate that one must look elsewhere to find the source of his popularity in the nineteenth century. This popularity must lie in the fact that he is a living dead. For from folklore to modern films, if we take away the vampire's essential quality, its *undeadness*, the character becomes considerably less compelling. Imagine Dracula, for example, as nothing more than a seductive and insidious foreigner. On the other hand, imagine Dracula as entirely supernatural, a mere ghost with no bodily presence. In short, the fascination of the vampire lies in his being both human and supernatural. When the possibility for revival seems most hopeless (when it has been decapitated, ashed, drowned, and eaten by worms), it can still pop up again, as much a nuisance as ever, almost as good as new, and significantly, with its individual identity intact.

True, one appeal of certain vampires lies in their breaking of various cultural taboos and their warnings about assorted dangers to the community. But we can and do have sensuality, brutality, arrogance, selfishness, intolerance, insidious evil, and even aristocratic bad manners in many Gothic villains like Ann Radcliffe's Montoni in *The Mysteries of Udolpho* (1794) or Hannibal Lector in the film *Silence of the Lambs* (1991), who seem very much like vampires but lack the essential element that distinguishes the vampire—that of being living dead. To some critics, vampire literature offers a means to understand the world we live in and to formulate our own identities or sense of identity within this world. In *Terrors of Uncertainty: The Cultural Contexts of Horror Fiction* (1989), Joseph Grixti argues that, to some degree, horror fiction defines reality for us by providing models and modes of thinking that form a "component of our culturally determined intersubjectivity" (7). The vampire, for example, embodies (so to speak) our response to "the horrors of death and corruption as well as those of earthbound immortality" (14).

However, Grixti regards horror literature negatively, as an inadequate response to the fear and uncertainty in the modern world, which is assuaged by a form of magical, as opposed to realistic, thinking. He generally regards it as a harmful "game" we are enticed into by commercialized horror literature (148) that exacerbates our fears and anxieties by mythologizing them in the form of various superstitions and then "proffering magical solutions and soothing (if ostrich-like) cures for the horrifying and disturbing states which they invite us to consider" (176). That is, rather than regarding these fears as innate to humankind and merely expressed in fiction (from *Gilgamesh* to the present), he regards them as *created* by a greedy corporate hegemony for the purpose, apparently, of driving us into the magical safety zone of escapist fantasy and superstition also for sale by that hegemony (182–83).

His solution would be for us to reassert our sense of rational control. But death (real and inevitable death—so unfair) seems to be the very area of experience that stymies rational thought. Grixti's approach contains two mistakes, in my thinking, which I hope to avoid. First, like a number of other critics, he assumes that whatever falls under the general rubric of "horror literature" (which is not so easy to define) is inevitably horrible and fearful to the reader or audience rather than, like most vampire literature, eerily and interestingly uncanny (or even funny). Second, he also apparently believes that the average reader has little self-awareness or sense of reality and is very easily led to respond to fantasies like the vampire with terror and anxiety rather than as a stimulus to speculation and understanding.

In contrast to Grixti, I prefer to take the approach that most people—peasants and scholars—pretty much know what they think and believe. This position is argued by the sociologist Kathy Charmaz, in an essay in the third edition of *Death and Identity* (1994). She regards human beings "as reflective, creative, and active" (30), who have, Charmaz says, "selves and minds" (32). Through conscious interactions, they construct a (more or less) stable reality shared by a social community. Changes in this constructed world occur as a result of individual choices and influences, generally based on a "rational and pragmatic bias," according to which "meaning is related to *utility* and to the *practical* aspects of experience" (34–35). A particular element of belief—about the meaning of death, for example—persists through cultural changes and diversions because it fulfills a significant function at least for some people (29). However, because individuals are free to make choices, we cannot expect everyone to think the same way. These choices will be reflected, for example, in the images by which they decide to represent death, as, say, an angel song, a violent struggle, or a vampire.

Writers like Nina Auerbach, Carol Senf, and Gregory A. Waller are concerned with how literary vampires, even Dracula, modify to reflect changing environmental circumstances and cultural assumptions, from the nineteenth century to the present. The vampire's most human quality—its infinite adaptability to people, place, and time—is a major reason for its persistence. This, along with its very un-human and ambiguous position between the flesh and the spirit, its mysterious comings and goings, and its variable forms and faces, allows it to be continually revived in different guises in our differing worlds. But as diverse as they may be, from the bloated peasant of folklore to the opera-caped Dracula to the bratty *Lost Boys* (1987), vampires address issues and attitudes about death and immortality that are meaningful in all times and places. However much the contexts and ideologies of death may have been modified over the years, the fact of death remains the same, inevitable, irrevocable, and final.

Death, these days, however, is not often clearly constructed or even discussed. We do not see dying people interviewed on Oprah or cheered up by Dr. Phil. We do not see dying old people at all if we can help it. We do not see death explained. Advertisements for "funeral parlors" or "homes" come discreetly in the mail; the word *die* is replaced by the phrase "when your time comes." For many today, especially the young, the only place even to find out about death is in the movies and on television, where there is plenty of it, mostly of the violent and thus preventable kind—car crashes or serial killers, for example. Apparently, we do not *have* to die. Death always has causes that can be treated and cured if we just know how. Thus Elisabeth Kübler-Ross shocked America with her book *On Death and Dying* (1969, 1997) based on her conviction that the denial of death, the refusal to acknowledge its inevitability and even its actual occurrence in family and friends, is a commonplace of modern living.[4]

A different kind of denial was manifested in John Edwards's weekly series *Crossing Over* (1999–2004) in which he supposedly communicated (in a very general way) with deceased relatives of audience members. In HBO television series like *Six Feet Under* (2001–2005), the dead appear as ghosts, asserting their continued existence somewhere and their continuing influence on the living as though they were not dead at all. Obviously, many people are fascinated with death, and almost everyone fears it, although most of us do not care to acknowledge it just yet. In the popular media, too, death is treated (when it is treated at all) either as a vague and mysterious existence in another world or as a horrifying and unfortunate mistake—one which, however, with healthy living, the right exercise, the right neighborhoods, or the right faith (sincerely held) might be avoided. We seldom admit that deaths, even among the very old, are unavoidable; someone must be to blame.

The vampire provides a fictitious and mythical focus for universal concerns about death and its reasons—as well as for a good deal of wishful thinking. In the first place, the vampire is often a bringer of death, even a personification of death itself—a mortal danger to the protagonists. And like the popular literature of natural catastrophes or serial killings, vampire stories and films offer means and methods by which this danger can be averted. More important, the vampire overcomes death and, in doing so, promises eternal life on a somewhat earthier and more comprehensible level than most religious faiths. It posits, at least, the *renewal* of life, very much like the archetypal dying god (very likely its remote ancestor). Possibly, it fulfills for some of its enthusiasts, on some level of consciousness, the role of this mythical figure, the vegetation deity, which dies and is reborn each year. Or it is itself a kind of goddess or god of the dead, or Death itself. As such, it is also the source of fecundity and new life, and its sexuality is that of the force that makes the dead nature bloom. Stoker's *Dracula* and many others like it can be regarded as retellings of the Hades and Persephone story or other pagan myths of underworld gods. Whatever it is, the vampire has mythical significance as an in-between creature of this and the "other" world, hinting to us that such a world might exist, for the very reason that the vampire refuses to go there. The vampire is popular because it will not die, and, however monstrous it may seem, unlike other monsters, it remains a human—who, by virtue of its immortality, becomes a god.

The primary effect of vampire literature is not to threaten readers with death, but to provide a symbolic and metaphorical means to apprehend, contemplate, and deal with death within the larger context of life. Dealing with death and the dead, moreover, involves thinking about the past. The literary vampire often comes out of an imaginary past more or less Gothic in nature, peopled with impressive mythical and supernatural figures, impossibly virtuous maidens, dauntless heroes, satanic villains, and fantastic monsters that we are familiar with from traditional stories, fairy tales, and Arthurian legends and that remain alive in the modern imagination. Because of this association and because popular Gothic literature found early expression in the Graveyard School of poetry, Gothic critics seem more likely than others to find in vampires various messages about death.

The Western vampire also has a tradition of its own that begins with folklore vampires of Greece and the Slavic countries. And in spite of seemingly vast differences (bloated peasant versus suave aristocrat), there is a surprising consistency in vampire behavior and function from these beginnings to the present. Folklore vampires provide important clues to understanding the meaning of vampires in modern popular literature. We are not, after all, so very far advanced from our own village origins of a few hundred years ago that we no longer need the comfort and solutions to life's mysteries that folklore and mythology provide. Nor, as we have noted, are our lives destitute of folklore figures, who survive and multiply in the myriads of fairies, ghosts, alien invaders, mad scientists, aerobatic superheroes, and, recently, angelic visitants, and other denizens of the New Age that fill the media. The modern literary vampire—although superficially advanced from his folklore peasant origins—arose, one might say, and flourished along with many other rather unorthodox supernatural beings, that, if not the objects of firm belief, at least allow the mind to dwell on possibilities beyond those offered by conventional religion or rational empiricism.

Sources

Unfortunately, before the twentieth century, reliable accounts of vampire appearances from people who claim to have actually seen them or experienced their effects are very scarce. Most folk accounts are either old but well-crafted tales or second- or third-generation retellings of village traditions. This is the case with the outburst of vampire activity in Eastern Europe in the eighteenth century that first aroused literary and scholarly—and theological—interest. Particularly, a lengthy report on this phenomenon by Augustine Calmet (1746)—a biblical scholar appointed to investigate its legitimacy—quickly became a best seller in Western European countries, primarily France, Germany, and England. This, along with other reports like that by Giuseppe Davanzati (1744), aroused interest in vampire folklore that—combined with appropriate mythical and literary figures, like Faust, Milton's Satan, and the Byronic Hero—eventually gave birth to the modern literary vampire, which now has a mythology of its own. Calmet's survey became a source for Romantic writers like Southey, Byron, and Stoker, and although many of his accounts are highly questionable, they provide considerable information about folk beliefs.

In addition, some Slavic and Greek villagers living until recently in isolated areas have preserved vampire folklore, which has thus been available for study in its own environment by modern folklorists and anthropologists aiming at some degree of objectivity. It is on their accounts that I have chosen to rely for the organizing principle and basis of my discussion, especially those who have gleaned their information from direct personal contact with the people they have studied. I have tried to avoid sources about folklore vampires that seem to be aimed primarily at creating sensational effects by tossing together all the "lore" they can come across, frequently citing questionable sources or none at all. This means I will be cautious in using *information* from the famous vampire expert Montague Summers, although I cannot resist commenting on his motives and influence.

Instead, in addition to Calmet, I have chosen to rely primarily on scholars like Jan Perkowski or Richard and Eva Blum, who show familiarity with the people and cultures that produced the vampire folklore we know, and who are objective enough to draw attention themselves to possible biases in their studies. For example, in *The Dangerous Hour: The Lore of Crisis and Mystery in Rural Greece* (1970), Blum and Blum recount the responses by Greek peasants and shepherds to a systematic survey designed to call up unusual or uncanny stories related to illness and death. Thus the responses may suggest a stronger role for these beliefs than actually exists (3–4). Gail Kligman's study *The Wedding of the Dead: Ritual, Poetics, and Popular Culture in Transylvania* (1988) derives from her firsthand observations while living among the people of the isolated area of Maramures in northern Transylvania. Her analysis of rituals and laments from weddings and funerals may be colored by her own feminist dismay at the position of women in this male-dominated culture. But she has clearly endeavored to report their beliefs and practices accurately and sympathetically.

Persistence and Belief

Accuracy is important because I began my study trying to figure out what the belief in vampires *meant* for these villagers. What good did vampires do? The folkloric accounts support my conviction that human nature, human motives, and needs remain very much the same across time and across cultures. This is not to dispute that vampires or other folk or literary figures modify with the times. Twenty-first-century vampires are often quite different from their Victorian precursors—but also strikingly similar—and just as undead. My discussion focuses on the similarities, moving freely among vampires of various kinds, times, and places. I include folklore accounts of ordinary, relatively unsophisticated people in those communities where vampires, along with other supernatural beings, make up part of the general worldview, particularly in regard to ideas about death and immortality. I do not regard these views as "primitive" or wrong or superstitious or magical simply because they do not concur with our own. (And, after all, what could be more superstitious or magical than wearing a lucky hat or expecting Jesus to help us win the lottery?)

In any case, because there are always skeptics in any culture, I will not be concerned with whether or not all individuals actually *believe* in every element of this worldview. Blum and Blum, studying Greek folkloric beliefs related to death, found extremes of belief and unbelief even within one family. It will be enough that, in general, they conform to community values and practice. Vampires also appear, even in rural cultures, as characters in suspiciously literate and familiar fictions (oral or written) that are obviously not intended to be taken as true, although they may have some effect on the social reality as expressions of a popular mythology.[5] Van Helsing's famous conclusion to Deane and Balderston's play *Dracula* (1927)—"remember that after all *there are such things*" (150)—may express the secret wish of many modern storytellers that their creations become real in the minds of their audience.[6]

And a few, like John Polidori and Bram Stoker, have had some success. Through them and other writers, vampires belong to a modern popular folklore that few will admit to believing but that has become part of a way of thinking about and ordering our vision of the world around us. Our modern vampires, too, fall into a rather loose popular mythology that offers meaning in those areas of life that are inadequately explained by more organized, institutionalized systems of science, psychology, or religion. For example, we may act as though black cats or broken mirrors can bring bad luck, or use the expression "an angel is passing over" to explain a pause in conversation, regardless of whether we actually believe this or not. This popular folklore comes to us not only through oral traditions (knocking on wood, crossing our fingers, ghosts, the tooth fairy), but also in written and literary sources like children's stories and Disney films that include such figures as Santa Claus and Cinderella, Peter Pan, Superman, ET, Darth Vader, the Big Bad Wolf, and now Harry Potter. Even the highly educated and sophisticated among us share in this vast, various, and complex folklore that helps to form and determine contemporary attitudes, ideals, and behavior—sometimes, often covertly, in regard to death.

According to most reliable accounts, the original vampire folklore occurs almost entirely in connection with rituals and beliefs about death and the soul. These concerns are no less vital today than in the past. Science, for all its accomplishments and its success in prolonging the *average* life expectancy, has not extended the *possible* life span beyond what it has always been. Moreover, moderns share with the folk a healthy skepticism about the explanations and solutions offered by institutionalized religion concerning death—if not open skepticism, then a certain inner fear or reluctance to embrace the peace or paradise promised as the rewards of dying. Yet open speculation about death has often been taboo either because it might offend a powerful public opinion or religious institution or because it is too appalling to contemplate.

To sum up: Setting out to focus on the undeadness of the vampire, I thought it might be fruitful to start my research with a look at the folklore studies to find out, if I could, what meaning the vampire had for the folk. How did they come up with this idea anyway, and what good did it do them? In taking this approach, I was led to a number of assumptions: (1) that (almost) all human beings share the same needs and fears and hopes, modified, of course, by their particular culture and circumstances; (2) that these are revealed in their various cultural productions; (3) that all people, even we educated and sophisticated moderns (or postmoderns, for that matter) have a folklore, even though we might be incognizant or incredulous of it, which also fulfills some function; (4) that a particular folklore, such as vampire folklore, persists because it satisfies some need or answers some question for those who repeat it and who may even believe it. Thus, (5) the vampire as living dead belongs to and has meaning in the culture in which it appears, whether this is a Slavic village or the cities of modern America; and (6) this meaning lies in the one characteristic that persists through all its various manifestations—that it is a human that does not die.

From Them to Us

Like us, the folk whose lore produced the vampire were not necessarily concerned to develop a coherent system. Their stories and examples are full of unaccountable inconsistencies and contradictions. Nor, apparently, did they specify or codify the relationships between vampires and other supernatural creatures. Moreover, vampire and similar folklore generally remains distinct from the accepted theology predominant in the area, whether Christian or Moslem, Roman Catholic, Orthodox, or Protestant. The folk know what they can tell the authorities and what they cannot—just as we do. They feel themselves under no obligation to regularize their beliefs into a consistent theology or even to write them all down in one place. Like those of the ancient Greeks, their beliefs may be diverse, contradictory, and chaotic—and still perfectly satisfactory to them. Thus, in discussing folk ritual and belief, I use the term *system* very loosely, to attempt to impose, from the outside, a kind of unity on a rather disorderly hodgepodge. In regard to modern folklore, we are no more consistent or rational than the Slavic peasant, no matter what we may tell ourselves. We all carry with us a whole array of literary and mythical figures that are part of our lives—that we refer to in everyday speech, tell stories about, try to emulate (the Western hero, for example), produce countless images of, and even include in our own rituals (Santa Claus, the Easter Bunny).

Folklore scholars like Blum and Blum argue that we should not study folklore only as an artifact of a lost culture that retains echoes and parallels in the present but should apply it to understanding our own ways of dealing with anxiety, misfortune, illness, and death. For "We too have our priests and healers, our magic and rituals, our omens and prophets, and our religions with their immortals and extraordinary dead" (376). But unlike the Greek peasant, we are ashamed of our superstitions or demonologies, or belief in magic. We must conceal our uncertainties and fears in order to maintain the pretense of rationality. Repressed, they become aberrant and perverse even leading to "fellowships of the irrational" like the many cults that have flourished in the twentieth century (377).

Although "our own irrationality is denied elevation to a dramatic folklore since few dare speak it and few dare listen," it still exists, Blum and Blum argue, "inherent within our psychological structure, and clearly emergent in response to life stress" (377). After all, we cannot always control the world we live in or even our own lives. Our fears of sudden and catastrophic failure, sickness, suffering, disaster, and death and our inability even to comprehend their meaning cannot be alleviated by some sort of rational stoicism or insistence that this is "the best of all possible worlds." Thus, many of "our cultural offerings" cater to these irrational but realistic fears and desires, even though in disguise or by purporting to counteract them (377–78). The modern literary vampire is one of those cultural offerings whose effect is pervasive and far-reaching through the network of imaginative and mythical experiences offered by the modern media.

What do vampires do in Greek folk culture? Vampires are people, citizens of a community, who, usually as the result of some failure in the complicated rituals surrounding burial and death, did not die but became living dead. These rituals are designed to protect and encourage the deceased while he is making the dangerous transition from the world of the living to the world of the dead. According to Loring M. Danforth (1982), the vampires help to bridge the chasm between life and death "by asserting that death is an integral part of life," for the funeral rituals emphasize "the continuity and meaning of life itself" (6). To Danforth, the vampire is one element of a symbolic system that endeavors to reconcile the desire to deny death through belief in a transcendent other world and the "common-sense perspective" that forces us to accept it (32). The commonplace idea that the dead hear and sometimes communicate with us is simply an elaboration of this same need to find continuity between the worlds of the living and the dead.

Gail Kligman, too, in her discussion of Romanian death weddings, reminds us that, even today, death remains "the consummate vampire who thrives on the bodies and blood of humans" (247). In Romanian beliefs and rituals surrounding death and burial, the human, the material, and the spiritual worlds are interrelated in "a culturally comprehensible framework" that gives them meaning and a sense of control (247–48). The weddings of the dead, she says, bring together themes of desire and death that moderns must find other ways to express. One way is through art, as in the popular figure of Dracula—both sexy and dead. To Kligman, to consider the meaning of desire (sex) and death is actually to consider the meaning of life—a meaning that modern science does not provide for us (247). However silly it may sometimes seem, the folklore vampire is not merely an expression of fear or ignorance or lack of scientific knowledge. Neither is the modern popularity of the vampire simply an egocentric masturbatory fantasy of power and rape or cultural superiority or even just irrational wishful thinking. The vampire implies an effort to explain and deal with the quandaries of life and death, however ineffective it may sometimes seem.

In this study I propose to apply these insights about folklore vampires, so far as makes sense, to the vampire in the modern world to show how and why the vampire has become part of a kind of general, culturally approved and accepted mythology. My sources cover a rather broad range: (1) folklore and folklorists such as those cited earlier; (2) vampire literary works including novels, stories, films, and television series; (3) literary critics who have been concerned with similar issues; and (4) some social and historical studies that provide relevant background and insights into the culture that has produced and responded to the vampire figure.

Organization

Folklorists have attributed to the vampire an assortment of *functions* related to beliefs and practices about death. These I found could be grouped into four general areas that provide the overall outline of my discussion. I should make it clear that these are not separate kinds of vampires but functions that vampires—folk, literary, past, and present—fulfill or at least seem to try to fulfill. Few vampires can be pigeonholed under one label or another. I am concerned with general uses and meanings attributed to vampires by their context or their authors. In some cases, one vampire—like the ubiquitous Dracula, for example—might illustrate all four of these meanings or functions. And we will find him discussed in every section of the book along with others. In other cases, a vampire might illustrate one approach more thoroughly than others and will be discussed only once in relation to, say, its social function—that is, its social function in relation to death and immortality, and not, say, to child rearing or good manners.

Perhaps I should call these, not functions, but promises, illustrations, or solutions related to issues of death and immortality—or manifestations of various approaches we might take or meanings that we might attribute to death. It is possible to do so because of the vampire's double nature, both alive and dead. References to or warnings against vampires or other revenants no longer appear in the public contexts of funeral rituals or shared formulas of belief. But they persist nevertheless as expressions of our underlying anxieties and fears—but also hopes—about death and eternal life. In surveying vampire literature, I found that these areas of experience could fall into four categories: scientific, social, psychological, and religious.

(1) Scientific: The folklore vampire often provides a practical understanding of aspects of life that simply do not seem to have any reasonable explanation—that is, illness and death—and provides practical means of dealing with them. As a scientific phenomenon, vampires no longer fill an explanatory function in relation to death. This is provided by science—at least in a limited way: this death was caused by this virus. Yet the vampire's ability to overcome the virus or bullet or whatever, to prolong life—or life expectancy—has had great appeal for modern readers and writers. Vampires have inspired some scientific speculation for a kind of science fiction "what if" scenario of both wishful thinking and serious thought.

(2) Social: Even in the modern world, death has social and community ramifications that vampire lore addresses. In both folklore and in modern literature, the vampire's existence reinforces a sense of community identity and of historical continuity with the past. The folklore vampire is usually an undead *ancestor* or *relative* who insists on maintaining relationships, usually

unwanted, with the living. In modern literature, the vampire embodies the not-so-dead past, insisting on the interconnectedness, for better or worse, of our origins and our present selves. As a living representative of history, the vampire tells us that we are not alone, that our past is not gone, our dead have not disappeared.

(3) Psychological: Vampires and the beliefs surrounding them provide a means of exploring and possibly dealing with personal loss and acceptance of death. In regard to the death of the self and others, vampire-related folklore consoles and comforts the individual by directing personal attitudes and providing a source of relief from personal guilt and sorrow that often accompany the loss of a loved one. In doing so, vampires assert the persistence of the individual and the unique self into the afterlife. The vampire's rebellious assertion of personal identity—of Self—against society, nature, and God was one reason for its appeal to the Romantics (as they saw it) who handed it on to us.

(4) Religious: Perhaps most important, the vampire, by its supernatural origins and godlike powers and its frequent identification with Satan (and sometimes God), makes a religious statement. It raises questions about the meaning of the soul and the existence of an afterlife; about the nature and existence of a god and the relation of this god to the created world; and about the nature of evil and the power of a devil or devils. It carries about with it its own mysterious and divine aura that derives from its origins in gods of nature and the underworld. The last three chapters of the book explore the religious and mythical functions of vampires that explain their popularity, particularly in regard to the persistence of dualistic thinking, the promotion of Christian beliefs, and more important, the urgent human desire for immortality and transcendence. This is the longest discussion, including the final three chapters (chapters 4, 5, and 6).

The fourth chapter reviews the implications of the early literary vampires from the Romantics to Bram Stoker and Montague Summers in regard to their pagan origins and to established Christian and popular theologies. The fifth chapter focuses on "Christian vampires" (or "Vampires for Christ," as I call them) in the twentieth century, whose stories promote a primarily dualistic version of Christianity. In the rage for order, for clear divisions and boundaries, this viewpoint entails a rather rigid division of the cosmos—and human nature—into spirit and body, dark and light, good and bad, angel or devil. Yet, whichever side they are on, these vampires speak for the immortality of the soul and the existence of an afterlife in more or less Christian terms.

And finally, the sixth chapter is concerned with the desire of much vampire literature to convey a sense of a transcendent reality, of religious awe and wonder, of sacredness—a sense of the numinous, as it has come to be called—that accompanies the appearance of this supernatural figure out of the ancient past. For the vampire still trails behind him the aura of the ancient god of the dead that was very likely his predecessor. He is Death itself, Ruler of the Underworld, but also, like almost all gods of the underworld, a fertility deity, a giver of Life. He is beautiful, powerful, active. If nothing else, he brings a kind of glory (or at least attention) to death that rescues it from the anonymity and disgrace into which it has fallen in the modern world. In short, I am primarily concerned, in chapters 1 through 3, with what *our* vampires (as Nina Auerbach calls them) have to tell us about the practical science, sociology, and psychology of death—and finally, in the last three chapters, with what they imply about the meaning of death in the universal order.

1

Vampires and Science

Folklorists believe that early folklore often constitutes a kind of scientific attempt to explain natural occurrences. Hungarian folklorist Tekla Dömötör (1981), for example, argues that, for rural people, "taking a keen interest in the supernatural was in reality also a means of conducting scientific inquiry" so that "thinking in terms of myths with their own symbolic systems supplied for them what the more privileged were able to imbibe from an advanced education" (14–15). Such belief systems, she argues, remained uncodified and disorganized because, otherwise, they may have seemed to conflict with the "official code" and have been suppressed as heresy (11).

Paul Barber, in *Vampires, Burial, and Death* (1988), asks: "Lacking a proper grounding in physiology, pathology, and immunology, how are people to account for disease and death?" A natural inclination is "to blame death on the dead" (3)—usually previously buried family or community members. In American history, we have a good example in the now famous vampires of Rhode Island toward the end of the nineteenth century when tuberculosis was killing people in large numbers. Desperate to stop epidemics within their families, some few people had recourse to disinterring recently deceased family members who they thought might be causing the deaths. In *Food for the Dead: On the Trail of New England's Vampires* (2001), Michael Bell tells the story of George Brown, whose son Edwin was dying of tuberculosis, which had already killed his mother Mercy Brown and two sisters. In each case, George Brown tried every known remedy, but Edwin became increasingly worse. On the basis of folk remedies, neighbors and friends proposed digging up the bodies to discover if the hearts and livers still had blood in them; if so, then this was the cause of the epidemic. The cure and preventative would be to remove the hearts and livers, burn them, and, as a further precaution, to eat the ashes (a not entirely unusual method to prevent the recurrence of vampirism). To prevent the death of his only son as well as to relieve the fears of the community, Brown carried out this procedure. The heart of one of the daughters, found to contain blood, was destroyed, and the community was hopeful that this would stop the spread of the disease (even though Edwin died anyway) (18–38).

In *The Darkling: A Treatise on Slavic Vampirism* (1989), folklorist Jan Perkowski reminds us that "contemporary man is by no means immune to such 'superstitions,'" pointing to the vast number of "urban legends" that are regarded as true by those who hear them, including a number of supposed vampire killings (146–47). He posits that the ultimate source is a deep psychological need to understand and to find hope in the midst of calamity that equilibrium will ultimately be restored (152). However comforting it may be, Christianity does not even attempt to identify, explain, or treat illness and death except by reference to the will of God and the efficacy of prayer. Vampires are part of a practical alternative, a folk science of death and the dead, which, like modern science, operates independently of accepted religious dogma and is often in conflict with it.

Even more important, for those who accept vampires as objectively real, the vampire offers irrefutable scientific proof that the dead are still in some way alive. For if reliable testimony affirms that the dead can sometimes get up and walk, then they must somehow retain consciousness. If vampires refuse to go where they are supposed to go, they assure believers that there is a place to go. The existence of vampires provides material verification of a belief that otherwise, then and now, must rest entirely on faith. Even today, visible ghostly appearances, poltergeists, and even vampires purport to prove with physical evidence that a spirit world exists and the dead are in it.

Vampires Come to Western Europe

In the eighteenth century, reports of a number of vampire "killings" in Eastern Europe appeared in the Western press. These consisted of cases in which families or communities, suffering from an unusual number of inexplicable deaths or sometimes even bad crops or thefts attributed their misfortunes to recently deceased community members who had returned as living dead. In such cases, respected members of the community, often accompanied by a priest, would make up a little task force to destroy the vampires and stop these depredations. Yes, they *were* killing dead people—by staking, decapitation, burning, dismembering, or drowning. And, in general, public opinion and, more significantly, church doctrine regarded this as a shameful desecration of the dead. But until this rash of vampire events, officials in Hungary, for example, often turned a blind eye. After all, *they* did not have any explanation for the epidemic or any cure. And most of these events involved uneducated peasants in rural villages and did not always come to the attention of government or church authorities. In the Enlightened West, among the educated who were reading about them in the press, creatures like vampires were regarded, of course, as the ignorant superstitions of isolated and barbarous peasants.

Well, not entirely. The accounts became numerous enough to motivate the Catholic Church to send two investigators. Archbishop Giuseppe Davanzati, reporting on his research in his *Dissertazione sopra I Vampiri* published in 1744, dismissed the subject as the superstition of the poor and illiterate. The outlandish *belief* in vampires was ascribed in rational terms to the effects of ignorance and panic. The other investigator, a French bishop Dom Augustine Calmet, also examined reports of vampire scares in Hungary. Both of these men were charged with discovering if there was any truth to the stories about living dead. For the existence of human beings who could raise themselves from the grave was clearly a serious matter for the church. Calmet's report, published in 1746, was based on thorough, painstaking, objective research through all accounts of revenants from the grave, including the acceptable reappearances of saints, for example, for holy purposes. In every case, he considered naturalistic explanations first, for example, (barring miracles performed by God) that vampires are apparitions caused by "prejudiced fancy" and "melancholy" (2:54–55) or are the result of premature burial (2:164–74).

Christopher Frayling (1991) reminds us that the early sources of vampire information were not Gothic horror stories, but accounts like those of Calmet and commentaries on them, that represented efforts by thinkers in the Age of Enlightenment to understand the nature of these supposed vampire predations in Eastern Europe (20). An example of such accounts is the case of Arnold Paul, published in *The London Journal* in March 1732 that had supposedly occurred about five years earlier. According to Calmet's account:

> [T]he people known by the name of Heyducqs believe that certain dead persons, whom they call vampires, suck all the blood from the living, so that these become visibly attenuated, whilst the corpses, like leeches, fill themselves with blood in such abundance that it is seen to come from them by the conduits, and even oozing through the pores. (2:37)

The report continues that "a certain Heyducq, inhabitant of Madreiga, named Arnald Paul" was crushed to death under a wagon. Thirty days later "four persons died suddenly" as if killed by vampires (2:37). The people recalled that Paul had said that, when in the military service in the East, he had been bitten by a Turkish vampire, but he had cured himself by "eating earth from the grave of the vampire" (2:38). Nevertheless, he became a vampire after his own death, which was discovered when he was disinterred and "they found on his corpse all the indications of an arch-vampire." That is, his body was red and bloated, his hair and nails had grown, and his veins were "full of blood":

> The Hadnagi, or bailli of the village, in whose presence the exhumation took place, and who was skilled in vampirism, had, according to custom, a very sharp stake driven into the heart of the defunct Arnald Paul and which pierced his body through and through, which made him, as they say, utter a fearful shriek as if he had been alive: that done, they cut off his head and burnt the whole body. (2:38)

Unfortunately, Paul had also bitten an ox that, five years later, was eaten from by another young man who became a vampire himself and managed to do away with seventeen people, all of whom were dug up and executed:

> All the information and executions we have just mentioned were made juridically, in proper form, and attested by several officers who were garrisoned in the country, by the chief surgeons of the regiments, and by the principal inhabitants of the place. (2:39)

This report was sent to an Imperial Council of War at Vienna, signed by the respectable villagers, the chief army officer, and several army surgeons (2:40).

In another example from Calmet, a man who had been dead over thirty years came back and "sucked the blood" from his brother, a son, and a servant, killing them. At the orders of the "Count de Cabreras," his body was disinterred and a large nail driven into his head. Later, the Count of Cabreras had another man burnt who had been buried for more than sixteen years, but had returned to suck the blood of two of his sons. Calmet's report tells us: "The person who related these particulars to us had heard them from the Count de Cabreras at Fribourg in Brigau, in 1730" (2:34)—suggesting the respectability of the witnesses and sources that caused Calmet to consider them seriously.

Such sensational publications created a variety of responses, most of which involved the effort to find reasonable scientific explanations. Frayling lists about twelve of these, ranging from premature burial to effects of plague to mass hysteria (25–26), none of which, however, assume the objective reality of the vampire. Calmet had recognized a number of these possibilities and favored them over the supernatural explanation.[1] But the force of the scientific viewpoint in Western Europe is evidenced by the fact that he was ultimately criticized for appearing to leave the subject open (Frayling 28–29) or, indeed, for even bothering about such superstitious nonsense.

Yet according to Frayling, the early vampire genre was based on this "very limited frame of reference" of the controversy surrounding Calmet's report (37). Very likely we would never have had Dracula or the vampire

Lestat without it. Paradoxically, for all its insistence on empirical evidence, science (natural philosophy—as it was called) provided encouragement for serious investigations into all sorts of superstitious folderol and strange phenomena. (This is still going on and comparable perhaps to searches for Bigfoot or the Holy Grail.) Increased travel and exploration brought new mysteries and "monsters" every day, even including the actual vampire bat in South America. Frayling cites an article of October 1784 in the *Courier de l'Europe*, that described a creature recently found in Chile, as "part-man, part-bat, part-lion" and insisted that this proved the real existence of supposedly legendary creatures like vampires and harpies (35).

Indeed, early fascination with vampires in Western Europe devolves in part from the ferment of scientific and pseudo-scientific interests that characterized the seventeenth and eighteenth centuries. Robert Darnton (1968), writing about the craze for mesmerism in eighteenth-century France, points out that science itself, which had called traditional Christianity into doubt and relegated God to the role of a clockmaker, had also discovered a new world of "unknowns," of powerful invisible forces like magnetism and gravity or tiny invisible beings that could cause a person to sicken and die (10). Conversely, one of the promises that mesmerism held out to believers was the eradication of all diseases and the extension of the human life span. Many believed that Mesmer's electrical and hypnotic cures might have tapped into the Vital Fluid or Life Force that animates all living things. Maybe this Force *was* electricity. Many even hoped to find empirical proof for the existence of spiritual and transcendent realities. A public that could embrace mesmerism as a sure cure for all illnesses was certainly not going to be averse to taking a look at what vampires might have to offer.

Mesmerism with its scientific pretensions, says Janet Oppenheim (1985), gave rise to the mania for spiritualism and the occult that characterized the nineteenth century and that strove mightily to find empirical scientific proof: "Each created a blend of theory and practice that could appeal strongly to a population wanting scientific authorization for its faith and the blessings of religion upon its scientific discoveries" (222). Certainly, the French upper classes in the 1770s and 1780s were ready to accept enthusiastically the shenanigans not only of Anton Mesmer but also the claim of a charming someone who called himself the Comte de Saint-Germain that he had lived over a thousand years. Claiming to be a prince from Transylvania, an alchemist who had discovered the secret of longevity, he made a sensation in the French court. He "lives" today as the central figure of a modern cult (Jenkins 97) that believes he ascended to Heaven like Jesus and still directs the course of history through alchemy, occasionally in the person of a great man.[2] He survives too as an elegant "good" vampire who passes through the ages in a series of popular historical novels by Chelsea Quinn Yarbro, based loosely on his initial self-characterization.

All these scientific and occult speculations were related to changing attitudes about the nature of life and death and the distinction between them. Death too had become scientific. Philippe Ariès, in *The Hour of Our Death* (1981), notes that, by the eighteenth century, the authorities on death and the dead were no longer clergymen but doctors. Death was now accepted and studied as a physical rather than a spiritual matter (353). Faith in the resurrection of the body into eternal life had waned. There was growing scientific interest in the pathology of death and dead bodies among lay people (Ariès 354); public dissections for entertainment became the rage, and the wealthy often purchased corpses for the after-dinner edification of their guests, leading to a shameful increase in the theft of cadavers (366–69). This was a perfect stage for the appearance of the undead.

According to Ariès, two opposing (scientific) views prevailed in both medical and popular belief as to the relationship between life and death: (1) that the corpse retains a "kind of life and sensibility" so long as some flesh remains and the body is not reduced to a skeleton (the same view that underlies vampire folklore: even a little bit of flesh *may* retain the soul); and (2) that there is no life in the cadaver once the soul has left, which occurs at death (355). The former view had long had the support of popular superstition, and many doctors preferred it because it seemed to explain those same phenomena that, in Slavic villages, were used to identify vampires, such as the natural movement of the corpse and the apparent growth of hair and fingernails after death (356).

The first view that there is life in the corpse was not such a new idea. According to Ariès, a whole range of medical cures, regarded as perfectly acceptable, were based on the belief that there was some efficacious sensibility in the corpse: an injured member of a living body could be healed by applying to it the same part from a cadaver (357). The soil of graves was also "rich in therapeutic properties," says Ariès: "Corruption is fertile; the soil of the dead, like death itself, is a source of life" (358). In the nineteenth century, this view of the cadaver was dropped in preference for the second opinion, that "death does not exist in itself but is merely the separation of the soul and the body" (360). Nevertheless, vampire folklore and most vampire literature would seem to adopt the sentient corpse approach. Edgar Allan Poe's returning dead—Madeline in "The Fall of the House of Usher" (1839), Ligeia (1838), and Morella (1835)—are clearly awake, listening, and plotting their return. Poe also explored the possibility of prolonging life by mesmerism, as in his story in "The Facts in the Case of M. Valdemar" (1845). A dying man is hypnotized to survive death and actually does so, only to collapse into decay when the hypnotic spell is lifted. Dracula in his coffin knows what is going on around him as do many twentieth- and twenty-first-century vampires.

Interest in vampires early in the nineteenth century was interwoven with scientific speculations about the nature of life and the possibility of prolonging or even creating it. In her introduction to the third edition of *Frankenstein*, Mary Shelley tells us about the stormy night in the summer of 1816 when her novel as well as Byron's "Fragment of a Vampire Story" and John Polidori's "Vampyre" were conceived. These works were inspired, not only by the reading of Gothic horror stories, but more important, by long discussions between Byron and Shelley about "various philosophical doctrines," including "the nature of the principle of life, and whether there was any probability of its ever being discovered and communicated": "Perhaps a corpse would be re-animated; galvanism had given token of such things; perhaps the component parts of a creature might be manufactured, brought together, and endued with vital warmth" (171–72).

In Shelley's novel, Victor Frankenstein is a scientist who creates a new being out of pieces of dead bodies and electrifies it into intelligent life. Both Byron's seeming vampire Darvell (who apparently will revive in the unfinished portion of the story) and John Polidori's vampire Lord Ruthven reflect this interest in the possibilities of reviving life from death. John Polidori had recently graduated from medical school, and Frayling comments on the "clinical" nature of his vampire story (17).

Science might or might not be able to create monsters or resurrect the dead, but it was now required to explain and verify monsters in literature. That is, within the context of a horror story, science (often misapplied and misunderstood) provides one means to achieve the suspension of disbelief. In such early vampire stories as the anonymous German tale "The Mysterious Stranger" and in Le Fanu's "Carmilla" (1872), medical doctors are brought in (rather than clergymen) to provide confirmation that this form of life after death, though undesirable, is indeed possible. It is *Doctor* Van Helsing in Stoker's *Dracula* who pleads for the others to keep an "open mind," that is (he believes), a scientific mind, and not to reject mysteries simply because they cannot yet be fully understood. Montague Summers, a real person who really believed in vampires, is certain that his open-minded acceptance of vampire accounts from Sumatra to the British Isles and from ancient times to the present is a truly scientific position.

Three Scientific Vampires

Three major vampire works of the nineteenth century reflect the influence of popular scientific speculation about the nature of death, immortality—and vampires: James Malcolm Rymer's *Varney the Vampyre or The Feast of Blood* (1847), Joseph Sheridan Le Fanu's "Carmilla," and Bram Stoker's *Dracula.*

All three make use of doctor characters to direct the readers' attitudes toward the vampire phenomenon: Chillingworth, Hesselius, and Van Helsing, respectively.

James Malcolm Rymer's *Varney the Vampyre*, a serialized "penny dreadful" written to entertain, does not show any confusion about what science can or cannot prove. Even after Varney has been seen leering over the beautiful and innocent Flora Bannerworth, the skeptical Doctor Chillingworth takes a rigorous scientific position: that the existence of vampires " 'is contrary to all experience, to philosophy, and to all the laws of ordinary nature' " (1:164). Later, as Varney terrorizes the Bannerworth family, the narrator too undercuts any inclination to take Varney seriously when he comments to the reader that the "human delights in the marvellous," and the less information there is about it, the more people are disposed to take it for truth. This, he complains, is how a "dim and uncertain condition concerning vampires" managed to spread "insidiously, throughout the whole of the civilized world" (1:188). Dr. Chillingworth affirms the need for plenty of recorded empirical evidence to believe in the existence of vampires. The doctor finally proves his point in regard to Varney by confessing that it was he who resuscitated Varney from a botched gallows execution by means of "galvanic" experiments, somewhat reminiscent of those used by Dr. Frankenstein (1:328–31).

Chillingworth's admission leads the reader to question if Varney is to be taken as a vampire at all. The hangman who delivered Varney's body later asks him scornfully why he has chosen " 'to *enact* such a character' " (1:331, [emphasis added]). Varney, who believes himself to be a vampire, takes the open-minded (and Shakespearean) view, that " 'there are truths connected with natural philosophy which he [Chillingworth] dreamed not of' " (1:354). Finally, even the victimized Bannerworths begin to doubt that Varney actually is a vampire. Only their friend Admiral Bell takes a pragmatic view: " 'He is a vampyre in his own opinion, and so I don't see, for the life of me, why he should not be so in ours' " (1:411).

In spite of a superficial silliness and various inconsistencies, Varney, like Dracula later, becomes a focus for a discussion about what and how we can know about reality—and the reality of death. When one character, Marchdale, accuses him of being " 'one who would doubt a miracle, if you saw it with your own eyes,' " Chillingworth replies,

> "I would, because I do not believe in miracles. I should endeavour to find some rational and some scientific means of accounting for the phenomenon, and that's the very reason why we have no miracles now-a-days . . . and no prophets and saints, and all that sort of thing." (1:38)

God means for us to employ reason to understand both Him and nature. When Henry Bannerworth asserts " 'the truths of Scripture,' " the narrator interposes to point out,

> Mr. Chillingworth . . . was one of those characters in society who hold most dreadful opinions, and who would destroy religious beliefs, and all the different sects in the world, if they could, and endeavour to introduce instead some horrible system of human reason and profound philosophy. (1:40)

The tongue-in-cheek tone of this statement puts the narrator on the side of the skeptical Chillingworth, as does Henry's realization that, once one accepts the reality of vampires, one is compelled to accept *all* the stories about them (1:48).

In any case, if vampires did exist, they must have been created by God for an unknown purpose and can therefore be considered "natural" and right. At one point, Marchdale asserts, " 'What is is natural' " (1:135). Varney agrees. He tells Flora that his miserable existence is fated and has a purpose " 'in the great drama of existence,' " a rational and benign natural order created by a wise and beneficent Deity (1:155). That is, Rymer employs his supernatural vampire to support a rational argument against the supernatural. We will see this argument repeated later by the vampire Carmilla in Le Fanu's story (further on) and by the vampire Lestat in Anne Rice's novels—but without Rymer's Enlightenment (pre-Darwinian) assumption that nature is good.

In Sheridan Le Fanu's "Carmilla," a father and daughter, recently arrived at a new home in Styria (a province in southeast Austria), offer temporary shelter to a young lady whose carriage has been smashed in an accident. The guest Carmilla begins to exhibit odd nocturnal behavior that, as in *Varney*, is at first given a rational explanation and attributed to sleepwalking (109–10) although she is actually out drinking blood from the neighbors as well as from her hostess Laura. Carmilla justifies her lifestyle: " 'All things proceed from Nature—don't they? All things in the heaven, in the earth, and under the earth, act and live as Nature ordains? I think so.' " By the end of her experience, Laura, the victim, believes in vampires, not only because of her own experience, but also because (like Calmet) she cannot ignore the "voluminous" amounts of "human testimony" about them (134). Her story supposedly can be found in the papers of a Dr. Hesselius, who—in contrast to Doctor Chillingworth—provides authority for its "truth" and testimony to the sanity of the teller. Attitudes toward nature have clearly changed since Rymer's enlightened 1840s: now, in 1872, Carmilla embodies nature's ruthless voraciousness. Carmilla is discovered in her coffin as the 150-year-old

Countess Mircalla and is destroyed there by means of staking and decapitation, and thus, within the story, proves that vampires are real.

In *Dracula*, Bram Stoker goes considerably further than *Varney* and "Carmilla" by making his Doctor Van Helsing a key figure in the story, whose supposed scientific knowledge becomes a major factor in identifying and eliminating the dangerous undead. In a letter from Dr. John Seward to his friend, Arthur Holmwood, he is introduced as "a philosopher and a metaphysician," an "advanced scientist," with "an absolutely open mind" (147), which means, we find out, that science deals not only with natural but also with supernatural phenomena. *Dracula* shows us how much the line between empirical research and occult inspiration had become clouded by the end of the nineteenth century. Van Helsing's idea of scientific open-mindedness has nothing to do with the strict reasoning and empirical evidence acceptable to Rymer's Dr. Chillingworth. Whereas *Varney* makes a strong case for rationalism and casts doubt on its own supernatural hero/villain, *Dracula* (in line with current trends in occult and psychical research) brings science into the metaphysics (or vice versa), positing an alliance of science, religion, and tradition, and even magic, in proving not only the existence of supernatural evil in the material universe but, on the upside, the possibility of achieving earthly immortality.

Van Helsing attacks contemporary science head on in an argument reported in Seward's diary (in Stoker's strange version of a Dutchman speaking English): that science " 'wants to explain all; and if it explain not, then it says there is nothing to explain.' " Yet, he says, many of the " 'new beliefs' " offered by science " 'are yet but the old, which pretend to be young.' " His own credulity extends to the occult phenomena of " 'corporeal transference,' " " 'materialization,' " " 'astral bodies,' " mind-reading, and hypnotism (235), in addition to vampires. When he asks, contemptuously, if science knows " 'all the mystery of life and death' " (236), he restates one of the nineteenth century's great disappointments: empirical science had failed to fulfill its early promise to understand—and prevent—death. The fault was, as many now saw it, that science had foolishly limited itself to what could be observed or measured. What science must do, as Dr. Seward records, is to learn " 'to believe in things that you cannot' " (237) and to " 'have an open mind and not let a little bit of truth check the rush of a big truth' " (238). Science *could* explain these mysteries, he implies, if scientists were not so closed minded. Yet, to defeat Dracula, Van Helsing finally resorts, not to science, but to magic, which he treats as some as yet unexplained science of yore.

In another conversation recorded by Mina Harker, Van Helsing, like the occultists and spiritualists of the times, uses "science" to shore up his speculations about Dracula as the product of " 'something magnetic or electric' ": " 'all the forces of nature that are occult and deep and strong must have worked together in some wondrous way. The very place where he have been alive, Un-Dead for all these centuries is full of strangeness of the geologic and chemical world' " (378). Or " 'some vital principle have in strange way found their utmost' " *without* " 'Diabolic Aid' " (379). Van Helsing repeatedly identifies Dracula with nature and natural phenomena—the cycles of day and night, for example, or mist and storm, or his native earth, or certain animals and plants. But, by the end of the nineteenth century, science has destroyed the Enlightenment view of nature as benign and orderly, and shown it to be cruel and death-dealing. Van Helsing's "scientific" explanations really warn the reader *away* from the natural world and point him *toward* the occult—or at least the conventionally religious—as a refuge from all this violence and death.

The Vampire Disease

Twentieth-century vampire literature carries on Stoker's association of vampires with voracious nature; in Murnau's *Nosferatu* (1922) and the 1979 remake, and in Tod Browning's *Dracula* (1931), Van Helsing is shown demonstrating a Venus Fly Trap, which acts automatically, according to its nature, as do the wolves invariably associated with Dracula and many other vampires. Natural evils—pollution, disease, and death—are the venue of vampires in folklore and literature, and the defeat of vampires is a defeat of these natural dangers. In Murnau's early film *Nosferatu*, the vampire is literally the plague itself, which ends with the destruction of the vampire. The "lesson" of both versions of *Nosferatu* seems to be that the plague—and other such evils—can be defeated by acknowledging it and taking practical steps. In Tod Browning's *Dracula*, as well as the numerous Hammer films, the vampire carries something like a virus that is contagious and that can be stopped only by destruction of the host organism. The disease idea persists in the occasional depiction of vampires as sort of nauseating half-decayed beings, as in the film *Bloodstone: Subspecies II* (1993). Brian Aldiss in *Dracula Unbound* (1991) suggests a connection between his prehistoric animal-like vampires and the mental degeneration brought on by syphilis (84). Even more scientifically, their mindless rapacity can be explained by the fact that they have not yet developed a neo-cortex (165). However supernatural and mysterious some of these vampires may seem, their restriction by rigidly specified sets of "natural" laws shows us, as Varney recognizes, that vampires do not exist or act at random or by chance. Their destructiveness, like that of a tornado or some devastating disease, remains within the realm of human understanding and control.[3]

The Upside: Vampire Promises of Immortality

Paradoxically, this fictional vampire "science" (we might call it) also offers a spur to believing in the possibility of achieving earthly immortality.[4] The (fictional) vampire as the key to immortality or how to get it takes an increasingly scientific turn in modern literature. After all, such a condition could be caused by viruses like HIV or genetic mutations. Two vampires introduced in television series, Barnabas Collins of *Dark Shadows* (1966–1971) and Nicholas Knight of *Forever Knight* (1992–1996) are convinced by lady doctors that they are suffering from medical conditions that can be medically cured (although they never are). In this approach, the vampire that began as a kind of explanatory scientific figure for the rural folk becomes a representation of (not scapegoat for) various modern physical illnesses—illnesses that might be cured, not by Nosferatu's dissolution in the face of moral perfection, but by medication.

Why they want to be cured is often hard to discover. For although some vampires, like Anne Rice's Louis in *Interview with the Vampire* (1976) or Nicholas Knight (*Forever Knight*), claim to be suffering deeply from their condition, it is not always clear that their lives are so miserable. Even vampires who eventually commit suicide—Nicholas Knight at the end of his series or Dracula in Kim Newman's *Judgment of Tears: Anno Dracula 1959* (1998)—hardly seem justified when given their intriguing alternative and all the fun they have been having. That is, these "diseased" vampires not only offer the fantasy of immortal life and considerable good times but they also suggest the way to get it—if we can just find the right virus. Science might yet fulfill its early promises. As the eighteenth and nineteenth centuries found promise in magnetism and electricity, the twentieth century looks forward to advances in genetics and virology.

For many vampires, excessive longevity, well managed, entails no penalty at all. Michael Romkey opens his novel *I, Vampire* (1990) with a direct appeal to the "yearning for life beyond the few years allotted" (6). In this novel, the vampire condition is not at all supernatural but involves a transmitted virus that apparently turns the vampires into a genetically "distinct species" from humans, similar except for superior capabilities and "enhanced regenerative powers on a cellular level," so that aging is slowed (95).

In Dan Simmons's *Children of the Night*, vampirism is caused by an inherited physical abnormality something like hemophilia. The biologist heroine Dr. Kate Neuman is a researcher at the Center for Disease Control. The novel dramatizes her excitement when she discovers that vampires really do exist and that she has gotten hold of a "vampire" child, Joshua, Dracula's offspring, who has the genetic mutation that allows vampires to resist death. These vampires, as Kate explains it, have a way of adapting human blood to repair their own inherited immunodeficiency, in some sort of " 'shadow organ' " " 'where the blood is broken down' " and then " 'disseminated throughout the body to catalyze the immune system.' " The child has a " 'retrovirus . . . something as persistent as HIV, only with life-giving rather than fatal consequences' " (133). This "vampire gene" along with the vampire virus might offer a cure for certain devastating autoimmune diseases like AIDS as well as a means of repairing injuries and resisting the ravages of old age.

Like Romkey, Simmons believes that the popular fascination with vampires expresses a natural and admirable love of life. Even his decrepit old Dracula, finally ready to succumb to death, rethinks his decision after taking some of Kate's experimental serum that restores his vitality. He thinks, at the novel's end,

> *I have given up thoughts of dying soon. Such thoughts were the products of illness, age, and bad dreams. I no longer have the bad dreams.*
> *Perhaps I will live forever.* (451)

Revitalized by this injection of a hemoglobin substitute, he cheerfully tootles off for a new life in Japan. The novel is full of Kate's enthusiasm—and even Dracula's at the end—that her research with his child can help end immunodeficiency diseases and prolong human life. This fictional search for ways to infect or genetically engineer humans with immortality may seem like mere fantasy, but we just have to glance at the news now and then or read some popular science journals to know that the prolongation of life and youth has become a large part of modern medical research.

In a recent book entitled *Merchants of Immortality: Chasing the Dream of Human Life Extension* (2003), science writer Stephen S. Hall reviews longevity research in the last hundred years, because, as he indicates, immortality is what everybody wants:

> We prick our ears at any breakthrough, whether marketed by clairvoyants or molecular biologists, that purports to arrest or reverse the inevitable process of aging, or even to extend the human life span in such a way that it no longer seems preposterous to speak of a certain, practical immortality. (11–12)

The title of his book suggests the market-directed nature of much of this research, which he sees as a combination of scientific ambition and greed feeding on the elemental fear of death.

Hall quotes serious researchers who burble enthusiastically about eliminating aging and prolonging life. Molecular biologist Cynthia Kenyon tells Hall she is working on a "'fountain of youth gene'" in nematodes and believes that the normal human life span will be dramatically increased in the twenty-first century (8). Kenyon's scientific work received little popular attention, she said, until she started work on aging and inquiries began pouring in: "'The public is absolutely fascinated by aging. They don't want to get old. And you can see—read Shakespeare. Read the sonnets. They're all about aging'" (11). Yet, after a long and detailed explanation of various and extensive research, Hall regretfully concludes: "No serious scientist believes victory over mortality is possible." Although we may be able to slow down the aging process, we are not likely to extend life expectancy significantly any time soon (345). Nevertheless, in vampire science fictions, some writers leap ahead in time to the achievement of immortality by wholly natural means.

Some Problems

Like much science fiction, vampire literature sometimes examines various possible failures and costs of such scientific investigations. In Whitley Strieber's *The Hunger*, the two main characters, Miriam Blaylock, the vampire, and Dr. Sarah Roberts, researcher on aging, try to discover the cause of Miriam's vampirism, which is linked to some sort of blood condition. But science fails. The vampire must transfuse her blood into her victims, who live forever but ultimately begin to age rapidly, finally falling into a state similar to that of Swift's Struldbrugs in book 3 of *Gulliver's Travels* or the eternally aging Tithonus of Greek myth. Their bodies are wizened into helpless, dried-up little bundles of cravings, while their minds remain more-or-less aware. Miriam carts them from place to place and era to era packed in little crates. They suffer for her misdirected effort to thwart nature. Her latest victim, Sarah, finally doomed to eternal decrepitude in one of Miriam's crates, ponders her own vanity in thinking that she could actually live forever: "What was death but a disease, she had asked herself. And she had told herself she would break the secret of death from within the shelter of immortality and give the secret to humanity. What a lie that had been!" (302). Through the vampire, Strieber's novel finally derogates scientific investigation into aging and longevity as arrogant overreaching beyond man's appointed lot.

The vampire character offers a familiar figure by which to examine this possible achievement of science. For as soon as a few people were to achieve immortality, then wouldn't everyone want it? What would the world do with all those old vampires? And anyway, if all the world were vampires, what would the vampires eat? Vampire authors have anticipated these problems, which are major reasons for the vampires' secretiveness and reclusiveness (in addition to the onus attached to their peculiar eating habits). Nancy Baker's novel *Kiss of the Vampire* (1993), for example, tells of a vampire who is hunted down like an animal by a succession of millionaires such as Althea Dale, who has imprisoned a group of scientists to study his blood and discover the secret. In Patrick Whalen's *Night Thirst* (1991) some "rogue" government scientists try to get hold of two wise old vampires to get immortality for themselves, as well as to create armies of zombie-like young vampires to take over the world (à la *Night of the Living Dead*).

As for the proliferation of vampires, not everyone regards this as a problem. In a collection of essays entitled *Immortal Engines: Life Extension and Immortality in Science Fiction and Fantasy* (1996), James Gunn writes that in spite of any drawbacks, "I did not for a moment buy the idea that people would not choose immortality if they had a chance . . ." (15). Very few could resist the opportunity to extend their lives beyond their "allotted time." In a comment on stories of failed resurrections (such as *The Hunger*), Steven B. Harris sees them "as fundamentalist reactions to the ambiguities gradually introduced by science" into the stable and comfortable worldview provided by Christian doctrine since the eighteenth century, ranging from hysteria over dissection to "attempts to suppress cryonics" (65). In "Longevity as Class Struggle," Fredric Jameson finds himself "appalled at the residual moralism still inherent in this topic." He is dismayed at

> the insistence of so many writers on the subject that it would be evil to live forever, that true human existence requires a consent to mortality, . . . that hubris and egotism are denounced as prime elements in this particular fantasy about the supreme private property, not merely of having a self but of having it live forever. (40)

This attitude reveals an "extraordinary puritanism" that finds it easier to rely on "simple religious and ethical paradigms" to condemn the fantasy rather than to figure out its social implications and consequences were it to occur (40).

Writing about his own vampire novel *The Empire of Fear* (1988), Brian Stableford regrets that immortality has received "a remarkably bad press" in modern fantasy and science fiction ("Sang" 79). Too much space is given to demonstrating the misery that would occur as a result. In *The Empire of Fear*, a widespread and easily attainable (for most people) vampire condition is ultimately brought under beneficial scientific and social control (the social control being the most difficult). In his novel *Vamped* (2004), David Sosnowski creates a world that is all vampires, who survive fairly contentedly on artificial blood and whose greatest difficulties are boredom, missing children and food, and, worst of all, ironically, fear of death.

A common denominator in "scientific" vampire works is the number of doctors and medical researchers that appear in them to confirm this natural phenomenon. In Colin Wilson's science fiction novel *The Space Vampires* (1976), he speculates about the possibility of a kind of natural (in a spacey sort of way) "benevolent vampirism" (211) for increasing the human life span. This all depends, however, on an occult concept of a "life field" or "life force" which exists in all living beings, but which can be vampirized, as it is by the bad aliens, to prolong life. Or it can be willingly and beneficially exchanged. Commander Carlsen and his crew find the vampires on an abandoned space ship in a state of suspended animation, and bring three of them back to earth. But of course they are not dead. Wilson provides *two* Van Helsings; one, in Doctor Hans Fallada, who establishes "beyond all doubt" that these aliens are "energy vampires" (69), and another, in the Swedish "psychologist and philosopher" Count Ernst Von Geijerstam, who has discovered the "benevolent vampirism" by which he prolongs his own life through the aid of three gorgeous and willing young ladies. (This is possibly the most male chauvinistic vampire novel I have read—and that is saying a great deal.)

Apparently, all humans have a certain ability to exchange energy; what is needed is the knowledge of how to make beneficial use of it. In the tradition of Montague Summers, all this wishful fantasy is supported by reference to previous vampires—Dracula and Count Magnus[5]—as though they had really existed, as well as to occult concepts, some conventional religion, and, of course, an astonishing amount of completely incomprehensible "science." We are asked to suspend our disbelief that all this is entirely natural, including the vampires' ability to live outside their bodies or to exchange bodies. The good aliens, who finally show up to save the world, however, are, in the spiritualist tradition, all mind and "shimmering purple" energy (197), kinds of "gods" (205). This is perhaps an extreme example in vampire literature of supporting a spiritualist agenda and belief in a transmittable "life force" as well as ordinary wish-fulfilling fantasy with allusions to contemporary popular science as though these could make it true.

2

Vampires and Society

Folklore: The Vampire and the Community

Folklore vampires serve the needs of their community, even when they differ from one another from region to region, in details of what they eat or do or how one kills them. But they are all living dead. As living dead, vampires and stories about them often inculcate important social lessons, reinforcing social solidarity and responsibility within the family and the community. Moreover, they reinforce communally shared beliefs about the relationship between the living and the dead, and, in doing so, they provide ties with the family and community past. Many literary vampires offer similar communal lessons for their readers, although the norms may be quite different and the past much broader. As living embodiments of history, modern vampires can offer a sense of continuity with a very ancient past as well as with an expanded, international community.

Folklore vampires often convey important social messages in that their undead condition is regarded as a penalty for mental, physical, or behavioral deviations from communal norms, willful or otherwise, during their lifetime. Involuntary deviations may include such abnormalities as being born with a caul or with teeth erupted or with red hair. During their lifetime, people may become vampires by the misfortune of having been bitten by a vampire or, after their death, by being buried carelessly without the proper ritual. Sometimes, the smooth passing on of even ordinary people may be blocked by some conflict in their community or family relationships, some unresolved business, unavenged wrong, or even a curse (especially parental). Usually, however, becoming a vampire involves more socially offensive deviations, such as being witches or werewolves or sorcerers, or drunks or criminals, or by dying violently or being excommunicated, by being just generally obnoxious, or too attached to this world to leave it gracefully.

In his *Essays on Russian Folklore and Mythology*, Felix J. Oinas (1984) points out that Russian supernatural beings have been created "in the image of human society" (94). The good spirits behave according to Russian peasant standards of acceptable social behavior, and stories about them are designed to set an example for humans. The wicked spirits, like vampires, tend to be identified with social outcasts, such as robbers, and behave in an antisocial way. In places where the two churches exist side by side, one can become a vampire by being a Roman Catholic as opposed to Greek Orthodox or the reverse, or by holding any other heretical belief. The line between the beliefs and attitudes of the living community and those attributed to the dead or to other supernatural beings may be very thin—and often just as varied and inconsistent.

Responses of Greek villagers to questions from Blum and Blum about folklore related to illness and death included a variety of stories: a man returned to sleep with his wife (and gave her two children); a boy who drowned in a well returned to tell his father that his aunt had pushed him in; a man became a vampire because he had burned another man to death and had never been punished. One respondent's statement tells us about the importance of proper burial ritual:

> "I learned from my grandmother that nothing, specifically nothing animal, bird, insect, or candle should be allowed to fly over, jump over, or be carried over the corpse because it will become a vorkalakas (a vrikolax) and will pollute the flour in the house. If this happens, then the relatives and the priest go in the night after the funeral and burn the body." (73)

A boy became a vampire because the priest failed to read the burial service through completely (74). One man died and returned to a different village where he married a new wife (72). And again, Blum and Blum were told,

> "One of the worst curses you can put on a man is to say, 'May you never decay.' One who is cursed that way can become a vrikolax. So too can someone who has been a drunk. Also a person who steals from a school or church will not decay, nor will the one who points the five fingers at his parents or otherwise does not behave properly with his parents." (75)

Vampire folklore demonstrates a terrible fate for those who affront community values. But it also offers them a chance for acceptance and reconciliation—and thus, says Gail Kligman, fear of the returning dead helps to close the social gap between the community and even the most violent outcasts. For one thing, rigidly prescribed funeral rites allow the living to make amends and express their sorrow and regrets through ritual laments; in turn, the deceased can ask forgiveness and say farewell, often through the agency of the officiating priest (Kligman 194). If this is properly carried out, even the angry and potentially dangerous dead will be placated and remain content where they are.

Funerals are social occasions that bring the dead and the living together: the previously deceased are believed to congregate to welcome the newcomer to the other world, and the living can then take the chance to talk to them, ask for favors, and keep them up with the local news (Kligman 204). The conversations, laments, funeral prayers, and speeches of the participants including the deceased (spoken for them) preserve continuity between the living and the dead and thus preserve traditional values (154).[1] For the living, paradoxically, these efforts to keep the dead happy while maintaining social relations serve partly "to humanize the other world" (158) and lessen "the stark reality of mortality" (155): "Without memorials, traces of the deceased are erased from cultural memory. It is in the interest of the living to keep the dead, and therefore themselves, eternally alive" (Kligman 196). Within the community, no one has to be just "gone and forgotten."

Although laments often urge the deceased not to die but to return, no one really wants them to do so. An important part of mourning includes providing food for the dead to take on their long journey ahead (Kligman 157). Although it seems not to have much appeal to modern writers of vampire fiction, the folk custom of dining and socializing with the deceased—not only at funerals but at frequent specified occasions in future years—is certainly the most common means of remembering them and keeping them happy where they are. (Before we turn up our noses at this provincial superstition, we might recall that, until the intervention of Christianity, the sophisticated citizens of Rome observed similar practices.) One reason the dead walk is that they are hungry; they just need to be fed; they *will* eat normal food (or it is eaten for them). In modern vampire literature, feeding the dead survives, perhaps, in the emphasis on the vampires' insatiable hunger, which, although antisocial, does force them into contact with the warm bodied.

In addition to maintaining community cohesion, the interaction between living and dead also reconciles generation differences. Juliet du Boulay suggests that fear of vampires originates "in the need for the young to look after the old" (234). In his article "Why Are Vampires Still Alive?" about Wallachian immigrants in Scandinavia (1986), Swedish anthropologist Carl-Ulrik Schierup focuses on this very practical "use" for vampires. Vampire belief is a form, he says, of "*worship of the dead*," which involves mutual duties and obligations. Failure to fulfill these obligations either before or after death can result in the return of the deceased to create problems for the living, to whom they can bring good or bad fortune (179). In the multigenerational family, the ancestor cult and the fear of postmortem revenge provide means by which the older generation maintains control over the younger and reinforces a sense of family obligation (189).

Even the young, who sometimes express contempt for these beliefs, may end up publicly adopting them to support their own right to community leadership positions (Schierup 194). Schierup gives an example of an educated man in an immigrant Slavic community who reported being tormented at night by his deceased mother, who was also causing him all sorts of bad luck. Confronted by a respected sorceress (medium), she complained that she had been neglected concerning his choice of her daughter-in-law. The solution lay in his performing the proper ritual to placate her. His doing so also indicated to the rest of the community, in which he was a leader, that he subscribed to the group morality (173–74).

Even a relatively docile vampire (and many *are* docile) is unwanted in the community. The vampire's soul does not go off to wherever souls are supposed to go but remains tied to the body, which generally becomes bloated, red, and unsightly, as well as a community pest, even a killer (in contrast to the pale, elegant, slender—unless a woman, then full-bosomed—aristocratic killer vampires of modern literature). Stuck in the transitional phase between this world and the next and unable or unwilling to travel on, the vampire's greatest affront to the community is this disregard for the impassable boundary between life and death. The living dead are dangerous because they threaten the natural order of things. Many burial practices such as driving a stake through the corpse or stuffing bodily openings with garlic are intended to cut off unnatural contact between the living and the rebellious spirit. Paradoxically, doing so "returns the individual to the fold of society and transforms perceived chaos back into order," says Kligman (245).

By rituals and burial practices, including burning and staking, social outcasts or deviants like witches or drunks can be reintegrated into the community after death by "undoing" their deviance (whether they like it or not). This willingness to accept deviations, says Harry A. Senn (1988), is a manifestation of "a reasoned acknowledgement of the universal existence of misfortune and individual transgressions" (34). Such practices emphasize the continued importance of each of its members (however drunk and disagreeable he was) to the family and the community. Moreover, fear of the return of the dead (a mother-in-law, for example) to right perceived wrongs encourages community and family members to see that this is done during her lifetime and thus promotes social harmony.

Social Lessons from the Literary Undead

The value of the vampire in teaching all kinds of social lessons has not been overlooked by modern writers. In some cases becoming a vampire is a punishment for wrongdoing. In the earliest complete vampire story in

English, "The Vampyre" (1819) by John Polidori, the vampire Lord Ruthven (based on Polidori's former employer, Lord Byron) is clearly intended as an indictment of aristocratic arrogance and disregard for others and is a warning to the young against being taken in by charm and sophisticated manners. Coleridge's Ancient Mariner is condemned to (and by) "Life-in-Death" for his wanton destruction of the spirit bird that gave hope to his fellow mariners (*The Rime of the Ancient Mariner* 1798). Byron's Giaour in the poem of that name (1813) will be cursed to an eternity of unrest for his contempt for human life and his affronts to community values.

Stoker's Dracula may have been a great leader in his day, but he was also a cruel and ruthless tyrant, who isolated himself from humankind by his pact with the devil. Dracula's failure of social accountability and his refusal to follow even the rules of God is why he is dangerous and why he is finally defeated, according to some readers like Gregory A. Waller (1986). Instead of being integrated (as in folklore), he must be totally wiped out as a pernicious foreigner. But his presence as a predatory outsider, says Waller, does arouse a new sense of social solidarity in the English characters so that the battle quickly becomes "the struggle between the values of selfless, unified community and the destructive excesses of egotistical individualism" (40).[2]

According to David J. Skal in *The Monster Show: A Cultural History of Horror* (1993), the proliferation of vampires and other horror figures in the twentieth century, like Dracula and Frankenstein and various zombies, were a response to the horrors of the War and the Great Depression (159). These monstrous images in twentieth-century literature, Skal tells us, like a modern folklore, "contain a rich, if hidden, culture of their own" (22), flourishing alongside the acceptable worldviews of both science and religion, not unknown to them but simply ignored or brushed aside as insignificant. They express two different "cautionary daydreams about failed attempts to overcome death" (83). Perhaps, in a more fantastic and manageable form, they recalled or reenacted for viewers who could not forget them or had only heard of them, the horrors that the 1950s cheerfully frothed over with *Mouseketeers*, *Archie Comics*, *Leave It to Beaver*, and glorious Technicolor images of the American Way of Life.

Moreover, they come back again and again, often in hordes, impossible to ignore. Richard Matheson's future vampires (of, well, the 1970s) in *I Am Legend* (1954) add a nightmare of the mass rising of the mindless and hungry dead—or ruthless Communists or the grasping poor. The panic and prejudice that characterized the Cold War era is still evident in Robert Neville, the one human left alive (rather than undead), who has lived so long with irrational fear and hatred that he cannot give them up when life is offered to him. Much more recently, in the television series *Buffy the Vampire Slayer* (1997–2003), the contented and prosperous citizens of happy

Sunnydale carry on their superficial lives ignorantly perched above a roiling pit of sudden apocalyptic destruction bursting out occasionally in a seemingly endless supply of the forgotten dead.

The folk beliefs and rituals related to vampires actually provide a means to maintain social awareness and community coherence even into the next world. Literary vampires often perform a similar function. For in his role as loner, rebel, or outcast set against the group, the vampire reminds us, by positive or negative example, that we *live in* and will be *remembered by* (that is, *live through*) other human beings, our families and friends, within a community of some kind so long as it persists.

Historical Vampires: Lessons from the Past

In their connection with the past, the literary undead play a most important—and popular—social role. For *dead* means *in the past*, and the modern vampire, from the past, starting with *Dracula* (and picking up the threads from folklore) comments on the failure of modern communities to preserve their traditional values and loyalties—or, in twentieth-century America, to acknowledge *any* past or adhere to any sense of community responsibility at all. In the twentieth or twenty-first centuries, ancient vampires sometimes awaken into a heartless society controlled by ideals of production and material progress, at best, and at worst, a dog-eat-dog world in which the struggle for success and self-gratification is all that counts, as illustrated by the rapacious lawyers in the firm of Wolfram and Hart in Joss Whedon's *Angel* series (1999–2004). Even as killers and destroyers, modern vampires often appear miniscule compared to the vast impersonal forces of war, big government, and multinational business. Moreover, many good vampires have blossomed in the second half of the twentieth century. Yarbro's long-lived and much-traveled vampire, the Comte de Saint-Germain, carries humane values from age to age and culture to culture (and novel to novel), making the point that genuine humanitarian virtue is timeless and absolute.

Not everyone is happy about these vampire reformations, and some are annoyed by the failure of modern vampires to at least *stand for* a vast cosmic evil even greater than that of Stalin or Ceausescu. Jules Zanger, in his essay "Metaphor into Metonymy: The Vampire Next Door" (1997), complains that modern vampires, by becoming more humanized and nicer, have given up the "absolute timeless condition of Dracula" in order to move "into time and history" (22). This, of course, is a matter of interpretation; no vampire could be more self-doubting than poor old (pre-Dracula) Varney. And Stoker's "timeless" Dracula, with three wives at home, we recall, is forced (by Stoker) to carry around ridiculous coffins of dirt that tie him, irrevocably, to his time and place. By definition, all vampires—good or evil—step out of the timeless world of Death into the time of Life.

Vampire literature plays with the slipperiness of place and time and our perceptions of it, and the conflict between our desire to stop time *now* versus our compulsion to barge on ahead. Bram Stoker's method of narrating *Dracula* carries us backward and forward in time and place, from a medieval castle in Romania to modern London but also, within the narrative, from one character's time to another's. Events that occur at different times and places blend into one meaningful account. Frank Langella's Dracula reminds his pursuers, "It is always daylight somewhere on earth" (1979), asserting his persistence through the eternal cycles of day and night. The film versions of Dan Curtis's *Dracula* with Jack Palance (1973) and Coppola's *Bram Stoker's Dracula* pick up a hint from Stoker to depict Dracula's new life as a partial recurrence and redeeming of the old. One of the most popular features of vampire literature is the way that it plays with the impingement of the past on the present—or even the future—while not entirely abandoning the conventions of realism. This is a function, of course, of the supernatural element common to all Gothic fiction, but a vampire (however dead) who can sit down and chat over a glass of wine about meeting Queen Elizabeth or Julius Caesar conveys a kind of meaningful materiality to history.

Fear of the Past

Stoker's Dracula sets the model for the vampire who represents the dangerous persistence of the past in the present, often unacknowledged and unrecognized, creating friction and conflict, for example, of the antique patriarchy with the New Woman or the traditional aristocracy with a new kind of democracy of middle-class heroes. And a kind of ironic joke seems to lie in the fact that the antique patriarchal Dracula—along with other aristocrats—does not seem fully to realize that he is dead. Dracula desires to restore not just his family but the whole social system in which such a family could rule, with its princes and peasants, warriors and serfs. A more recent example is Kim Newman's Dracula, who, with his barbaric rage for power and sense of entitlement to it, drags nineteenth-century England back into a rigid and hierarchical Middle Ages with himself as lord of the manor—the same Middle Ages that lay under the surface of Victorian yearnings for authority and romance. In these works and others, vampires stand for all the failures and errors of the past that we had thought were gone forever.

To some readers, critics, and moviemakers, vampires embody our fears of falling back, of degenerating entirely into mindless barbarism. The vampire hunters, in general, represent modernity, civilization, social order, and progress; the vampires represent superstition, brutality, chaos, and degeneration. The defeat of Dracula, then, stands for the triumph of modern science and civilization. Yet the figure of the vampire illustrates how fragile are modern achievements, how easily the present can become seduced, paralyzed, and corrupted by the past—a past that ought to stay dead. In Stoker's *Dracula*, Jonathan Harker's visit to Dracula's medieval castle early in the story becomes a "horrible nightmare" (23), in which he barely escapes being lured into unseemly sexual excesses and corrupted into animalism by Dracula's frisky wives.

An extreme extension of Stoker's description of Dracula as an evolutionary throwback with hairy hands and pointed ears appears in Brian Aldiss's *Dracula Unbound*: most of Dracula's army of vampires (although not Dracula himself) go all the way back to the Mesozoic era, the age of the dinosaurs, before humans, before the development of a conscience or kindness or sense of social responsibility (or God?). Some writers have recreated other kinds of ancient-creature-vampires, like, for example, the disgusting parasitical blob of Brian Lumley's *Necroscope* (1986). Even earlier, in M. R. James's "An Episode of Cathedral History" (1919), a strange, formless creature, accidentally released from a tomb during the remodeling of a church, provides a lesson against carelessly digging up the past.

But fear of the past is also a fear of death. Gothic literature is about the horror of death and the dead combined with an irresistible charnel-house fascination, even necrophilia—which is the source of the repulsiveness of Dracula, Frankenstein's monster, and all the living dead. In vampire literature, we literally dance with death and feel its cold hands and its cold eyes watching and its thin voice calling. An extreme example of this fascination is provided in the books of the prime vampire enthusiast of all time, Montague Summers. In *The Vampire in Europe* (1929), Summers declares his intention "to trace back the dark tradition of the vampire to its earliest beginnings" and its unfortunate persistence as "man marched towards civilization" (xi). In his efforts to prove the actual existence of vampires, Summers became himself a kind of living anachronism, who revived in his own person the horrors of medieval superstition as he gleefully totted up the various manifestations of vampire vileness.

Love of the Past

Contrarily, enthusiasm and respect for the past also underlie much vampire literature, especially enthusiasm for a highly romanticized and idealized Middle Ages invented by the nineteenth century. This imaginary Golden Age of chivalry and faith was both a fictional refuge from and a condemnation of the muddled moral values and aesthetic bleakness of nineteenth-century Victorian England and America. In *A Dream of Order: The Medieval Ideal in Nineteenth-Century English Literature* (1970), Alice Chandler writes about the Victorian creation of a "partly historical but basically mythical Middle Ages" that stood for "a metaphysically harmonious world view" that no longer existed (1). According to Chandler, this new mythology offered both "a social and political ideal" and a "metaphor of belief" in an ordered and meaningful cosmos that provided an antithesis to the disorder and lack of faith that many perceived around them (10). Moral clarity and faith required clear distinctions between right and wrong; and these were provided in this mythical re-creation of the Christian medieval story of the cosmic combat between good and evil, God and Satan.

In *The Return to Camelot: Chivalry and the English Gentleman* (1981), Mark Girouard demonstrates the pervasiveness of attempts to recreate the Middle Ages in almost every facet of Victorian life, from tournaments, to costume, to literature, art, and statuary and the construction of medieval castles. Ideals of chivalry, as the nineteenth century understood them, including purity, high-mindedness, piety, self-sacrifice for the common good, loyalty, aristocratic sense of honor, patriotism, and enmity to all forms of villainy and wrongdoing, found their way into the charters of organizations from sports clubs to the Boy Scouts (Girouard 255–58)—and of course, into Stoker's heroic vampire killers. For, if the vampires are the medieval villains, the killers are the knightly heroes who show us how to teach them a thing or two.

A persistent sense of ancient supernatural evil, sinister and exciting, undefeatable even by Enlightenment rationalism or Victorian science, appears in nineteenth-century Gothic literature even when not set in the Middle Ages. Extricated from his folklore origins and dressed up, Stoker's Dracula, for example, takes the place of the old villains—infidels, black knights, devils, or dragons—in this revised popular mythology. In *Dracula: The Novel and the Legend* (1985), Clive Leatherdale says that Stoker saw his age as "undergoing a profound philosophical and moral crisis" and, in his novel, expressed a longing, shared by many, for a return to a time of piety and shared beliefs based on faith, before rationalism and science cast their stark light on them (201). Medieval and Arthurian values are represented in various ways, from Jonathan Harker's nostalgic fantasy of virtuous medieval womanhood (almost immediately undercut by the erotic shenanigans of Dracula's wives) to the pious vows of the band of "heroes" in their knightly quest to destroy Dracula.

After Stoker, this "placing" of his vampire was well established; most modern Dracula films show how good people should react to his supernatural malevolence with medieval heroism, high-mindedness, and the code of chivalry as it was more or less invented by the nineteenth century. Like folklore vampires, these modern descendents provide a link with perceived communal history and, in their defeat, offer assurance that what are imagined to be the old ways and old ideals—patriotism, courage, loyalty, for example—still hold true although they may have seemed to many in both the nineteenth and twentieth centuries to be sadly neglected.

It is the pseudo-medieval trappings and ambiance that count: the vampires need not be evil. Some modern vampires eschew villainy and opt for the knightly virtues. In Michael Romkey's *I, Vampire*, the vampire Mozart (the composer) trains new vampire disciple David Parker like a medieval squire so he can become a "knight" and join the good vampires' continuing battle against evil in the world. The showdown between Good and Evil takes place in a Bavarian castle out of a Gothic horror story, "a setting poisoned by centuries of violence, treachery, and an impenetrable darkness of spirit" (257). The vampire hero, like St. George, finally destroys the vampire villain, who actually appears in the shape of a dragon. On television, the courageous and high-minded vampire police detective in the popular television series *Forever Knight* is actually *named* Nicholas *Knight*.

The Romantic Past

In addition to ideals of virtue and order, the vampire—good or bad—carries the excitement of medieval romance, of the "olden days," into our humdrum world. In *Our Vampires, Ourselves* (1995), Nina Auerbach, praising the Lugosi portrayal of Dracula, says that "this soft-seeming foreigner possessed his century. He did so by giving the bleak decade of the 1930s a romantic past it had never had" (116). Bela Lugosi and Christopher Lee—not to mention Frank Langella—play the irresistible dark knights who swoop the excited maidens off for erotic thrills and chills, temporarily (at least) rescuing them from tedious respectability and propriety and some really boring men.

The vampire's subversion of contemporary expectations is what Auerbach admires most in vampire literature. She finds this admirable subversiveness in the vampire's *pastness*, his old-fashionedness; she says of Dracula that he "stands apart, an alternative to mass society, a cultivated remnant of a stately past our country never had, a forbidden lover in times that claim to forbid nothing, the king Americans are not supposed to want" (112). In the 1950s and 60s, says Auerbach, Hammer Films' *Horror of Dracula* and sequels burst into well-kept households, contemptuously ignoring all the maidenly and womanly virtues of modesty and diligence, of loving wifehood and motherhood, of shining kitchen floors and healthy meals. Instead, Christopher Lee's aristocratic Dracula "provided an image of disobedience," liberating these "good" women from dehumanizing domestic duties and responsibilities.

"Opening windows beyond the family and, in the guise of vampire victims, surging into themselves," says Auerbach (125), they willingly leap from their comfortable households and well-advised womanhood into the spontaneous romance and earthiness of a lost past.[3]

By their very pastness, vampires, good or bad, romantic or dull, create historical links. For us today, Stoker's *Dracula*, about a late-Medieval count, written in the late nineteenth century, and dramatized in the twentieth and twenty-first, encompasses all these time periods. Our awareness that he will surely turn up again very soon, in his own person or a barely concealed imitation, also offers us the reassuring promise of an endless future of cyclic returns. Within their stories, romantic vampires like Yarbro's Saint-Germain or Anne Rice's Lestat carry us along with them through their lengthy and varied existences. When they are not actually time traveling, they move back and forth in mind and memory, like Nicholas Knight or Angel, sometimes with nostalgia, but also to draw comparisons with their current circumstances and reinforce the lessons learned from their mistakes, say, in the seventeenth century. As living dead, they stand for both the loss of all that is past and its paradoxical aliveness in the present. As readers or viewers, we are free to identify with their histories and take them up as our own. Through the living dead, we acquire a sense of the past that we did not have before.

For we moderns neither wish to restore the past nor to bury it for all time. What we wish is to *have* a past. Our need for a past, real or fictitious, is as much a part of our humanness as our anticipation of the future. And many recent vampire works, like Kostova's *The Historian* or even Coppola's *Bram Stoker's Dracula*, are partial tributes to both the real and the fictitious past.

Some vampire writers shamelessly teach history lessons. In Chelsea Quinn Yarbro's works, the same vampire protagonists reappear from novel to novel in different well-researched centuries, involved with actual historical figures and events. In *Hotel Transylvania* (1978), Yarbro introduces us to the vampire "le Comte de Saint-Germain" in pre-Revolutionary France, but he shows up in an earlier age, a friend of the Medicis in Renaissance Italy in *The Palace* (1979), and in ancient Egypt in *Out of the House of Life* (1990). Olivia Clemens, the vampire protagonist in Yarbro's *A Flame in Byzantium* (1987), is able to contrast her restricted life as a woman in Byzantium in the sixth century with her previous freedom and authority in imperial Rome. Yarbro's protagonists, male or female, are fully involved in the cultural, social, and even political events of their current era. But as survivors from previous places and times, remembering and comparing, they experience a sense of historical change and continuity that we follow along with them. Yarbro is not alone in this historical awareness. In Elrod and Greenberg's collection of eighteen vampire stories, *The Time of the Vampires* (1996), each story is by a different author and each is set in a different historical era. They are arranged chronologically from ancient Greece and Rome to a modern hematology research lab in America. Many of the stories are followed by authors' comments on the historical accuracy of the events and/or settings.

In Kim Newman's vampire trilogy, both Kate Reed (the protagonist) and Dracula, among others, survive from Victorian England to World War I to Rome in the 1950s. The works of novelists like Yarbro and Newman are based on a thorough knowledge of time and place, even when modified by the insertion of fictitious characters and events. For example, in Newman's *Anno Dracula*, Dracula has not died but has married Queen Victoria and is now Prince Consort and actual ruler of England. But, given this premise, we see an England that we might expect, with its familiar citizens, fictional and real, behaving as we think they might under such appalling circumstances, with only some surprises.

In retelling history, vampire novelists like Yarbro and Newman not only revive the past but offer the reader a chance to view it from different perspectives involving different possibilities. Moreover, by peopling the novels with both fictitious characters and actual historical figures, they make a complex statement about the relation of art to life and the way fiction(s) may replace or even supersede history, as, for example, Newman's Bram Stoker is executed by Stoker's fictitious Dracula. It is often surprising how well the two mesh or how, as we know in many cases, fantastic fictional occurrences make as much sense as actual ones. Newman also demonstrates the extent to which fictional figures like Dracula and Sherlock Holmes become integral to our own image of this earlier age, so that visitors to London line up for the vampire tour or eagerly search Baker Street for the apartments of Sherlock Holmes.

Such works also draw lessons from history. Newman's *The Bloody Red Baron*, about World War I, is a scathing indictment of the English people's deliberate ignorance of the slaughter taking place on battlefields while officers sat smugly behind the lines. Dan Simmons's novel *Children of the Night* gives us a good deal of accurately researched history of Dracula and Romania and of the country's dreadful misery under the tyranny and downfall of the monstrous Ceausescu and the Communist government. Like Newman and many other writers of vampire literature, he reminds us that the real evil of this world has not been perpetrated by supernatural beings. The novel's historical message underscores the importance of knowing a country's past in order to understand its present, especially when that country is still very much trapped in its past. Both past and present are embodied in the lives and minds of the Romanian vampires. Like the nation itself, they must resolve, in themselves, the conflict between old ways and new possibilities. For this is another lesson: whether we are aware of it or not, we all, even Americans, stand drawn between the tradition and security of the past, the comfort of the present, and the risks and enticements of the future.

Yet these authors also caution against romanticizing and sentimentalizing the Middle Ages or any other past. Newman's Dracula is a Gothic villain who cannot understand that medieval tortures are not generally popular in nineteenth-century London and may incite revolt. Ensconced as the new Prince Consort to Queen Victoria, he still lives in medieval chaos and squalor in Buckingham Palace, and his heavy-handed approach to government, supposedly so effective in fifteenth-century Transylvania, creates poverty, crime, and disorder in nineteenth-century England. Through Dracula, Newman disparages the Victorian (and modern) romanticizing of medieval heroics that pervades Bram Stoker's novel and that got England into the horrors of the Great War in the first place (and we might add, in the guise of John Wayne and "kicking butt," has mired the United States in another hopeless mess). Dracula is not killed by heroic knights, but flies from England as a giant bat—to show up again in *The Bloody Red Baron* as Graf von Dracula, behind the scenes manipulator of the German air force, for which his crude brutality and contempt for life perfectly suit him; however, his use of medieval war tactics proves disastrous for him and the German offensive. Another vampire, Lord Ruthven in *Anno Dracula*, mocks Dracula as " 'festering in medieval superstition' " (48) while imagining that he is modern. Ironically, the revolution against Dracula's control of England is "a minor Arthurian revival," which Dracula combats by banning Tennyson's *Idylls of the King* and William Morris's *Defence of Guenevere* (*Anno* 258).

Elizabeth Kostova's *The Historian: A Novel* is *about* history and its continual reemergence in the here and now—toward which she expresses an ambivalent attitude. The unnamed narrator leads us through a tangled search from present to past and back, pursuing her father as he seeks out the still rapacious and destructive Dracula. Ironically, Dracula himself turns out to be a ruthless historian with a truly enviable library of ancient and modern documents collected throughout his long lifetime. The whole book frolics in the love of historical research and the discovery of obscure historical connections as the narrator draws us through various libraries, monasteries, villages, palaces, and ruins from France to Greece to Romania and Bulgaria, and even Istanbul, to locate Dracula's burial place and discover the truth about his death.

The author's research is so thorough and convincing that we are in danger of being lost between what is real and what is fantasy, especially as she adopts Stoker's fiction that the historical Vlad Dracula *was* actually a vampire—who yet survives, a danger to all, but particularly to librarians and historians, whose services he covets in his own pursuit of a place in history.

She also creates a new fiction that Vlad has at least one actual descendent, an innocent victim of his heartless and egotistic machinations. In this novel, Dracula *is* history, both a lesson and a danger to the present (and happily is brought to bay, for once, not by knights or priests but by librarians and academics). Yet at the very end, we know he lives on and are glad of it. History, both its reality and its myths, is an intricate all-pervasive continuity that survives in remote places, secret letters, mysterious documents, and personal recollections. It impinges on all our lives, sometimes in unexpected ways, telling us of vast networks of relationships we could never have guessed at, but which make up our present selves.

Continuity with the Past

Carrying with him the folklore, culture, and literature of his past, the vampire embodies a historical continuity that we have ostensibly abandoned. In the United States, we have been raised to believe, almost as a religion, that the American Way of Life was founded on a complete break from our European past. We apparently believe that such breaks are endlessly repeatable, even now, even from our own (relatively meager) history. We are eager to blot out custom and tradition in favor of the "latest thing" and to contemn those who will not follow. In our public primary and secondary schools, the only history we really teach is American history, and very little of that. We rewrite European songs and stories and even movies and call them our own without reference to their origins (not to mention foreign discoveries and inventions). Yet, in much vampire lore and literature, history is everything. No doubt the popularity of the vampire in its many forms derives partly from its ability to convey this "sense of the past" that Henry James so often noticed is missing in the United States—and is increasingly missed today as the young become more aware (ironically, through modern technology and the media) of their ties to the greater world beyond their personal lives and local stories.

Much of vampire literature strives to recover this sense of the past—literary, mythical, and historical. According to Gregory A. Waller, the typical vampire story inculcates "the importance of traditional wisdom, symbolic and sacred objects, and ritualized action" drawn from previous vampire literature (7). Those who would destroy the vampire, for example, must learn, says Waller, "that the present struggle—the story they are living—must be understood in relation to previous struggles, previous stories" (8). Thus, Waller insists on the "larger cultural significance" of this genre in the "history of ideas and shifting ideological assumptions" (10). Although Waller focuses primarily on examples of the vampire as enemy, all vampire stories, even those about "good vampires," draw on and operate within this extended narrative, even when it is most innovative. Ever since Dracula related his family history to Jonathan Harker, vampires have continued to expound on their origins, their families, their loves, their travels, their suffering, and on and on, from, say, ancient Egypt, right down to the present—a performance that would be impossible if they had died like ordinary people.

Moreover, many vampires are said actually to *contain* the knowledge of the ages in the lives and deaths they have passed through and to carry it with them. In his book of essays on the Renaissance (1893), Walter Pater praises Leonardo da Vinci's *Mona Lisa* as a "vampire" because "she has been dead many times, and learned the secrets of the grave; and has been a diver in deep seas, and keeps their fallen day about her . . ." (99). In Barbara Hambly's *Those Who Hunt the Night*, the vampires absorb the psyches of their victims along with their blood so that their minds become "abysses of dark memory" (241)—"so rich, so deep, so filled with the colors of living, and so thick with the overtints of all the lives it has taken" (265). It is this persistence of memory that confers immortality, after all, along with the expansion and enrichment of the self that would be one of the perks of being immortal. Failure to remember is what makes Weyland in Suzy McKee Charnas's *The Unicorn Tapestry* (1980) so disappointing as a vampire. He has immortality and the enviable ability to learn very fast, but if he forgets when he hibernates, he might as well be dead, for his *life*, as we understand life, with its relationships and contexts, is gone.

In contrast, in *I, Vampire*, Michael Romkey also plays with the vampires' ability to encompass past and present within their own minds. At one point, one of the old vampires (Mozart) admonishes the new vampire narrator David Parker to study history (198), to exercise his vast powers of mind to become, eventually, a creature of "high culture" (124). Vampires from various historical eras interact in the present time. Although living in the twentieth century, Parker finds himself consorting with a "rescued" daughter of Czar Nicholas, and with Rasputin (84), whom he joins in the old battle against evil vampires like Cesare Borgia and Jack the Ripper (Prince Albert Victor, in this version).

Christopher Golden's *Of Saints and Shadows* (1994) is full of (not particularly convincing) historical vampires from Genghis Khan to Buffalo Bill, going back even to Lazarus, few of whom even know each other, much less compare histories. But Peter Octavian, the vampire protagonist, born in 1420, the illegitimate son of Constantine the Eleventh, is said to be "a living piece of history" in the modern world (123). So, in all these works, at least the *sense* of a history is there, and the modern world appears as floating on a river of space and time to which it ever belongs. In all these novels, the continual moving backward and forward in history, however muddled or haphazardly drawn the history might be, allows readers vicariously to transcend time, to take an objective perspective that assures some interrelatedness and meaningfulness in its progression. Past, present, and future become one. And the vampire, as Octavian points out, can remember it all (127).

Within the texts, from "The Mysterious Stranger" to *Buffy*, the more traditional lore the protagonist knows, the more capable he or she is of defeating the vampire. The more previous vampire literature the audience knows, the more it can appreciate what is going on. Thus, through the vampire, the past is given an authority that modern American culture often denies it—the authority to know something worth knowing. Yet, while free movement in time and space is common in vampire literature, only a very few writers are concerned to be factually accurate. Radu Florescu and Raymond McNally have shown us how Stoker and the cinema have distorted the history of Romania and turned a national hero into an undead, blood-drinking Gothic monster. Anne Rice's vampires move all over space and time but in a fantastic world that often seems to be drawn from old movies like *The Mummy* or *The Phantom of the Opera* rather than even casual cultural or historical research. But perhaps it is not so important that the past be realistically portrayed as it is that the work conveys a *sense of a past* that, in the person of the vampire, continues to act on the present. This is the most important lesson from the undead: we are all trapped in the flow, or cycle, of history, tumbling along with others—dead and undead—whether we like it or not.

3

Vampires and Psychology

Body, Soul, and Self

We die into history, but we die away from ourselves, our family and friends, and they from us. On a personal level, vampire folklore and literature function to assuage the fear of our own death and to lessen sorrow at the loss of loved ones. In doing so, it must appeal to and express our ideas about individual psychology, concepts of the soul and the self, their relation to the body, and their possible survival after bodily death.

Vampire lore and literature offer a chance to explore and deal with—accept or deny—the inevitable horror of decay and death that nature imposes. The vampire stands for the impossible "what if": "What if I do not have to die?" "What if natural law—or God's law—*can* be broken?" The vampire embodies (so to speak) our instinctive, "Oh, no! Not me!" to the threat of ultimate nothingness. According to sociologists Robert Fulton and Robert Bendiksen in the introduction to their collection on *Death and Identity*, the conviction that the individual does not die—that there is ultimately no death—that in some way, somewhere, he or she will continue to exist, is innate and universal. It derives "primarily as a result of the way the human mind fundamentally functions" (5). Fear of death and the search for alternatives are not neurotic symptoms or mental aberrations or moral weaknesses.

However, even some vampire fans believe their preoccupation to be to some degree delusional. Clive Leatherdale, for example, in discussing folklore vampires, hints that because the living cannot imagine themselves as physically and spiritually nonexistent, they cannot imagine the dead as nonexistent either, but project their own desires on them, including the desire to come back (17–22). Human beings, he says condescendingly, have "always held a morbid preoccupation with the deceased" (17). But Leatherdale also reminds us (as did Calmet in the eighteenth century) that the folk who believed in vampires had ample encouragement in the stories of reanimated saints and in the rising of Christ and the promise that, by consuming His body and blood, they too could live on somewhere, somehow (21)—a belief still very widely held. The greatest appeal of Christianity, after all, is the promise of personal immortality based on the idea of an invisible but very real, individual soul that thinks and feels and functions in the other world very much as if it had its body.

Soul and Body

The idea of the soul and its relationship to the body is basic to vampire folklore and literature. Sometimes, it can be quite independent. Veselin Čajkanović points out that, in some Slavic folklore, even in life the soul can separate from the body and float about on its own or transfer from one body to another (270–71, note***). Such ideas survive in some modern vampire movies: In Mario Bava's movie *Black Sunday* (1960), the vampire strives to rise from the tomb to live again in the body of her descendent Katya; and again, in *Planet of the Vampires* (1965) outer space vampires succeed in coming to earth disguised in the bodies of astronauts. In Joss Whedon's television series *Buffy* and *Angel*, souls seem to come and go and move around all the time, especially Spike's and Angel's. Perhaps the most extreme example of a "wandering soul" in a literary tale occurs in John Metcalfe's "The Feasting Dead" (1954): the vampire soul variously inhabits dolls, a scarecrow, and a little dog.

Nevertheless, in much vampire folklore, even an ordinary soul cannot immediately and entirely exit the body at death but remains in the area, suspended between this world and the next, until decomposition is complete. Until this happens, according to Danforth, the recently deceased are thought to be "sentient" in their coffins and able to hear what the living are saying and doing. Their ultimate aim, however, is—or should be—to set out on their destined journey to the other world (127). There is a parallel between the decay of the body and the departure of the soul; the faster the body decays, the sooner the soul can reach its destination (49). A person may become a vampire simply by the failure of the body to decay properly. Or, the willful persistence of the soul can, in some cases, lead to the survival and reanimation of the flesh.

These conflicting views that the soul of the deceased is both *in* the body and *out* of it find echoes in popular belief today that, from the moment of death, the souls of the dead live on somewhere, sometimes sleeping but often fully alert to what is going on in the living world. Philippe Ariès in his study *The Hour of Our Death* shows how this belief revived in the seventeenth century and became widespread in the nineteenth and twentieth centuries. Even today, we are aware of the common practice of saying goodbye to the recently deceased in their caskets, as though they can hear and understand. In the HBO series *Six Feet Under* (2001–2005) about the operations of a funeral parlor, the deceased are often shown to respond to these addresses (even those of the embalmer), no doubt to convey the perception of the bereaved that they have been heard and understood. The popularity of mediums, like John Edwards on the Sci-Fi Channel's *Crossing Over* (1999–2004) suggests that even the not-so-recently-dead really can communicate, even in television studios, no matter where their bodies may be. In both cases, the soul is assumed to retain the unique personality of the deceased. The soul *is* the person. It is not such a far step from this to assume that a strong soul might be able to climb back into its body—or *some* body—and make it work.

In folk cultures, as we know, various funerary practices are aimed at encouraging the soul to move on as quickly as possible. The bereaved address the deceased personally, by name, as they knew him in life. Danforth tells us that, following a death, the soul of the deceased is believed to wander around the area for a number of days in something like its human form (45–46). He quotes a Greek mourner as saying:

> "At death the soul emerges in its entirety, like a man. It has the shape of a man, only it's invisible. It has a mouth and hands and eats real food just like we do. When you see someone in your dreams, it's the soul you see. People in your dreams eat, don't they? The souls of the dead eat too." (46)

The laments addressed to the dead are personalized. Personal items are included in their graves, and they are offered their favorite foods to take on their journey. These practices maintain awareness of the individual identity of the deceased, not as a misty wraith, but as a personality with an ongoing history.

This interaction with the souls of the recent dead allows for the tying up of loose ends in the personal lives of both deceased and mourners, such as reconciling disagreements, reestablishing friendships and family relationships, apologizing for wrongs, and completing other unfinished business. Explaining the strange practice of the "wedding of the dead," which is the focus of her book, Kligman tells us that people who leave behind unfinished personal matters, like an unfulfilled love affair or some hiatus in the usual progression of life, may return in the bodies that they no longer inhabit as *strigoi*, the unwanted living dead. Thus, in case of the death of an unmarried person of marriageable age, a symbolic wedding with a sweetheart or a volunteer member of the community or Christ is performed as part of the funeral. The deceased is dressed in wedding clothes in the coffin and something like a wedding service is performed as part of the funeral (Kligman 216–18).

Kligman suggests that these weddings and the laments that accompany them explore the relationship between marriage and death as major life-changing events (see 215–48). More important in my view, the link drawn between marriage and death "humanizes the eternity of death by locating it (via kin obligations) in an ongoing web of human social relations" (Kligman 244). A married person is a full adult member of his or her society that she will join in the other world. The death of self or other thus seems less frightening and less final. In a note, Kligman reminds us that there are "inversions" of death weddings in Stoker's *Dracula*, between Arthur and Lucy, and Dracula and his victims, whom he regards as his "family" (357, note 42). In her view, such literature, like folklore and its ritual context, provides a means by which taboo topics may be thought of although not actualized—an opportunity provided in various ways by almost all vampire literature.

But the main function of these funerary rituals is to make sure that the dead will stay dead. The bereaved are consoled by knowing that their loved ones are happy, for death does not mean abandonment of one's unique identity but instead is a comfortable extension of it into another world. Continued interactions between the living and the dead through periodic ritual meals, for example, remind the living that the dead are *actually* still with them, taking an active interest in their lives. Moreover, Perkowski tells us, in the case of vampires, "The dead who seem not to be totally dead, are killed to the survivors' full emotional satisfaction, wiping out feelings of guilt, fear, and false hope" (*Darkling* 123). The freed soul of the (staked or beheaded or etc.) vampire is sent off on its journey at peace with those left behind. Finally, the vampire's "fate worse than death" assures the living that, after all, a normal passing is for the best.

Many fictional vampires also emphasize the misery and grossness entailed in not dying. "Life-in-Death" is a terrible punishment for Coleridge's Ancient Mariner. If his enemy's curse against him holds, Byron's mysterious Giaour will survive in an earthly torment of his own making, hunting and destroying those he loves the most. Varney's prolonged life in Rymer's *Varney the Vampyre* is so stressful that he finally (after 868 pages in 220 chapters) jumps into Mount Vesuvius. And, of course, in Stoker's *Dracula* (and most dramatizations of it) Lucy's vampirization illustrates the wrongness—or at least the tawdriness—of surviving in this unnatural life. In Tod Browning's film of Stoker's novel (1931), Bela Lugosi's Dracula says with conviction, "To die, to be *really* dead—that must be glorious!" Of all its meanings, then, the most obvious function of vampires like Dracula is to reconcile the reader to God's incomprehensible intentions in letting us die.

Death Personified

The natural horror of death can be minimized somewhat by personifying it—as a malevolent devil figure or as a lover and friend—or as a god. Lawson tells us how the Greek peasants he studied imagine death as Charos, the god of the lower world (98), sometimes cruel and sometimes compassionate. Danforth says that, in some Greek funeral laments, Death becomes the spouse (81): "Just as a man at death is said to take 'the black earth' as his wife, so a woman at death is said to take Haros, or less frequently Hades, as her husband" (82). Like Kligman, Danforth sees such "marriages" as an attempt to reconcile the opposition between life and death (83). Kligman says that to the Romanian villagers she studied, "Death is active; it involves passage and transformation. At the same time, death is objectified; it has form in time and space" (174). To these villagers, death is a woman, and they sometimes curse her like an actual person (175). As an active being with bodily functions, death has physical needs, including an insatiable appetite; very much like a vampire, she "devours the living to maintain her physical well-being" (207).

Widespread folktales about playing games with Death or buying Death off in some way express the wish to exert control over it. The vampire, too, often plays this role and like Charos, humanized into a familiar figure, might easily be thwarted or mollified—with garlic, a good meal, or a stake, or might even be outwitted. Vampire literature demonstrates many ways that death-dealing vampires might be warded off or defeated—and more important, assures us that it *can* be done.

Although in many folklore accounts of vampire attacks, the deceased heads straight for home to "embrace" his spouse or lover, garden variety folklore vampires are almost never sexy or seductive. Kligman's Romanian death weddings are social occasions marking life stages, not romantic trysts, and the spouse is not a vampire. Links between sex and death occur primarily in vampire folktales of the demon lover kind as retold by writers like Johann Wolfgang Goethe in his poem "The Bride of Corinth" (1797). The dead fiancée returns to claim her betrothed:

> "From my grave betimes I have been driven,
> I seek the good I lost, none shall me thwart,
> I seek his love to whom my troth was given,
> And I have sucked the lifeblood from his heart." (26)[1]

Demon lovers do, no doubt, provide models for some obsessive modern vampires who, even after centuries, return in a sort of frenzy to claim their lost loves, like the two movie Draculas played by Jack Palance and Gary Oldman. As for *seducing* victims to their deaths (like Keats's "La Belle Dame sans Merci"), well, folklore village vampires are not, after all, the attractive and elegant aristocrats of modern literature, but rough peasants in rural communities—and not usually the most popular ones either. And when some occasionally do assault their spouses (even to asphyxiation), they are, after all, just going home.

Nevertheless, many modern critics continue to believe that *all* vampires, folkloric and literary, are sexual—overtly or covertly. Along with a few vampire authors, they interpret the vampire as representing the unacceptable sexual Other within us—or without—that we do not wish to acknowledge. Such views generally appear in the context of modern depth psychology, Freudian or Jungian, or possibly feminist or queer theory, and define the vampire in terms of unconscious sexual desires and fears. The sexual interpretations have become so prevalent that they seem to have established themselves for many as the one and only explanation for the vampire's existence. For this reason, we need to say something about them here—and for another reason as well. The other reason is that they have a great deal of legitimacy, even when they contradict each other; for the vampire *is* a sexual figure, whose sexual energy, as I wish to show in a later chapter, is intrinsic to his (or her) very meaning as a god of death.

Sometimes, however, we may feel that these sexual interpretations go a bit far: they find a lot of sex where the rest of us did not even notice it and then insist that this is the reason that we enjoy the works. Ernest Jones, in his psychoanalytic work *On the Nightmare*, published in 1931, discusses the psychological basis of vampire folk belief (98–130): "It may be said at the outset that the latent content of the belief yields plain indications of most kinds of sexual perversions, and that the belief assumes various forms according as this or that perversion is more prominent" (98). Most psychoanalytic criticism related to vampires focuses on Bram Stoker's *Dracula*. Maurice Richardson, in "The Psychoanalysis of Ghost Stories," says: "From a Freudian standpoint—and from no other does the story really make any sense—it is seen as a kind of incestuous, necrophilous, oral-anal-sadistic all-in wrestling match" (427). Phyllis A. Roth finds Bram Stoker's neurotic fear of sex and women to be the clue to his novel's popularity; it allows readers "to act out" their own "essentially threatening, even horrifying wishes," based in the "lustful anticipation of an oral fusion with the mother" (*Bram Stoker* 111). Judith Weissman concurs: "The vampire, an ancient figure of horror in folk tales, undoubtedly represents in any story some kind of sexual terror . . ." (392). Others, like Christopher Craft and Andrew Schopp, regard vampire literature as a disguised opportunity, as Schopp says, "for acting out socially prohibited roles, and for reconfiguring desire" (241).

In fact, many recent critics take as a given that the vampire is first and foremost "a source of both erotic anxiety and corrupt desire," and that this is the primary source of its popularity (Gordon and Hollinger 1). In literature, the vampire often appears as a kind of wicked double of a "good" and innocent character. Carmilla becomes the darkly sensual double of her victim Laura, seducing her nearly to death; Dracula appears as the evil double of the harmlessly lecherous Van Helsing. Whatever external threats the vampire may pose are enhanced by its appeal to inner needs and desires. Polidori's Lord Ruthven, for example, draws out his victims' secret vanity, lust, and greed; he is the ultimate enabler of self-destructive vices, flattering and cajoling his victims into gambling, debauchery, and crime. Sometimes we feel that his trick is being played on us, for, taking the hint from these earlier works, some later writers cram their stories and films with graphic sex and violence, in the effort, apparently, to draw out—and profit from—any (and every) possible repressed wish-fulfilling horrors of their readers. Examples abound. In the fifties and sixties, Hammer Films introduced the handsome and sexy Christopher Lee and his erotic women, who shocked and delighted audiences by splattering around huge quantities of bright red blood while terrorizing and sexually assaulting their (often willing) victims—just a precursor to the bloody sexual frolics of movies like *Bordello of Blood* (1996) or *From Dusk Till Dawn* (1996).

In S. P. Somtow's novel *Vampire Junction* (1984) the youthful vampire Timmy Valentine regards himself as a focused image out of Jung's collective unconscious (16), a "distillation" (17) of the shadow side of all humans, their "death wish" (51). Scott Baker's *Ancestral Hungers* (1995) moves us into a violent and erotic interior world, a kind of Freudian/Jungian wet dream of incest, torture, murder, and assorted sexual perversions. A French movie *Two Orphan Vampires* (1996) equates the bloodthirsty little vampires, Henriette and Louise, with "your dreams": "We are you, and you are us," they tediously intone. The effect of these psychological approaches is to portray the vampire not as a dead member of a community, but as a threatening personification of the internal Other and its vicious, unconscious, and not-so-exclusive desires.

Vampire literature is hardly alone, of course, in equating sex and death. Philippe Ariès comments on the tendency of the nineteenth and twentieth centuries to combine "Eros and Thanatos," in what he calls "a new category of disturbing and morbid phenomena" (369). This has its origins as early as the sixteenth century, when images of death "become charged with a sensuality previously unknown" (370). For love and death, "corruption and fertility," are nature's two assaults against human order, reason, and sense of self. By the nineteenth century, people were forced to recognize that nature was inside them (395), corrupting them from within.

In *The Gothic Imagination: Expansion in Gothic Literature and Art* (1982), Linda Bayer-Berenbaum criticizes Gothic literature for its over-preoccupation with extremes of experience—nightmares, insanity, sexual excess, and death—that challenge the sense of an integrated and rational self (30–31). Worse still, she points out, barriers between the self and the world, the real and the imaginary, civilization and nature, the physical and the spiritual are often unclear or broken down. The most subversive tenet "beneath the Gothic gimmicks" is "an expansion of consciousness and reality" (21). To Bayer-Berenbaum the most attractive and terrifyingly ambiguous figure is the vampire, who crosses forbidden barriers and threatens essential categories (all, we might point out, without losing an iota of his own self-awareness and self-control). For whether the vampire stands for the unconscious or for a suspicious foreigner or a dominating father figure or just death, it threatens the genetically and culturally constituted identity of the victims and their own self-concepts. Once attacked, the vampire's victim is never the same again.

In contrast, Terry Heller, in his book *The Delights of Terror: An Aesthetics of the Tale of Terror* (1987), argues that the vampire's ambiguity of identity *helps* us to formulate and maintain our own sense of a self in the world against assaults from the unconscious, from our "unsatisfied natural desires" (81). In defeating Dracula, Mina and Jonathan reaffirm and strengthen their own conscious identity threatened by the vampire. For the reader, the pleasures of *Dracula* are those of risking and then reasserting control over the ego or identity (83–84). Both Bayer-Berenbaum and Heller put forward a modern secular dualism in which the *desires* (nature, the body) remain distinct from the *self*, which is somehow higher and better—or at least individualized and our own. In these approaches, we are assumed to identify with the actual or potential victims threatened by the vampire (which I suspect is not always the case).

But of the two consuming dangers to the self, sex is temporary and intermittent (and often unavailable). Death is unavoidable. Christian promises of a vague spiritual immortality hardly seem to make up for the loss of *life*—personal identity and solid physical presence in this familiar world. Folkloric burial practices, acknowledging this human regret, are designed to assure the deceased (and themselves) that she remains the same person, only going on to a different place. Moreover, if she refuses to go, she faces an even more devastating loss of personal identity as a zombie-like, predatory undead that no one wants around. In the folklore surrounding vampire belief, a dead person can remain in contact with his self and his familiar world only by graciously leaving it. And of course, as an additional bonus, the folk also have the promise of the church assuring the ultimate resurrection of the body as well. Yet the folklorists Richard and Eva Blum consistently found a good deal of dissatisfaction among the Greek peasants regarding the church's teachings. Their formulation of an elaborate system of supernatural creatures like vampires to explain illness and death indicates their desire for something more concretely manageable than the mysterious Will of God and the promise of a remote paradise.

Doubts and fears about death do not belong exclusively to Greek and Slavic peasants. Among the educated in England as early as the sixteenth century, Robert N. Watson finds that, in spite of church teaching, much literature and even religious writing indirectly reveal the writer's fear that death meant not salvation but, instead, annihilation and loss of self. We fear the loss of our unique personality, says Watson, which we have "so tentatively and laboriously carved out of the world" (20). By the nineteenth century, with the spread of Protestantism and the rise of a contradictory scientific worldview, traditional Christian teachings were necessarily much modified or rejected entirely. Faith, no longer supported by strong community or institutional authority, seemed to have become merely a matter of arbitrary choice or hopeful believing.

In the meantime, the Romantic Revolution had encouraged assertion of individualism and exploration of the self. We have only to think of Wordsworth's insistent exposition of the growth of his own thoughts and feelings in *The Prelude*. In Byron's *Manfred* (1817)—like *The Giaour*, a study of a single melodramatically tormented soul—the protagonist, before he dies, declares the predominance and persistence of the individual mind beyond death:

> "The mind which is immortal makes itself
> Requital for its good or evil thoughts,—
> Is its own origin of ill and end—
> And its own place and time— . . ." (3.4.129–32)

—an approving restatement of a sentiment with which Satan condemns himself in book 1 of Milton's *Paradise Lost* (1:254–55), where he sets his own will against the will of God. But to Byron, man need no longer be a passive victim; he has the greatness of mind to formulate his own spiritual destiny. The persistence of self becomes the very meaning of immortality.

In the meantime, according to Ariès, popular religion was already anticipating and leaping over the complications created by Christian theology and the tension of Byronic rebellion to come up with a new and mellower view of the self as an independent entity that simply lives on in another life after this one, only better. The increased emphasis on the individual in the nineteenth century resulted in two new and significant elements in what Ariès calls "the romantic death": (1) the view of death as a joy, a release from earthly suffering into "the immensity of the beyond" (as opposed to undergoing an awful judgment), and (2) the eventual reunion with loved ones in the afterlife (as opposed to an impersonal spirituality no longer affected by the needs and attachments of the living) (436). These popular but unorthodox ideas of a joyful and purified soul, free of earthly hardships and sins, are oddly in accord with the folk beliefs in the cultures that gave rise to the vampire in the first place, and many of them find expression, as well, in modern vampire literature (and, I would suspect, in much modern thinking—although recently there have been some loud huzzahs in favor of harsh punishments for others).

Along with them came a new but widely accepted unorthodoxy about the separation of the soul from the body at death. Instead of traditional doctrine about the eventual resurrection of the soul and the body on Judgment Day, the soul becomes the true and complete identity and the body only a temporary residence that it leaves behind forever at death (Ariès 457–58). It is the soul that has uniqueness and meaning in and out of this life, not the body; however, the soul often appears as a ghostly form of the body, like the dead Catherine and Heathcliff traipsing about the moors in Emily Bronte's *Wuthering Heights*. In the popular social phenomenon of occultism, especially spirit rapping and ghostly séances, the already resurrected and happy dead (they are always happy) can communicate with their living relatives and even become visible through a recognizable misty or ectoplasmic form.

Indeed, nineteenth-century dead are every bit as social as those of the Slavic peasants and every bit as much in need of human company. And it is in this social milieu that the vampire rises again. Death, says Ariès, has become not a time of wrenching separation or terrifying judgment but "a step toward the reunions of eternity." Popular consolation literature of the time taught readers to look toward the "heavenly home," says Ariès, where "people found everything that made them happy on earth—that is, love, affection, family—without what made them sad—that is, separation" (452): "In the beautiful death of the nineteenth and twentieth centuries, the room of the dying man is filled with disembodied friends and relatives who have come from the other world to assist and guide him in this first migration" (460)—much like the family gatherings at Slavic and Greek funerals. Whereas in folklore the soul can be loosed only by the total dissolution of the flesh, in nineteenth-century popular belief, the soul's release happens automatically and immediately upon death. For the soul no longer needs the body, says Ariès; it has come to be viewed as "the essential principle of the individual, his immortal part" (456).

Paradoxically, along with belief in a free-floating soul came a new interest in cemeteries and tombs—an interest that perhaps explains their prominence as vampire "homes." This too has folklore parallels. Blum and Blum point to the inconsistency in folklore: "Concepts of a separate abode of the soul from which it could not return . . . blended without apparent conflict into concepts of the lasting power and influence of the dead in the neighborhood of his grave-site . . ." (318). Similarly, in the nineteenth century, says Ariès, we find two views of the dead: "Memory and immortal soul on the one hand; vague subterranean survival on the other. The first could dispense with the tomb; the second turns the tomb into the scene of a physical presence" (526). The latter view is expressed in the nineteenth century in the excessive displays of mourning, elaborate funerals, and almost palatial tombs for those who could afford them. In either case, the *self* lives on. In Stoker's *Dracula*, for example, Lucy, after being staked, and other normal dead like her mother apparently pass quickly into immortal soul-dom while Dracula's coffins provide him with the "subterranean survival" from which to maintain a physical presence. (The need for "native soil" was Stoker's idea.)

Soul and Self

If, for all of us, the soul (and the self?) can live on in eternal bliss and even fuzzy visibility, the vampire's attachment to his cadaver is a kind of indecency. In folklore, for example, once the vampire's soul has completely departed, the body (the skeleton, really) is left without a self, that is, without a personal identity. It is just a cadaver. In the journey to the other world, the soul and the self are the same. No real attempt is made to distinguish between them.

Most modern writers also have difficulty with this distinction. For some writers, to leave the undead with a fully functioning personality would seem to be unacceptable. A simple solution is to portray their vampires as soulless and self-less brutes. Ambrose Bierce begins "The Death of Halpin Frayser" (1893) with this distinction between ghosts (souls) and vampires (bodies):

> For by death is wrought greater change than hath been shown. Whereas in general the spirit that removed cometh back upon occasion, and is sometimes seen of those in flesh (appearing in the form of the body it bore) yet it hath happened that the veritable body without the spirit hath walked. And it is attested of those encountering who have lived to speak thereon that a lich so raised up hath no natural affection, nor remembrance thereof, but only hate. Also, it is known that some spirits which in life were benign become by death evil altogether—HALL. (145)

Other mindless zombie-like vampires are ruthless predators, as in Frank Norris's "Grettir at Thorhall-Stead" (1903), whose attacks require no other explanation. In movies, brain-dead soulless vampires are often replaced by their close relatives, cannibalistic zombies, as in *Night of the Living Dead.*

The distinction between soul and self, spirit and personality, is a very tricky thing, and it is interesting to see what modern vampire literature makes of it. In folklore, the soul/self (even retaining an invisible appearance) floats around a bit and then goes off to join the family in the other world. In much vampire literature, however, the word *soul* is tossed about a good deal without giving us any clear understanding of what it might mean—probably because Stoker did it. Stoker took some old pagan rural folklore and padded it over with assorted Christian implications that it never had. He did not seem to understand what Davanzati and Calmet recognized immediately, that these old superstitions and the practices that accompanied them had almost nothing to do with Christianity or its Heaven or Hell—any more than putting out food for Santa Claus or throwing salt over one's shoulder to avoid bad luck. Folklore vampires are not necessarily damned to Hell (unless they were heretics or excommunicated, and these conditions were easily remedied by a priest with a little holy water). Official inquiries into the disinterring and staking of supposed vampires were concerned with the issue of desecrating the dead, not with finding and punishing vampires. Like elves or fairies, vampires were only interesting to religious authorities if they turned out to be real or if belief in them interfered with or contradicted Christian doctrine.

But writers like Polidori or Stoker did not want to write about soulless liches. They wanted to write about satanic villains like Byron, who, to be suitably dangerous and interesting, must have vital force and supernatural powers. But in calling their vampire villains *soulless,* modern writers leave us wondering, in this modern world, what that means. Obviously, their personalities remain intact. David Punter calls Dracula "a manic individualist" (2:19), who offers his victims the immortality of the body, "but disunited from soul," in a kind of inversion of Christianity (2:20). Apparently, to Punter, the survival of a unique and assertive *self*—of reason, passion, and will, not to mention memory, experience, and superpowers—is bought at the cost of loss of a sort of amorphous *soul.*

One author who recognizes the problem and tries, at least, to define *soul* is Brian W. Aldiss. In his *Dracula Unbound,* our *soul* lies in "an inner consciousness, detached from daily happening" (125; funnily enough, what the hippies used to call the *self,* as in, "I am dropping out [of society] to find my*self*"). To Aldiss, Christ brought to humankind the idea of "the value of the individual," "the idea of individual salvation," which was "consciousness raising" (125). In this approach, the sense of the self and the idea of an immortal soul turn out to be the same thing, after all, and Aldiss illustrates this by making most of his vampires rather generically mindless and monstrous (but not all of them—or where would be the interest?). However, this supposed distinction relies on a dubious historical proposition that, before Christ, among the Greeks or Romans, for example, no such concepts of individuality or soul existed, but did exist in the undernourished, dulled, and stunted minds of Christian medieval serfs.

The Triumph of the Self

Clive Leatherdale discussing Stoker's *Dracula* sees the difference between self and soul as a matter of free will. He argues that because Dracula adheres so strongly to his physical existence, he lacks free choice. He is only "a driven machine, with Satan behind the wheel" (189). But Stoker never makes this point. Throughout the novel, Dracula appears to be making choices on his own; he is never shown receiving instructions from the devil as Van Helsing imagines. Dracula may not have a soul, whatever that may mean, but he certainly has a Self. Indeed, Leatherdale proposes Dracula as a candidate for Nietzsche's superman, standing for the "will to power," without the weakening mitigation of Christian compassion or love (190), or, we might add, guilt (Are these the soul?).

This powerful superman quality is certainly a major reason for Dracula's popularity although he is often given just enough attractive or sympathetic qualities to allow us to identify with him rather than with foolish old Van Helsing or his bumbling young "knights." (However there *is* good reason to admire the strong-minded Mina.) For if we have the active body and we have the assertive *self* and we do not have to die, then what do we need with a *soul*?

Well, perhaps along with many others, we may *believe* that the soul is the only part that can live on without the body—although it must do so in another world. But we *know* that the powerful and immortal vampire striding the earth for all eternity is just a fantasy. Perhaps the best definition for *soul* as Stoker uses it is that part of us that gives us spiritual immortality—along with our identity. Like others of the nineteenth century, Stoker reconciles his readers and, no doubt himself, to Christianity because it offers the consolation of the immortal soul. It is the meta-fantasy that finds support and authority in tradition and general public acceptance. We need a soul because only a soul can live forever—and perhaps even drag the body and the self along with it. It is a spiritual promise that cannot be confuted or denied or even found wanting, as Dracula's is.

Moreover, this spiritual afterlife frees us from the sordid physical needs and interactions required of our faulty and unreliable material selves. Stoker meant to show the readers of his day that Dracula, emblem of mere physicality and of the survival of the fittest, denies us that hope. In the end, Stoker did not mean to tell us how to defeat some abstract concept of Evil (however concretely represented) but to remind us how to accept the very real fact of death by imagining something worse. However, what he succeeded in doing was to recreate and perpetuate for the modern reader the very epitome of a *self*-assertive and *self*-aggrandizing Byronic rebel against the constraints of mere human mortality and the status quo.[2]

In the same spiritually practical approach, in her series Anita Blake: Vampire Hunter, Laurell K. Hamilton brings vampires, along with werewolves, zombies, shape-shifters, and witches, to life in modern St. Louis. They are a mixed lot, some good, some bad, just like the humans. But vampires are not human, Anita Blake tells us, because they lack souls, even though most of them have a strong sense of self. But, without a soul, however long they may live, when the vampires are finally dead, they are just dead; they lose both self and soul, whereas humans, she believes, will go on to some sort of heavenly afterlife (*Guilty Pleasures* 122). Having a soul apparently is like a ribbon or a certificate that entitles one to personal immortality in the other world, and she will not give it up even to join the attractive (though often quarrelsome) vampires. That is, without propounding a religious message of physical versus spiritual or devil versus God, she does appeal to the popular belief in another spiritual world in which only the insubstantial soul (and presumably *self*) lives on forever.

And who would actually care if they had the chance to live on as they are—only stronger and richer? In Baker's *Kiss of the Vampire*, the wealthy Althea Dale declares she wants to live forever as a vampire: " 'Everyone does. And they'd pay for it. They'd give their souls for it' " (270). Yet, in this novel as in so many others, there is really no question of losing one's soul by becoming a vampire in a world where so many humans appear evil and soulless. And what does God do with *their* souls? Michael Cecilione does not like this whimsical god. In his novel *Thirst*, in order to become a vampire, the heroine Cassandra Hall must overcome the "anti-life, the will to die," the self-hatred, moral squeamishness, and sense of guilt inculcated in her by convention and religion (326). Rather, she has to learn to assert her *self*, her innate innocence as a created being, and her love of life. That is to say, not all vampire authors preach self-abnegation and soulfulness, but admire the vampire's assertiveness and solid earthiness.[3]

Many writers choose to avoid serving their vampires in a Christian pudding and omit the idea of soul altogether. Instead, their character complications turn on the problem of *identity*. In Richard Matheson, in *I Am Legend*, some vampires have died from an unknown virus but later arose and walked and hunted—but with no apparent identity or sense of identity. Another type, after contracting the vampire disease (with the vampire's peculiar problems), did not die, but retained normal human consciousness, self-awareness, and sensibilities. They are ready to rebuild civilization as best they can. Jean Lorrah's novel *Blood Will Tell* (2001) also seems to equate soul with self. When her vampires fear the loss of their souls, they are not referring to damnation or some nebulous spirituality but to the loss of their personal identities—their memories, their experiences, their character traits, and their acquired knowledge and skills—under the control of a kind of "master" vampire, whom they call a "Numen," who is capable of leeching off consciousness and leaving them walking vegetables. In the case of many modern "nice" vampires, this distinction between a socialized, morally responsible, and even spiritual self and the vague concept of a soul seems pointless. Besides, even strong-willed vampires do not have to be selfish or socially irresponsible. They do not have to kill people. They can be superheroes, like Saint-Germain or Angel or Nicholas Knight, who give us the fantasy of immortality along with the heroism.

Even if we do not care much for goodness, most of us moderns are tolerant of a diversity of religions, lifestyles, and moral views—even vampires, so long as they are not harming anyone. As for morals, the vampire traits of self-assertive individualism, aggressiveness, even ruthlessness comprise our idea of a successful person as opposed to humility, contentment, and modest reserve. Lacking theological or moral quibbles, we can have the imagination of earthly immortality without the imagination of punishment for it. As for ourselves, instead of a soul to be saved or damned, we now have a *self* to be developed. Grocery store checkout counters carry a women's magazine frankly called *Self* (not *Soul*). *Self*-improvement means losing weight, or learning French, or getting a better job, not enhancing our spirituality or becoming more humble. In *Religion in the Modern World: From Cathedrals to Cults* (1996), Steve Bruce discusses the popularity of *self*-enhancing religious cults in the twentieth century like scientology and transcendental meditation or Rajneeshism, that aim to increase "self-regard and self-confidence" (179, 184, 173–87), which is also the primary aim of many New Age cults (204).

Whatever else it may do, most vampire literature affirms the Romantic ideal that individuality and a sense of self are the very meaning of being human. Loss of faith in religious authority and tradition has resulted in the multiplication of religious "truths" about the nature of God, the soul, and the afterlife. Science has shown us an ever-changing natural world, which must continually be reexamined and relearned by the only beings capable of doing so. Streams-of-consciousness, Existentialism, a plethora of confessional and autobiographical outpourings, "personal saviors," along with postmodern insistence that we can never know reality (if there is one) and that the world is what we say it is, individually or collectively—these intellectual (and otherwise) endeavors of the past century—have done nothing to mitigate the individual's natural inclination to believe that his or her conscious, perceiving self is, after all, the center of the universe. Vampire literature confirms the significance of this self either through the powerful, independent figure of the vampire or through the defeat of the vampire by a human who thus imposes the authority of his own being in the face of death's proffered annihilation.

The modern world does not discourage self-interest or even reward selflessness in a way that would lend force to the heroic message of Stoker's *Dracula*. We scarcely reward spiritual triumphs over material ones. In watching the 1922 *Nosferatu*, we find Mina's romantic sacrifice rather quaint. In other *Dracula* spin-offs, we find ourselves rooting for the imposing Dracula rather than for any of the hunters, except perhaps for Mina (up to the point that she will lose herself in the self-abnegating demands of a quaint Victorian marriage to a stodgy solicitor). Perhaps, if Stoker and his imitators had included a ghostly visit from Lucy after her "true death," we might have had some sense—also rather quaint—of her continued personal existence in a happier world. But all we have is a contented looking corpse, doing nothing and going nowhere.

Instead, we admire the rebelliousness of the vampire, its willful defiance of even the laws of nature. Ruthven, Varney, Carmilla, and Dracula and hundreds of others hold on tenaciously to life, enduring their hardships and limitations with a ferocious will. Edgar Allan Poe indulges in the wishful fantasy that the dead might revive by will power alone. In their eponymous stories, Ligeia and Morella by fierce acts of their own will take over the bodies of others—Ligeia that of the narrator's second wife and Morella that of her own daughter—in order to return to life, even briefly. Ligeia, characterized by "gigantic volition," "stern passion," and a "fierce energy" (571), exclaims, " 'Man doth not yield him to the angels, *nor unto death utterly*, save only through the weakness of his feeble will' " (574). And Morella, whose "powers of mind were gigantic," also holds strong opinions about personal identity, which resides in the mind and intellect and "which makes us all to be that which we call *ourselves*—thereby distinguishing us from other beings that think, and giving us our personal identity." Before she dies, she and the narrator-protagonist talk constantly about "the *principium individuationis*—the notion of that identity *which at death is or is not lost for ever*" ("Morella" 588).

In Barbara Hambly's *Those Who Hunt the Night*, the vampire Don Simon Ysidro comments that " 'to be a vampire is to have an almost fanatic desire to command absolutely one's environment and everyone about one,' " because the vampire is " 'necessarily selfish and strong-willed to begin with' " (163), and possesses an " 'all-consuming desire to continue in consciousness at whatever the cost' " (304–05). Dracula too has a powerful will that becomes more forceful as he exerts it, causing Van Helsing to marvel at the " 'mighty brain' " and " 'iron resolution' " (Stoker 291) that brought him out of his grave and over the sea. He does not die and he does not want to. He is an unabashed and unqualified embodiment of self-interest and self-preservation. With all this, what does he need with a soul? His powerful will has, indeed, kept Dracula alive down to the very present in novels like Dan Simmons's *Children of the Night* and any number of movies, in which he asserts himself over and over again: "I am Dracula!"

The vampire is the ultimate Self before whom all other things, even death, must make way. For whatever death may hold, a glorious Christian union with the Godhead or annihilation and eternal oblivion, these vampires would rather be alive. Carmilla and Dracula and their many modern cousins may be ravenous and sexually voracious, but we are aware that their appetites are the appetites of life itself. And we are less likely than the nineteenth century to deplore this fact, especially when heaven seems unconvincingly vague and remote. Even if we could believe in that happy home in the sky or that perpetual spiritual ecstasy, we might not want them. Do we really want an eternity spent in incessant adoration or an inane euphoria? We are internally programmed to hang onto and to perpetuate this life by those very appetites and passions that religion, custom, and even much vampire literature decry as low and vile. More important, beyond the life instincts we share with the beasts, there is our own carefully programmed consciousness of self. And it is hard not to envy this character who refuses to short circuit the programming. For most of us, whether the self is the result of external forces or our genetic makeup, we are familiar with it and fond of it. However contradictory, confused, muddled it may be, most people have a pretty good sense of having a distinct identity of their own. It is the only identity they know.

4

The Religious Vampire

Reason, Romantics, and Victorians

Vampires are both real and supernatural. They alone cross an impassable boundary between the worlds of the living and the dead. They ought to be able to tell us something about those worlds—about what they mean and how they are related. What do they signify, for example, for the actions of humans—for our concepts of right and wrong? For God (if there is one) and nature, and the order of the universe? Where do we fit in? And do we have to die?

These are, on one level at least, questions about religion, about the existence and nature of transcendent realities that complement, perhaps permeate, and guide this universe and give it meaning. Vampire writers must at least touch on these issues in creating a world in which these vampires can exist in a way that we cannot. But vampire literature is seldom pure fantasy; in most cases, the vampire is the only supernatural element in the story, and most vampire stories are set in (more or less convincing) realistic worlds. The narrative then takes place partly in the divide between natural and supernatural, this world and the Other.

Vampire literature, in its appeal to so many, must tell us something about what that audience enjoys, but also what it thinks and believes. For example, the vampire's undeadness certainly contains and relies on *our* presumptions about death and the afterlife, about body and spirit, this world and the next. And what it tells us must have validity as a cultural artifact even when it disagrees with—or more likely ignores—the more acceptable views of science and religion—and even when it is set before us as pure fantasy. For to be accepted, fantasy must coincide with our idea of reality and our desires (or our hopes) at some points—like the desire not to die (even though religion and science tell us that we must).

The literary vampire became popular in Western Europe in a time of increasing doubts about religious promises of everlasting life, and it seems to have proliferated and diversified as doubts broke up and scattered into hundreds of little differing skepticisms and beliefs—spirit rapping, for example, or séances. In the nineteenth century, vampires joined ghosts and elves in the search for an Other Reality to counteract the vulgarity, materialism, and crassness associated with the burgeoning of business and industry. For like other literary excursions into the supernatural, the vampire inspires a sense of mystery and transcendence. In *Dracula*, for instance, the presence of the vampire is the only evidence for the existence of an Other World, and he serves as a kind of roundabout argument for traditional Christianity and a Christian view of the afterlife. For some people, like vampire-hunter Montague Summers, the denizens of the Other World are apparently as real as for any Slavic peasant and seem to provide assurance of the reality of the supernatural. (In *Varney*, we recall, belief in vampires is associated with belief in miracles). Vampires fit into the temper of the nineteenth century—and the twentieth—appealing to the widespread desire to communicate with the dead. The modern fascination with the occult and spiritualism posits—and attempts to prove—a continuing, timeless community including the dead as well as the living.

We cannot always avoid this religious dimension by saying that vampires represent the patriarchy, sex, even wicked aristocrats, subversive foreigners, or rapacious capitalists for the reason that we do not need a supernatural being, a walking corpse, to stand for these mundane considerations. As Calmet realized, by its very existence, the vampire breaks the laws of nature and the laws (traditional Christian ones, at least) of God. We can hardly expect a creature who has defeated death to observe conventional rules of propriety or even of property (although some do keep an eye on the fashions). Moreover, in the case of many literary vampires, the religious issue is foregrounded within the text itself; the vampire is set within a larger, usually Christian, context of belief about transcendent concerns that give meaning to its actions.

For the most part, his function is to be *not* mundane, ordinary, normal, or well adjusted—and certainly not "accepted." Indeed, the participation of an undead being in an evil—or a good—action automatically sets that action into a different realm, more powerful and more cosmically significant than if it is just another action by an ordinary mortal. The seduction and "ruining" of an innocent maiden by a vampire, for example, has different implications than an ordinary seduction, for the very reason that it involves her soul. His actions, for good or evil, are given power and authority by his supernatural origins (just as a rescue by Superman—flying in with *his* cape—confers a kind of honor that a rescue by Clark Kent could never give). He elevates the event beyond this world, making it an issue in the understanding of the nature of God and the universe—even if only to deny that there is any such meaning at all.

There is no doubt that, within its context, the vampire plays this religious role, along with other supernatural beings, Christian or otherwise. In writing about the folk beliefs involving vampires and other supernaturals in rural Greece, Blum and Blum see them as part of a broader and more profound religious experience through which people attempt to define and explain their own place in the material and spiritual world, to avoid the dark and the dangerous, on one hand, and to call to their aid the forces of purity and goodness, on the other. From the practical side, the vampire helps to define and maintain an orderly universe within which one can exert a modicum of control by taking certain actions and avoiding others. According to Blum and Blum, this order is not the product of a scientific or theological system. Because folk belief tends to deal with "experiences that are intimate, personal, and emotional," it does not "require consistency, rationality, or the presence of elaborated integrated, and impersonal institutional, technological, or intellectual structures." Yet, say Blum and Blum, certain constants must exist in the "spheres of crisis and mystery" from antiquity to the present (354). These constants are the needs and desires of human nature that do not change, even for modern man. It is in response to these needs, I would argue, that the vampire maintains its popularity.

Folklorists tend to regard the vampire as part of a sort of supplemental system, filling in the gaps where institutional religion apparently does not function, at least in the minds of the ordinary people. For example, the funeral rituals described by writers like Kligman take place within the context of, and along with, traditional Christian services. In many cases, the clergy tolerate or even participate in the folk elements. And when Blum and Blum surveyed Greek folk narratives or villagers' personal experiences with the supernatural, they found that non-Christian supernaturals played the predominant role. They conclude that we must recognize the important role of the pre-Christian religion even today in directing the way these people experience and interpret the world (183). One reason for the persistence of these beliefs, they argue, is that they "are deeply satisfying and, as such, reflect natural or typical ways for the human mind to function" (184). That is, they survive in the modern imagination, too, not merely as anachronistic holdovers from the past, but as satisfying constructs in their own right. The vampire's undeadness must contain and rely on *our* presumptions about death and the afterlife.

The modern literary vampire performs a similar function, although it has not had widespread community recognition. Since its rebirth in the nineteenth century, it has, however, taken a place among a range of diverse constructs for understanding the relation of this world with the other—only sometimes adapted to or integrated into the predominant religious belief. The matter of *actual* belief may be no more relevant for moderns than for the folk, so long as they in some way act or talk as if these constructs are meaningful, even in metaphorical terms or with deprecation. An example of such a world-ordering construction has already been discussed in regard to the nineteenth-century invention of an imaginary Middle Ages, which was taken as a model of chivalry and honor, of social order, discipline, and of true faith. In nineteenth-century England, moreover, fictional vampires appeared at a time when serious research on ghosts and other revenants was being conducted by highly educated people—like the members of the Society for Psychical Research.[1]

A present-day offshoot can be found in popular speculations about the possibility of communicating with the dead or calling up revenants or in popular television series where psychics purport to be solving true crimes. Norine Dresser's *American Vampires: Fans, Victims, Practitioners* (1989), for example, indicates that superstitions about vampires do survive among the ordinary population. She cites various interviews and a blind survey in which twenty-seven percent answered *yes* to the question "Do you believe it is possible that vampires exist as real entities?" (69). She probably would have gotten a similar response about angels or aliens or demons and werewolves. For the modern vampire falls into the large group of well-known semi-mythical figures that are often referred to as though they were meaningful, even real, from Snow White to Darth Vader, who is, after all, just another reworking of Lugosi's caped Dracula. Associations accrued by the vampire throughout his long and varied history give depth and resonance to this modern sci-fi villain (not to mention the "good" vampire Batman).[2]

Ancient Vampire Dualism

These modern figures also draw their force from the much deeper associations of the vampire's remote past: Folklorists speculate about the vampire's ancient origins, not only in the veneration of ancestors and of household gods, but also in echoes of the worship of gods or goddesses of death, darkness, or the underworld. Jan Máchal points out parallels with a popular Easter ritual called the "Driving out of Death," in which a wooden figure representing death is "killed" in ways similar to those used with modern vampires (74). This custom of killing or carrying out death is treated at considerable length by James Frazer in *The Golden Bough* (1890). Personifying and then killing Death—by drowning, burning, or dismemberment—will keep the people free from plague, or bad luck (1:260). Frazer suggests that this figure of Death might also, conversely, "be endowed with a vivifying and quickening influence" (1:266), might be an "embodiment of the . . . spirit of vegetation" (1:269). The ritual "killing" of Death in various guises also acts positively to promote good crops and even general good fortune. Such rituals may be followed by ceremonies of bringing in the spring, or sometimes by the resurrection of death itself (1:264, 266–67). In these cases, the figure of Death is clearly a personification of vegetation in its yearly cycle of growth and decay (1:319). (And why do we, at the end of every year, invariably, in the media, celebrate a baby in diapers pushing out a decrepit old man holding a reaper's scythe?)

Frazer notes that gods like Isis, Demeter, Adonis, Osiris, Thammuz, Dionysus, and Attis represent both the death and the revival of vegetation (1:295ff.): "Deities of vegetation, who are supposed to pass a certain portion of each year underground, naturally come to be regarded as gods of the lower world or of the dead" (1:325). Ritual killings of death (often in the form of the divine king or a representative thereof) might also be carried out in times of general suffering, like drought or epidemics, in hopes of hastening the desired rebirth. As descendents, however distant, of these vegetation deities, vampires retain their compelling virility and power—not only that of death, but of life and life-giving forces—as part of their very nature.[3]

Some scholars carry this association between vampires and the ancient gods even further than these parallels. In his introduction (1970) to the reprint of *Varney the Vampyre*, Devendra P. Varma melodramatically suggests an Eastern origin for the vampire myth in Europe, in "the Nepalese Lord of Death, the Tibetan Devil and Mongolian God of Time," with their "vampire-fanged images," going back to the Hindus of ancient India (xiv). Frescoes of the "vampire-god" that appeared in the Indus Valley civilization of the third millennium BC portray him as a "fierce deity," whose "terrifying figure characterized the night-side of its aspect of fertility and salvation" (xiv). In *The Darkling*, Jan Perkowski fills in the connections between these gods and the vampire. He suggests that the vampire derives from a pre-Christian dualistic religion of Indo-European origin, in which death is the province of the Dark as opposed to the Light side of things. After the adoption of Christianity among the Eastern and Balkan Slavs, the older religion survived side by side with a Christianity that characterized its gods as devils (*Darkling* 23). Understanding Perkowski's thesis about dualism is, in my opinion, essential to understanding the appeal of the vampire even today.

This dualistic survival was supplemented by another religious belief of Iranian origin, Manichaeism, preached by the Iranian prophet Mānī in the third century. Beginning in the fourth century, a wave of Manichaeism spread throughout Southern and Central Europe, especially in Bulgaria, Greece, Serbia, and Bosnia. It remained popular until the fourteenth and fifteenth centuries, when, at the same time, what Perkowski calls "the vampire cult" also appeared among the Slavs (*Darkling* 24). In the later waves, it came in the form of a Christian heresy, whose basis was the Iranian concept of dualism:

> There are then two separate forces in the world: God vs. Satan, Good vs. Evil, Mana (i.e., God's grace) vs. Matter. In this system, man is dual: his soul is divine and his body evil. The body serves as the tomb of the soul. Satan seeks to imprison light in the darkness of matter and to prevent the soul from returning to heaven. Redemption is the release of the soul in death. According to the teaching of Mānī man is a microcosmic mixture of Light (Good) and Darkness (Evil). Just as Light and Darkness are separated at his death, so too will there be a total and final macrocosmic separation of Light and Darkness at the end of the world. (*Darkling* 25)

A similar heresy was that of the Bogomils who came to Bulgaria with traders from Armenia in the ninth century. It survived in Bulgaria and among the Serbs in Bosnia until the fourteenth century in spite of increasing persecution (*Darkling* 26). And although condemned as diabolical, some of its religious practices entered folk customs among even Orthodox Slavs (*Darkling* 29). Perkowski sums up several motifs from Bogomilism that we can find in later vampire folklore—as well as modern vampire literature:

> the opposition of a good, creative god to an evil, destructive god; an evil god hounding man and sapping his strength, symbolic interplay of water, air, fire, and earth; sunrise and sunset as times of transition; association of light, fire, the celestial bodies, and men's souls with the god of good; association of darkness, men's bodies, and the material world with the god of evil; interface between man and meteorological elements and phenomena, and finally the migration of souls. (*Darkling* 29)

Perkowski finds echoes of these heresies in Slavic folklore in the association of evil, darkness, night, and death, on the one hand, and good, light, and Christianity, on the other, in a continual struggle against each other. "The pattern," Perkowski says, "is clear": "Dualistic elements, viewed as diabolical, combine with Christian and, in some instances, pagan elements to form Slavic vampire belief structures" (*Darkling* 32).

The dualistic worldview, especially in the extreme form of Catharism, was well known and influential across much of Europe at various times, where it was ruthlessly suppressed by the church. The possible connection between vampires and the heresy of Manichaeism explains the interest of church authorities, like Dom Augustine Calmet, in the vampire scares of the eighteenth century. Calmet, in his study of vampire reports, takes great pains to refute any possibility that vampires might act on their own or under the authority of Satan. Instead, he recognizes the need to locate vampire appearances in a context of similar supernatural reanimations, like those of saints, for example, sanctioned by the church as the workings of God. For to allow the vampire—or any demon masquerading as a vampire—any independent will or authority is clearly to fall back into the Manichaeism that the church had fought so hard to counteract. Calmet repeatedly insists that such affronts to natural law can occur only with God's permission or at God's behest, to fulfill God's will. Thus, an important consideration for Calmet in trying to decide if vampires are real is to figure out why God might permit such a phenomenon. For if God allows ghosts to appear, demons to create illusions, and corpses to rise as vampires, He must have some purpose in doing so, and, in these cases of vampires, Calmet is quite at a loss to find one. Calmet's orthodox Catholicism does not accept any grand supernatural Evil capable of opposing God's will, no Dark Force that balances off the Light.

Nevertheless, the Christian insistence on an entirely good and loving God, a God of Light, has left an opening for another figure, a God of Dark, who variously reappears, usually in the form of Satan, throughout history. As a result, an only partly suppressed dualism persists in the modern world, possibly exacerbated by the weakening of faith in a strongly established, widely shared theological position. Certainly, the invented medieval world of the nineteenth century (in which Dracula abides) makes a sharp distinction between Good, Order, Decency, Godliness, and the Spiritual, on the one hand, and Evil, Chaos, Treachery, Earthiness, and the Debased, on the other. In the late twentieth century—and the twenty-first—the frequent references to Satan in the popular media, the belief that some people practice "Satanism," the increasing tendency even among those who ought to know better to demonize America's "enemies"—all suggest the persistence of dualism in popular thinking. The apprehension of the world as a continual battle of the virtuous—or at least the innocent—besieged and undermined by a hellish and ungodly evil is the basis for countless popular films, from *The Exorcist* to *Blade*. The vampire, as a kind of evil Christ—that is, both human and supernatural, both dead and yet alive, both offering a kind of redemption of humankind into another life—is a popular representative of the Dark Side in the endless cosmic struggle.

Vampires of the Nineteenth Century

Early writers of vampire literature were aware of the vampire's complex religious associations and their pagan and Manichaean implications. The nineteenth-century vampire, along with other Gothic figures, was a symbol of the Dark Side in the Romantic reaction against the Enlightenment rationalism that chose to ignore the role of the fantastic and the occult, even death and evil, in man and nature. And conversely, like any Gothic villain, the vampire gave readers the pleasurable experience of vicariously trouncing Puritanical morals and social conventions, the self-satisfied and conventional "good." Moreover, some Romantic writers almost immediately understood that in bestowing on the vampire physical and mental superiority to mortals, supernatural powers, unlimited immortality, good looks, and social and economic position, along with cosmic associations with Satan and the underworld (which took him far beyond the minor nuisance of the folklore vampire), they were restoring the vampire to its proper origins—as a deity, a god of Death and the Dark Side, but also of Life. Under the influence of such literary figures as Milton's Satan, Faust, and the Byronic Hero/Villain, the new vampire grew into a "worthy adversary" identified with great cosmic powers, with Satan and the underworld. It has retained this adversarial role into much of present-day vampire literature—even in many of those cases of "good" vampires.

In their earliest appearances in German Romantic writers, literary vampires reflect their folklore and pagan sources. In Heinrich August Ossenfelder's "The Vampire" (1748) and Gottfried August Burger's "Lenora" (1773), vampires are typical demon lovers. In Goethe's "The Bride of Corinth" (1797), based on an ancient Greek folk story, the vampire maiden represents pagan sensuality in a brief triumph over Christian austerity. These seductive vampires embody not only what Freud has called the Death Wish but also the sensuality of a pagan fertility deity. In contrast, the more conventional Englishman Robert Southey in his long poem *Thalaba the Destroyer* (1801), carefully avoids any affront to Christian doctrine by including selections of Calmet's discussion in an extensive note (8:103–21), ending with the account of a Greek vampire slaying by Pitton de Tournefort, who ridicules the peasants as ignorant and superstitious (see Calmet 2:113–19). Within the poem, Southey avoids the issue of dualism by making the vampire an illusion, a demonic reanimation of the hero's deceased fiancée, devised by God as a test.

The Byronic Vampire

Beginning with these early literary appearances, the vampire gradually moves up in the world, but the literary vampire's rebirth on a higher social plane than his folkloric origins owes most to Byron and to the Byronic Hero that he both created and, to some extent, lived. Byron himself made the connection between his Hero and the vampire in his long poem *The Giaour* (1813), in which he demonstrates his familiarity with Greek folklore vampires. The Giaour is a likely candidate according to folklore standards: he is a violent man, a social outcast, and he has been cursed. Like a folklore vampire, he will attack his own family (not helpless maidens) and will be cut off from the Christian afterlife. In addition to these folklore elements, the Giaour, as a Byronic Hero, carries the complexity of that romantic figure, his sorrow and his anguish, his potential and actual good, his human dignity and mastery over his suffering, and a kind of godlike grandeur. These sympathetic qualities have followed him into modern literary vampiredom.

Byron became the model for later vampires, however, not because of *The Giaour*, but because, in connection with the famous evening at Lake Geneva in the summer of 1816 (which also gave birth to Mary Shelley's *Frankenstein*), Byron wrote a piece of a short story. Later, his one-time friend and physician John Polidori (who was at the Geneva gathering) rewrote the story and completed it, replacing Byron's protagonist with a derogatory picture of Byron as an attractive but evil vampire. The publication of Polidori's story "The Vampyre" in April 1819 in *New Monthly Magazine*, at first attributed to Byron, was followed closely by the publication of Byron's fragment in the same journal, and the two have been associated ever since.

Although in Byron's fragment the protagonist Darvell is never identified as a vampire, a few allusions indicate that this was to be the gist of the story. Darvell has many of the characteristics of the Giaour and other Byronic Heroes like Manfred (in Byron's closet drama of that name). The narrator describes him as an older man of "ancient family," "a being of no common order," a sensitive man of mystery, of "irreconcilable contradictions" and "morbid temperament," driven by a "shadowy restlessness" ("Fragment" 2–3). In addition, allusions to goddesses and animals associated with ancient mysteries of death and rebirth offer clues that some sort of revival will occur. Most important, they demonstrate that Byron understood the connection between the vampire and ancient vegetation deities.

The first clue appears early in the brief fragment. Traveling together in the East, Darvell and the young narrator arrive at a desolate Turkish cemetery, a "city of the dead," near the ruins of the temple of Diana (the Greek Artemis) at Ephesus—where Diana was worshipped as a goddess of fertility. Darvell reveals that he has come there to die, which he does, as he predicts, when a stork standing nearby eats the snake it is holding in its beak. He tells the narrator to bury him where the stork stands. Both storks and snakes are traditionally associated with the cycle of life and death. Not only do storks appear to return to the same nest each summer, but they have long been associated with the arrival of babies in European folklore.

With his knowledge of Roman and Greek culture, Byron must have been aware that snakes were a ubiquitous symbol of the souls of the dead, appearing on numerous funerary urns and other commemorative objects (Harrison 325–30, 332).[4] Moreover, in many cultures, because of its seeming ability to regenerate, the snake has been regarded as a symbol not only of fertility but of healing and immortality. The snake's ability to make its body into a circle is also an image of cyclic return, as is the ring that Darvell gives the narrator. "On the ninth day of the month," he must throw this ring into "the salt springs which run into the bay of Eleusis" (in Greece). On the following day, he must wait in "the ruins of Ceres," Darvell tells him. Ceres is the Roman equivalent of the Greek Demeter, goddess of vegetation and fertility. Eleusis was the site of the celebration of the Greater Mysteries of Demeter, which lasted for nine days, commemorating Demeter's search for her daughter Persephone when she was abducted by Hades to be queen of the underworld. The Mysteries celebrated the cyclical return of the maiden from the underworld and the consequent rebirth of vegetation (Hathorn 91–92).

In his adaptation of Byron's fragment, Polidori completes the link between the vampire and the Byronic Hero by renaming his main character Lord Ruthven. That was the name that Lady Caroline Lamb had given Byron in her lurid fictionalization of their adulterous affair, *Glenarvon* (1816) (in which Lamb contributes a good deal to the public image of Byron at his most exciting and reprehensible). But Polidori, in belittling Ruthven, omits the mythical allusions that associate the vampire with cyclical vegetation goddesses, except for Ruthven's revival by moonlight. The serpent image recurs in Polidori's version, but only as a metaphor for Ruthven's deceit and cunning and perhaps for his almost hypnotic power over the impressionable Aubrey, who tells the story.

Superficially, Polidori's vampire serves as a rather commonplace warning against fascinating but evil companions (like Byron). So, although, unlike Byron, Polidori does not provide obvious mythical associations to give his vampire cosmic or heroic dimensions, he does leave him his personal attractiveness, his compelling power over the minds of others, and his aristocratic bearing. The popularity of Polidori's story established the vampire as a Byronic Hero/Villain, whose malign intent is belied by a charming exterior. Far more than Byron's Darvell, Polidori's Ruthven brings into question the optimistic rationalism of the Enlightenment and reminds the reader that inexplicable evil and inevitable death remain realities, operating against—and within—the everyday, pleasant, and apparently rational world.

Nevertheless, without Byron, without the public knowledge that Ruthven was Byron, Polidori's "Vampyre" would never have enjoyed the enormous popularity that it did or spun off the hundreds of imitations, adaptations, and parodies that followed it, especially on the nineteenth-century stage starting in Paris with a sold-out melodrama.[5] Without Polidori, we may never have known of Byron's fragment, which restored the vampire's divine ancestry and (no doubt, unintentionally) reestablished him as a lord of the dead in a

Manichaean universe. In addition, Polidori's portrayal of Byron as a vampire (or vampire as Byron) set up the model for the modern vampire as an elegant rebel who rejects the dictates of man, nature, and conventional religion. The popular literary vampire takes as its point of departure the Byronic Hero as he appears, for example, in Byron's dramatic poem *Manfred*. This conflicted superhero confronts and defies even Arimanes, the tyrannical ruler of the physical universe and hell, for in the Manichaean tradition, Manfred will bow only to "the overruling Infinite—the Maker" (2.4.47–48), a remote spiritual being beyond the physical world. The vampire, both human and demon, is torn, like Byron's Manfred, between lofty aspirations undercut by degrading bestial needs, amazing powers constrained by trivial inconveniences and limitations. He inspires and compels us to consider the great paradoxes of the human and cosmic mystery.[6]

Varney the Vampyre

Having said this, I have to admit that the first fully developed vampire in English literature—and a very influential one—does not entirely fill this bill. Rymer's Varney the Vampyre may be the most ambiguous and ambivalent vampire in literature—and the most uninspiring. For a start, neither he nor we are ever entirely sure that he *is* a vampire. Briefly, at first, he appears as an almost Satanic figure, a Gothic Hades lusting to carry off his Persephone (Flora Bannerworth in the story). But this and other attempts at predation are so inept and ineffectual (although he improves toward the end) that as a fearful agent of the Dark Side he is a resounding failure. Nevertheless, timely religious issues, including dualism, science versus faith, and the nature of the soul, are debated directly in *Varney*. Three positions are represented: rational Deism represented by Dr. Chillingworth; rational and tolerant Christianity (Anglican) represented by Mr. Bevan, a clergyman, toward the end of the novel; and the third, popular ignorance, which includes both the unthinking collection of religious platitudes which passes for religion with many people, and the superstitious hysteria represented by the vampire-chasing mob.

In the first case, belief in vampires is subjected to scientific skepticism and "materialism" and related to belief in miracles. Chillingworth, who is doubtful about the truth of scripture and flatly rejects supernatural phenomena like vampires, states the case as " 'judgment' " versus a " 'fearful and degrading superstition' " (1:18). Chillingworth believes in a rational Deity who created a rational universe (although we may not always understand it) that operates invariably according to His wise laws. Thus, he regards belief in vampires as " 'an outrage upon Heaven' " (1:24). That is, the Deistic Chillingworth rejects the dualistic supposition of a monstrous supernatural evil acting independently of God and nature. Varney too is a rationalist, who, although he persists in believing that he is a vampire, sees himself as having a place (1:155) in an orderly and purposeful universe ordained by a Good God. In *Varney*, the vampire is demystified and shown to be amenable to natural laws.

As we have seen, Chillingworth is opposed by popular, accepted religious belief—including a certain amount of superstition—represented by Henry Bannerworth's and Marchdale's indignant arguments for belief in miracles and "the truths of Scripture" (1:40). Their own self-contradictions plus the scorn of Chillingworth's responses underline the thoughtlessness of their conventional faith. Meanwhile, the ignorant and superstitious mobs, whenever they hear of the vampire, go rampaging up and down the countryside in a panic, burning buildings and causing far more death and destruction than Varney ever could. Ignorant and excitable, they are easily led "to cast off many of the decencies of life, and to become riotous and reckless" (1:203).

Toward the end of the novel, the material and spiritual, reason and passion are reconciled when Varney meets the kindly clergyman Mr. Bevan, who takes a moderate Christian position based on belief in the soul and a happy afterlife. The story becomes more serious here. Varney admits that he has indeed (and finally) caused the deaths of some innocent people, but these misdeeds, he complains, are compelled by his own fear of dying. Mr. Bevan is not afraid of Varney because, as a devout clergyman, he too takes the view that Varney, " 'dreadful existence as he is, was fashioned by the same God that fashioned us' " (2:851). Mr. Bevan, described as "completely free from sectarian dogmas and illiberal fancies of superstition," is willing to believe that Varney's existence " 'accomplishes better things' " in spite of his misery (2:846).

Moreover, he argues that death is not evil or frightening or even mysterious as is often thought, for " 'there is a pure spirit that will yet live, independent of the grovelling earth' " (2:847). Even Varney has an immortal soul that will be released, sinless and free, in another world. Mr. Bevan's optimistic faith apparently motivates Varney to seek this happier world by throwing himself into Mt. Vesuvius. Thus, *Varney* ends on a conventionally moderate Christian note in regard to the immortality of the soul and its continuance into the afterlife. Nevertheless, *Varney* illustrates the growing tendency of the age, as Ariès points out, to ignore the traditional Christian conception of resurrection of the body and lean toward a dualistic view of the body, not as an evil, but as a useful shell that the spirit will transcend in death. In spite of its many contrived visions of Gothic horror (including poor ugly Varney himself), the novel is essentially anti-Gothic, ignoring the "Dark Side" and having fun with the vampire idea within a determinedly rational context.

Poe and Others

In contrast to *Varney*, Edgar Allan Poe's exploration of the vampire myth is deadly serious, driven by the obsession with transcending death that pervades his works. According to Camille Paglia, "Poe's vampire tales are religious literature, like Donne's Holy Sonnets. They confront ultimate realities, shocking and unconsoling" (574). On the one hand, death is physical and final—as in the case of Monsieur Valdemar. On the other hand, his female revenants like Madeline, Ligeia, and Morella, possess powerful souls, though not godly ones, that survive in suspension somewhere after death to grasp the first opportunity to return in a body. Poe's revival of dead heroines suggests a desperate longing to transcend the "nevermore" of personal annihilation without consideration of Christian scruples—or of Christian promises. Poe's vampirish women are shocking but not evil in their urgent desire for continued life in the body, whatever the cost. Moreover, their revivals *can* be taken as hallucinations of the demented lovers who tell their stories. In spite of all their Gothic paraphernalia, Poe's vampire stories may be most "shocking and unconsoling" because of the strongly rational element that ultimately denies these women—or himself, or us—any kind of immortality. For Poe credits the rational element, the intellect and will of these women, for their intense but brief survivals of bodily death, rather than some supernatural intervention or magic.

In contrast, other nineteenth-century writers retain the Gothic fascination with dualism and the Dark Side in a Christian context. Their ungodly vampires, with their insidious malevolence and contempt for the Good, demonstrate the reality of Evil and its danger to those too innocent to recognize its existence. In the anonymous but influential German tale "The Mysterious Stranger," the aristocratic vampire Azzo von Klatka, like Polidori's Ruthven, has an uncanny ability to fascinate and lure his naïve victims, whom he despises. The stipulation that he must be killed by a victim in a reverse crucifixion with three nails while the "Credo" is read "in a loud voice" (64) emphasizes the hellish wrongness of his kind of immortality as an anti-Christ in a dual universe.

In some cases, vampire ungodliness is indicated by their un-Christian sensuality attributable to their disreputable pagan origins. The beautiful Roman bloodsucking maiden from Anne Crawford's "Mystery of the Campagna" (1887) lurks in her dark tomb forgotten under a crumbling Medici mansion, slinking out occasionally through the ages to seduce and destroy any susceptible young man (in this case, the weak-willed sculptor Marcello). In Vernon Lee's "Marsyas in Flanders" (1900), set in the Middle Ages, a stone effigy of this wild Greek satyr, found on the beach after a shipwreck, is mistaken by the peasants for an image of the crucified Christ. But it manages, periodically over the years, to writhe and twist itself off the cross, which it then destroys, all the time making strange noises, playing the panpipes, and wreaking a kind of carnival havoc on the church and vicinity. Finally, the prior and abbot lock it up underground with an iron stake pushed through it, after which the wild performances cease. Unrestrained animal sensuality (of the kind the pagans enjoyed) can only be a danger to order and civilization.

Sheridan Le Fanu's "Carmilla" also pursues the Gothic theme of the sensual assault of the thirsty vampire on helpless innocence. In the prologue, the narrator quotes the fictional Dr. Hesselius, in whose papers the story was discovered; Hesselius asserts that the subject of vampirism involves "not improbably, some of the profoundest arcana of our *dual existence*, and its intermediates" (72, my italics). Hesselius does not specify the nature of this dualism, and it remains somewhat ambiguous since the author has left it open to us to interpret the vampire Carmilla as a projection of the repressed adolescent sexuality of her victim Laura. In this case, as Hesselius implies, the dualism lies within the character's own psyche. Although Le Fanu avoids heavy-handed Christian imagery, the ruthless and insidious malevolence of Carmilla, absorbing into herself the very being of her friend, prevents our taking a *merely* psychological view of the threat of annihilation and dark destruction she portends.

Nevertheless, Carmilla herself argues, like Varney, that she is simply a natural being following her own nature, and thus cannot be blamed for doing so. This is also the case in William Gilbert's "The Last Lords of Gardonal" (1867), in which the young maiden vampire is only doing what she must; the evil lies in Conrad, Lord of Gardonal, and his ruthless lust that brings her out of the grave. In this story, the message lies in the ill-advised attempt of the bereaved to override death. Justice is brought about by a mysterious wizard and astrologer named Innominato, who, along with Rymer's Chillingworth and Le Fanu's Hesselius, might have influenced Stoker's creation of Van Helsing. In this tale, however, evil lies in the humans, and the good wizard has the supernatural vampire on his side. These stories take a rational position in which nature is neutral, and evil and good reside within the protagonists. Dualism persists, however, for evil is clearly associated with the physical, that is, sexual, desires of Franziska and Laura. In "Mystery of the Campagna" and "The Last Lords of Gardonal," as well, evil comes close to being identified as lust, a reflection of the nineteenth-century obsessive dualism in matters related to sexuality.

Dualism: Stoker

In Bram Stoker's *Dracula*, the vampire is a powerful supernatural figure in a Manichaean universe. He stands for Satan against God, Evil against Good, the Body against the Soul, Darkness against Light, and Death against Immortal Life. Yet Stoker's harsh dualism is somewhat meliorated by the milder and more cheerful influence of popular Christianity and even spiritualism and their belief in the indestructible soul. Through his Gothic vampire and his knightly heroes, Stoker intends to call up into the nineteenth century a romantic past when people understood the reality of Evil and Good in the world. Nevertheless, in making Dracula into the Antichrist, Stoker inadvertently recreates a dualist context in which, in actions and influence, Satan and his agent Dracula often seem to have the advantage over God, who never shows up.

For this reason, in spite of Van Helsing's tedious ravings about God's will, and all the medieval romance trappings and crosses and holy wafers, Stoker's story has the effect of calling traditional religious faith into question. Margaret L. Carter agrees. In her book *Specter or Delusion? The Supernatural in Gothic Fiction* (1987), she notes that, in spite of the continual Christian allusions, God never seems to be fully in control: "If the vampire can damn even souls of otherwise innocent victims, he must be operating independent of Divine permission." Thus, she argues, the novel seems to depict "a Manichaean world where Evil seems to be as self-existent as Good," reflected in the many inversions of Christian doctrine and sacraments in the character and behavior of Dracula (102, 116).

Stoker may have been aware of this theological lapse in his presentation of Dracula, for he deflects possible criticism in two ways: First, we know Dracula only as he is perceived and understood by the other characters, who may be wrong. It is they, not Stoker, who create the character of Dracula. And second, these obviously sincere and conventional people often express doubts about falling into wrong thoughts as a result of their failure to comprehend. Jonathan Harker, on his way to Dracula's castle, for example, imagines himself in a realm of heresy and pagan superstitions, a nightmare world where evil things arise at night to threaten the Good. But, he records in his journal, he reminds himself that, as a rational "English Churchman," he has been taught to regard such fears "as in some measure idolatrous" (9). Nevertheless, by the end of his visit, Harker has managed to establish Dracula in our minds not only as an agent of Satan and the Dark Side but as a pagan deity of vile earthy appetites, a formidable adversary of the civilized and the good. And at the same time, all this speculation has been called into question as a kind of heresy or superstition on Jonathan's part.

With the coming into the novel of the great "philosopher" and "metaphysician" (147) Van Helsing, the Manichaean motifs become clearly defined—although he too occasionally has doubts. For example, it is Van Helsing who introduces the purity/pollution—soul/body dichotomy, no doubt from his reading about vampire folklore. It is Van Helsing who reports to

Mina Dracula's "'dealings with the Evil One'" in the famous school in the Scholomance (291). There, according to Emily Gerard (whom Stoker had read), the devil in person teaches "the secrets of nature, the language of animals, and all magic spells" (Gerard 198). In this allusion, Dracula is indirectly identified with Satan as an ancient weather god, a pagan threat to Christian orthodoxy, *who is still able and active.* But even Van Helsing (and Stoker, we suppose) is not always comfortable with this heresy. At one point Van Helsing briefly retracts—or muddies—his own pagan and satanist theories by suggesting that Dracula's occult powers derive from his superior force of will—without that "'diabolic aid'" that would have to yield to the power of good (379) (perhaps inadvertently suggesting that Dracula is stronger than God *and* Satan). Or his powers come from nature: "'Doubtless, there is something magnetic or electric in some of these combinations of occult forces which work for physical life in strange way . . .'" (378).

Van Helsing is introduced by John Seward as an advanced scientist (147), which means that, unlike Rymer's Dr. Chillingworth, he accepts and studies both natural and supernatural phenomena equally. But, for Stoker, unlike Rymer, the physical world no longer provides evidence of benign and rational purpose but rather of a pointless and dismal Darwinian struggle—"red in tooth and claw" like Dracula himself. In some ways, Van Helsing reminds us of some occultists and spiritualists of the late nineteenth century who also insisted on scientific open-mindedness in their pursuit of the supernatural, especially in his exhortation to Dr. Seward that he "'believe in things that you cannot'" (237).[7] But, whereas the spiritualists sought for proof of the continued reality of benign spirit pervading the cosmic order, Stoker's novel insists on the importance of recognizing the constant threat of chaos and the annihilation of spirit in a world in which God is frighteningly remote and unresponsive and whose very existence seems dependent on rather trivial human actions, like the brandishing of crosses, rather than on sincere faith and goodness.

And, for all his supposed devout Christian feeling, the philosopher and scientist Van Helsing seems all too often like a cult leader cajoling and threatening his followers with whatever comes to hand. Many of his assertions are based not on scientific evidence or Christian theology but on the heresies and superstitions of the past, "'the lore and experience of the ancients and of all those who have studied the powers of the Un-Dead,'" as he admits to Dr. Seward (261). Moreover, it is Van Helsing's explanations that elevate Dracula into the immortal god of the Dark Side, of the dead, of the elements and of "'the meaner things,'" who, with very little effort, can transform virtuous English girls and boys into "'foul things of the night'" forever shut off from heaven and "'abhorred by all; a blot on the face of God's sunshine; an arrow in the side of Him who died for man'" (287–88).

Van Helsing attributes to Dracula not only the power of life or death but also of salvation or damnation.[8]

God does not give his Christian heroes much help. The power of Christian symbols and Christian faith is only weakly manifest in temporarily warding off Dracula. Most of the time, the heroes of Christ must combat Dracula's supernatural physical and psychic powers with only human resources, aided mostly by assorted physical *things*—garlic, crosses, magic circles, and sturdy stakes and knives—as opposed to *Varney*, where the vampire is ultimately defeated by sweet reason and Christian love. Indeed, the power of virtue or of faith seems to play a very small role, except in keeping the vampire hunters on task. Although the virtuous Mina, damned by Dracula's kiss, is the only one capable of taking the Christlike attitude of forgiveness and pity, Van Helsing warmly assures her that, unless they defeat Dracula (with sharp weapons), she will be damned until the Judgment Day when "'God sees right to lift the burden'" (353).

Stoker's dualism does find meaning and purpose, though not necessarily a Christian one, in a continual and savage battle between Good and Evil. And this, I think, is part of the popularity of Dracula, this imagination of a great cosmic drama in which each person can be a player, even a hero, and win the ultimate reward of the Father's eternal approval. Toward the end, Van Helsing says, "'This battle is but begun, and in the end we shall win—so sure as that God sits on high to watch over His children.'" And Jonathan Harker is briefly comforted to hope, "There is something of a guiding purpose manifest throughout" (374). Full of righteous emotion, Van Helsing and his four knights go forth like the old Knights of the Cross to die, if necessary, "'for the good of mankind, and for the honour and glory of God'" (380). But, best of all for many readers, even after Dracula is done in, there is no assurance that it is all ended. In his school in the mountains of Transylvania, Satan remains to turn out more agents of his Evil cause, and Mina and Jonathan are already producing a new little potential innocent victim. In Stoker's dark Manichaean world, we will always have someone to stick a stake into.

A similar dismal ambiguity appears in Stoker's treatment of death and the afterlife. The theme of death is introduced early in the novel along with paganism and heresy, in Jonathan Harker's "unknown night journey" to Dracula's land of the dead (16). Meanwhile, back in England, Mina is drawn to contemplate death in the Whitby graveyard, where the doomed Mr. Swales expounds on the Judgment Day, when, he believes, the bodies of the dead will rise up carrying their tombstones (89). His literal orthodoxy about death and the resurrection of the body sets the background for the other kinds of death represented in the novel: Lucy's "true death," apparently one of those immediate spiritual translations of the soul into the other world, and Dracula's life-in-death.

The contrast in the novel between the "true" deaths and the vampire's un-Christian alternative is anticipated by the insertion into the text of a newspaper article about the strange arrival of Dracula's ship, the *Demeter*, with everyone on board dead. The article contains an allusion to Coleridge's *Rime of the Ancient Mariner*, also about a ship in which all die but one lost soul condemned to a perpetual "Life-in-Death" (*Dracula* 103). The ship's name Demeter, Greek goddess of the corn, recalls Byron's allusion to the Eleusinian mysteries, which hint at the prospective revival of his protagonist Darvell. Demeter and Dracula, pagan nature gods, share the gift of eternal return, and we are reminded in advance that Dracula's existence threatens not only English maidenhood but their deepest religious beliefs about the linear progression of the soul at death from this sinful world to a glorious resurrection in the next.

Much of *Dracula* seems like a desperate effort by Stoker to make death acceptable on Christian terms, to assure himself and readers that they *can* have immortality—and oddly enough, that this may not depend entirely on saintliness but can be achieved as well by certain prescribed rituals and actions, as in folklore, performed by other people. Lucy's soul must be freed in "true" death so she can be pure enough to " 'take her place with the other Angels,' " says Van Helsing (261). When, by the grisly and entirely unspiritual methods of staking and decapitation, Lucy *is* restored from a "foul Thing" to her original "unequalled sweetness and purity," her body reflects this change as well; her face displays a "holy calm," a "symbol of the calm that was to reign forever." Van Helsing says, " 'No longer she is the devil's Un-Dead. She is God's true dead, whose soul is with Him!' " (264) And if they chop her *body* up, it can be made to stay there. For she is both damned and saved through no action of her own.

In the entire work, only Mina—the strongest character in the novel other than Dracula—is consistently able to maintain a Christian vision of a loving and forgiving God who offers immortality to all when the soul leaps from the body into the spirit world, free from earthly pollution and pain. At one point she rejoices even in Dracula's prospect of salvation: " 'Just think what will be his joy when he, too, is destroyed in his worser part that his better part may have spiritual immortality' " (367). The worser part is apparently his physical body, the source of his evil. Stoker is not terribly specific on this dualistic division nor on the spiritualistic transcendence of the instantly cleansed soul—as usual leaving his characters (and us) to fill in. Even Van Helsing cannot be trusted to present a reliable viewpoint. For in spite of his rantings about eternal damnation, hope for salvation apparently extends to everyone. As they crumble into dust, even Dracula's wives look "placid each in her full sleep of death" (438), and Dracula too has "in the face a look of peace" (443).

Stoker had good reason for fudging on the tricky questions of soul and body, salvation and damnation. According to Philippe Ariès, hell and damnation were not so popular with the general public in the nineteenth century; Christian faith was in doubt and threats of eternal hellfire were not likely to appeal to those seeking comfort elsewhere, in spiritualism, for example, which promised a happy cleansing of the soul at death. Ariès comments that whereas in earlier ages death had been regarded as a time of confrontation between heaven and hell for the soul of the deceased, "in the nineteenth century, people scarcely believe in hell anymore: except halfheartedly—and then only for strangers and enemies, those outside the narrow circle of affectivity." What seems evil—"suffering, injustice, unhappiness"—is bound with the body and disappears with its death: "In the beyond, in the world of spirits, there is no more evil, and that is why death is so desirable" (473). Numerous experiments with séances and spirit rapping offered proof for many people of the survival of the spirit, contented and full of good will. *Dracula* carefully avoids offending this popular belief that the soul was innately good once free of its corrupting worldly existence.

What is the point of all this? John R. Reed reminds us that the use of supernatural phenomena in defense of religious belief was quite common among late-Victorian writers like Rider Haggard, Edward Bulwer-Lytton, and Bram Stoker. They "wrote to scold an age that refused to believe in mysteries which it could not explain" (100), which is, of course, exactly the job Van Helsing takes on himself, the job of making us believe, as Reed says, in "the probable reality of the Unseen" (102), and thus to provide "some means of escape from a depressingly materialistic existence" that "seemed drained of meaning and feeling" (103). For, in an entirely materialistic existence, death, for humans as for all life, must be final and absolute. Even Dracula, in his corrupt body, dies every day. Our only hope lies in the promises of spiritual immortality, probably Christian, but not necessarily.

Stoker appeals to the nineteenth-century quest for religion, spirit, immortality—and, what's more, for proof. Janet Oppenheim reminds us that, in the nineteenth century, research into the Other World was a "very serious business to some very serious and eminent people" all over England "hoping to discover the most profound secrets of the human condition and of man's place in the universe" (3–4). They had not had time, she says, to adjust to a universe without God or without meaning that cared nothing for humankind:

> If they turned to spiritualism and psychical research as refuge from bleak mechanism, emptiness, and despair, they did so as part of a widespread effort in this period to believe in *something*.

> Their concerns and aspirations place them—far from the lunatic fringe of their society—squarely amidst the cultural, intellectual, and emotional moods of the era. (4)

If much of this seems confused and self-contradictory both in popular thought and in literature like *Dracula*, we must remember that the spiritualism, folklore, Manichaeism, superstition, heresy, and just conventional Christianity in vampire literature do not necessarily constitute a well-thought-out program of theology; they come together variously as elements in a modern folk literature that is apt to have a haphazard and ambiguous relationship with any specific dogma. We are not looking to make a list of Stoker's actual beliefs about death and the afterlife as set out in *Dracula*, but to point out the concern expressed in this novel, often anxious and confused, about the human soul and its chances for immortality.

Montague Summers

The full ascendancy of the vampire to a height of gloriously ubiquitous iniquity is achieved in the beginning of the twentieth century in two books by Montague Summers, *The Vampire* (originally *The Vampire: His Kith and Kin* 1928) and *The Vampire in Europe* (1929). Although his vampire works were published in the twentieth century, I am including him here not only because of his Victorian high seriousness, but because, after *Dracula*, Summers has probably had more influence on subsequent vampire lore than anyone else for the reason that he has been cited by so many who have accepted his accounts at face value. And he would be delighted to know this because he believed every word of them.

Summers attributes the revival of interest in vampires in the nineteenth century to a revival of interest in occultism (*The Vampire in Europe* 99). Summers himself seems to be a kind of "node" of vampire thought. His sources are *all* the folklore and literature that he could possibly have found and packed into his two books, and through him, make up an international panorama of vampires—which would be all right if writers had not retold his tales without apparent awareness that many of his sources are outright fiction, like *Varney the Vampyre*, for example, or even *Dracula*.

Summers is a kind of Van Helsing, obsessively intent on impressing his readers with the existence of these unspeakable supernatural horrors. Like Van Helsing, he is sure that science is on his side:

> the careful investigations in connexion with psychic phenomena which have been so fruitful of recent years, and even modern scientific discovery, have proved the essential truth of many an

> ancient record and old superstition, which were until yesterday dismissed by the level-headed as the wildest sensationalism of melodramatic romance. (*Vampire* 8)

He insists that in spite of some exaggerations by the "country folk," "the Vampire tradition has a very genuine substratum, and something more than a substratum, of truth" (*Vampire in Europe* 272). He attributes most vampire activity to a "Satanic source" (176) although, as a good Christian, he asserts that "the Supreme Being *may* make wicked Spirits his Instruments of Punishment here, as well as Plagues, Wars, Famines &c. and, that he *actually has* done so, is sufficiently apparent from Scripture . . ." (*Vampire in Europe* 158). This is why Christians, according to Summers, have much less trouble from vampires than those other "unhappy people" of distant nations who so easily "become the sport and the prey of fiends and cacodemons" (*Vampire in Europe* 320). He consistently trounces any attempt at natural explanations, even by Calmet. Nor does he explain what purpose God might have in creating all those monstrous creatures—from Malaysian flying heads (*Vampire* 251) to the Apocryphal Lilith to our own Dracula.

His accounts remind us of present-day tales of flying saucers and alien abductions. No alternative explanation or lack of evidence will dampen his enthusiasm. In *The Vampire in Europe*, Summers repeats approvingly the tales of ghosts and vampires told by William of Newburgh and Walter Map in the twelfth and thirteenth centuries (79–99). Attributing the authorship of *Varney the Vampyre* to "Preskett Prest," Summers accepts this supposed author's statement that it was founded upon "seemingly the most authentic sources" about a vampire incident in 1713 (anon. preface to *Varney*) (104). Although he cannot trace this account, he finds it "exceedingly interesting to find a case of vampirism in England at this date . . ." (105). He retells at length the story of the vampire at Croglin Grange (111–15), even though in his introduction he has admitted that "there is no place styled Croglin Grange," and no suitable tomb in the vicinity from which the vampire could have come. But to Summers, "These discrepancies do not, of course, militate against the essential truth of the tale" (xii). As for the dearth of such tales in his own day, "One thing is plain:—not that they do not occur but that they are carefully hushed up and stifled" (xii–xiii).

Like Van Helsing, he knows that our ignorance of evil makes us susceptible, and that the vampire is the most evil of all the supernatural beings in the world: "He is neither dead nor alive; but living in death. He is an abnormality; the androgyne in the phantom world; a pariah among the fiends" (*Vampire* 6). In *The Vampire*, Summers asserts: "The vampire is one who has led a life of more than ordinary immorality and unbridled wickedness; a man of foul, gross and selfish passions, of evil ambitions, delighting in cruelty and blood" (*Vampire* 77). But even worse, he is timeless and universal:

> Assyria knew the vampire long ago, and he lurked amid the primaeval forests of Mexico before Cortes came. He is feared by the Chinese, by the Indian, and the Malay alike; whilst Arabian story tells us again and again of the ghouls who haunt ill-omened sepulchers and lonely cross-ways to attack and devour the unhappy traveler. (*Vampire* ix)

He patches together all this hodgepodge of vampires or vampire-like creatures into a "philosophy of vampirism" (*Vampire* xii) that becomes a kind of unifying element of human experience—an extended, complex, and elaborated tapestry of ubiquitous supernatural evil in the universe. Within the context of Summer's world, the vampire is by no means whimsical or idiosyncratic.

Most important, perhaps, is his hope to prove, by sheer enumeration of cases, the actual existence of a supernatural world and thus, like Stoker, offer an indirect consolation for death. Even for the pagan, says Summers, death is a peaceful sleep: "How fearful a destiny then is that of the vampire who has no rest in the grave, but whose doom it is to come forth and prey upon the living" (*Vampire* 7–8). Thus his belief in the reality of vampires, along with all sorts of supernatural creatures—incubi and succubi, sorcerers, witches, demons, goblins, and werewolves—is, for him, a necessary part of his belief in the spirit world and in the Christian promise of immortality. It is a religious belief. To deny the existence of vampires, to Summers, is tantamount to atheism (*Vampire* 148).

Both Summers and Stoker have a serious purpose: to affirm the existence of God by demonstrating the existence of evil. Evil is necessary to move us toward God. Neil Forsyth reminds us in his study *The Old Enemy: Satan and the Combat Myth* (1987) that John Wesley said, "No Devil, no God" (qtd. in Forsyth 7). But, Forsyth goes on, "this idea is not a peculiarity of the devil-soaked Protestant imagination, it is basic to the Christian story" (8). Forsyth treats the Devil as a character, "the Adversary" (4) in an ancient and ongoing narrative of the "myth of combat with a supernatural adversary" (14). "In a Christian context," says Forsyth, "God is understood as the ultimate author of this narrative reasonableness" (16) and thus transcends it.

Forsyth begins his account of this myth with the discovery of the stories of Gilgamesh and Huwawa and the first appearance of "a character named Satan" in early records, many of which survived only in "Ethiopic or Greek translations, and have had continuing impact on subsidiary or other local forms of Christianity, particularly in the Slavonic churches" (18). Huwawa is described, very much like a vampire, as a "devastating monster" and a "death-dealing demon," a common character in such myths, says Forsyth (26), who represents, like Dracula, "the ambivalence of the human attitude to death" (34) as well as a vegetation god that protects sacred trees.

Forsyth's book traces the influence of these early stories in the origin of the character of Satan and its gradual changes and development through various forms of Manichaeism, into Judaism and the Christian concept of the Antichrist. This dualistic myth, which gives so much power to the "Angel of Darkness" (212), reappears in the vampire as characterized by Stoker and Summers. We might say that the vampire story is one vehicle by which this cosmic drama has been carried on and made meaningful in the twentieth and twenty-first centuries.

5

The Religious Vampire

The Twentieth Century

Most vampire literature involves some sort of religious element. In the first place, vampires are not only supernatural but also real and human, existing between this life and the next, the material and the spiritual, like no other creature. Unless the entire work is pure fantasy, this existence must be explained or excused in some way, usually related to commonly accepted beliefs about death and the afterlife. Within and without any vampire story, the writer must deal with the problem of belief—not only in the vampire and in the (created) context that allows it to exist, but also, often, in a specific dogma or faith, usually Christian, or a worldview that provides the story with a larger significance in the reader's mind and imagination.

The usual vampire story involves a conflict of good versus evil, with the vampire representing evil or at least something antagonistic to the accepted nature of things. Even a good vampire compels the author to deal (with greater or lesser success) with potentially complex moral and metaphysical issues, regarding, for example, what constitutes good and evil and how they are related to death and the otherworld. However trivialized they may often be in their various fictional manifestations, vampires appeal to the human desire for knowledge, transcendence, and control over this life and the next. For, as a powerful immortal, the vampire takes on a godlike role in our modern mythology. In doing so, it offers meaning, consolation, and wonder in a vast, mysterious, incomprehensible though ultimately purposeful universe.

Dualism: The Cosmic Battle

A number of critics and writers choose to follow Stoker and Summers in locating this meaning in a traditional Christian dualism of clearly demarked opposites. The folklorist Jan Perkowski suggests that the modern appeal of

Dracula lies in its dualistic implications, with Dracula at one pole and Santa Claus at the other (*Darkling* 13–15). In this view, the vampire, along with similar figures of evil, like Dr. No, Darth Vader, and Damien (in the movie *The Omen*), stands for recognition of the cosmic Dark Side, of the Devil and his continuous assaults upon God's good creation. Humankind participates in this battle by its free choices for one side or the other, and this participation gives human life meaning and direction. Each choice has an effect, and the accumulation of these effects is rewarded or punished in the afterlife, Heaven or Hell, according to the decision of God. The vampire's choice to reject and disrupt God's universal plan puts him on the side of the Devil. As Stoker shows us, the sacrifice even of our lives in the fight against Satan or his minions is not a meaningless death but a significant event in the great cosmic battle between absolute Good versus absolute Evil. This traditional Christian dualism offers us a way to come to terms with otherwise inexplicable evil in the world, as well as with suffering, chaos, and death, by accepting these as aspects of a meaningful (although mysterious) cosmic order.

Historian Jeffrey Burton Russell believes that the modern world is desperately in want of such a sense of direction and purpose. In his four-volume history of Satan, he deplores the loss of a coherent vision of good and evil within a providential world order. He favors inclusion of a powerful devil figure in our belief system in order to remind us of the reality of evil in the world (in spite of the obvious dangers, like witch-hunting). Russell says, "The Devil is as much of a manifestation of the religious sense as are the gods" (*Devil* 34). And his comment that "we ignore the radical evil that Satan symbolizes at our extreme peril" (*Prince* 276) reminds us of Van Helsing's frequent warnings that "the doubting of wise men" "in this enlightened age" (*Dracula* 380) serves only to protect and strengthen Dracula (and, by implication, the "radical evil" that he represents). Unfortunately, Russell is considerably less clear about what constitutes evil than Van Helsing is—or than dualistic folklore, for that matter. He neglects to specify how personifying evil and then hunting for it can be prevented from becoming *doing* evil (as it so often does).

In his book *The Death of Satan: How Americans Have Lost the Sense of Evil* (1995), Andrew Delbanco argues that the popular revival of Satan, the proliferation of grisly horror films, as well as novels about vampires, witches, and serial killers, reveal a confusion about the nature of evil (16–17). Since the Enlightenment, Delbanco argues, the various redefinitions of human beings as animals or machines or computers responding primarily to biological and physical "input" has called up a good deal of resistance like that expressed in Romantic and Gothic literature, as well as in occultism, spiritualism, assorted alternative religions, and various outbursts of Christian fundamentalism. The objectifying of the individual as the end product of forces of history, inheritance, and environment has had the effect of setting the self as the center of each person's existence, in which he must find meaning that can be found nowhere else (106).

I have argued in a previous chapter that part of the appeal of the vampire is his stubborn assertion of an Immortal Self in the Byronic tradition. Delbanco argues that the modern elevation of the self to "America's uncontested god" (106) has proven unsatisfactory to many people, first, for the definition of good and evil in any terms other than those of expediency and self-advancement, and second, for the formulation of a coherent worldview in which human life and death become meaningful. As belief in God and "providence" disappeared, he says, it was replaced by ideas of "sport, chance, luck, fortune" (148) leading to "the driving fear of modern life: the fear that the world is not invested with meaning but is a place of speechless, pointless death" (157).

This plaint, in fact, runs through Joss Whedon's *Buffy* and *Angel* television series, in which the main characters, finding themselves engaged in the great battle for what seems to be good against what appears to be evil, desperately try to clarify the issues and to find a beneficent providence behind it—or any providence at all. One episode of *Angel*, "Epiphany," brings Angel to this conclusion: "If there is no great, glorious end to all this, if nothing we do matters, then all that matters is what we do. Because that's all there is. What we do now . . . today" (season 2:16). Angel and his crew find meaning in doing good, in preventing and alleviating, when possible, the pain and suffering of others. Yet this existential self-formation is often inadequate, off target, and unfulfilling in their chaotic and dangerous world. Although they persist heroically, the two series become more and more melancholy and pessimistic. Obviously, *Buffy* and *Angel* do not convey a message of Christian faith. Their message seems to be that being good and doing good are in themselves a noble purpose. The personal self-sacrifice of even a few is, in itself, a triumph against the forces of Darkness—even when there is no God to help out or no heavenly reward—for there will be no other triumph. Their sense of aimlessness and confusion, however, illustrates the loss of faith in a providential universe that Delbanco and Russell deplore.

Delbanco (like Summers, focusing on the evil) ignores the positive explorations of the nature of Good that is everywhere evident. In contrast to his gloomy list of what he views as modern religious aberrations, we might call attention to the plethora of material on the side of the good—of angels, visits from the Virgin Mary, ecstatic near-death experiences, and countless optimistic doers-of-good in fiction and actual life—set against fascination with psychotic robots, serial rapists, hostile aliens, and abstract concepts of evil. We have plentiful films about supernatural manifestations of goodness, like Superman and Spiderman, and Harry Potter, who defeat very specific embodiments of potential worldwide chaos and destruction, not to mention human heroes risking their lives against super earthquakes and giant meteors. The cosmic battle is reenacted again and again, even in outer space, and Good (as understood within the context of the film) always wins. Audiences apparently prefer this and, moreover, accept it as a truth. So then, what do we need the Devil for? Or vampires? Or all those psychopathic villains? The answer, for many people, is that we need them to *confirm* the existence of the Good, of the supernatural and transcendent Force or Providence that compels all life toward a worthwhile and rewarding future.

More important for many writers (and critics), we need them to confirm the truth of Christianity, to make us *believe*. Anne Rice's vampire Louis, toward the beginning of *Interview with the Vampire*, tries to explain this when he tells his interviewer, " 'People who cease to believe in God or goodness altogether still believe in the devil. I don't know why. No, I do indeed know why. Evil is always possible. And goodness is eternally difficult' " (12). The Devil helps us to believe in a good God because, like Milton's Satan (and Dracula), he makes evil easier to define and locate, and thus he makes it easier to comprehend the opposing goodness of God—and of the happy immortality He promises.

In a study of the causes of witch hunts from the fourteenth to the seventeenth centuries, Walter Stephens (2002) argues that the underlying reason for these horrifying persecutions was a sincere effort to *prove* the existence of spirits and the spirit world. Stephens quotes from the *New Catholic Encyclopedia* of 1967: "The Church is committed to a belief in angels and demons, but the meaning of this belief in terms that are both comprehensible and relevant to modern man has not been adequately presented" (176). Vampire literature seems to offer these comprehensible terms. In fact, the character of Van Helsing in Stoker's *Dracula* is doing exactly what the Inquisitors and witch-hunters (Protestant or Catholic) were doing: trying to offer scientific evidence in the form of witnesses, confessions, and physical effects that supernatural beings exist, albeit evil ones. For if the church could prove the existence of witches (or vampires) and their vile practices and if the church could effectively—and publicly—get rid of them, this would affirm the rightness of the church's teachings about the existence of God and His Providence—while hopefully avoiding the heresy of Manichaeism (Stephens 205). This practice is not so different from the recent mania among seemingly good people for exposing and persecuting supposed Satanists and Satanic cults. In a world of growing doubt, the teachings of their religion seem to be affirmed.

Stephens says: "A desire to be convinced of the reality of spirit was the psychic glue that held the witch myth together," even though it may appear to be "a bundle of unrelated, even contradictory beliefs" (366). If we remember that vampires—under the name of *incubi*—were included in Heinrich Kramer and James Sprenger's infamous witch-hunters' handbook, the *Malleus Maleficarum* (1487) (translated, by the way, by Montague Summers) and that sporadic vampire scares in Eastern Europe resembled the witch hunts of the sixteenth and seventeenth centuries, we can understand better the attraction of the wicked vampire and his continuing role, in literature at least, as Satan's corporeal and visible agent.

Those critics and writers like Stoker and Montague Summers who portray the vampire as an enemy of God and the Good actually assign him a powerful position in the universal order. In his "Preface: Bram Stoker and His Vampire" (1997), Patrick McGrath expresses amazement at the vastness of Dracula's moral "transgression" as he strives to replace God's creation with his own undead beings: "Like Satan, his real father, Dracula's argument is with God, and with the biological arrangements God made for humanity" (45). McGrath places the vampire in the position of Satan, the great Opposite and Opponent of God—as in the ancient dualistic versions of the cosmos. Neil Forsyth tells us that Satan grew out of ancient Near Eastern creation myths about the formation of the world in a fierce cosmic combat of gods versus monsters—standing for the forces of Creation versus Destruction, Light versus Dark, Order versus Chaos. As this myth developed in the West, Satan remained the "Old Enemy" by which the Christian God is defined (4). Satan's real crime (and function) is being the "Adversary" to the orthodox God. The search for Satan (or Dracula, à la Van Helsing) can be taken as a search for God.

Many twentieth-century vampire tales can be read as retellings of this ancient Near Eastern story that has been given, through the ages, a Christian meaning and intention. Forsyth says:

> Whatever disguises Satan, or Christ, might adopt for their various local encounters, they retained their main narrative functions as opponents in the Christian variant of a full-bodied cosmic myth, pitting gods against gods, in which the human condition was at stake. (6)

Eventually, however, Christianity, under the influence of Augustine, managed to incorporate the old Manichaean dualism into a monist system (437) in which God is shown to be all-powerful and without equal. By the Middle Ages, Forsyth says, the power of Satan had declined: "The death-dealing adversary of the ancient combat myth had become the windy and deluded opponent of God, and Satan's vice-gerent, death, was now God's way of recalling man from sin. The enemy himself was now the means of conversion" (440). Through Satan or his agents, now reduced in stature and dignity, we become aware of the wonder and majesty of God. The wicked vampire becomes the proof of and unwitting proselytizer for the Christian God.

Evil Vampires for Christ: The Battle Continues

A surprising number of modern vampire fictions recreate this combat myth with the aim of promoting Christian faith in the reality of evil and damnation and, through them, in a benevolent God and a happy reward in another life. These works usually abound in Christian references and allusions to make the point almost embarrassingly clear. Following Van Helsing, the vampire is said to be damned, an agent of the Devil, and an enemy of God and mankind. The immortality he offers is false and filled with suffering and despair in contrast with a "true death" leading to God and Paradise. The vampire's role is partly to illustrate the unmitigated evil of defying God's laws. The mortal protagonist may be portrayed as a hero, or even a kind of Christ figure who is willing to sacrifice him- or herself to save Christianity and humankind, like Mina in Murnau's *Nosferatu*. This conflict recurs in many of the reworkings of *Dracula* on stage and screen, beginning with Deane and Balderson's play in 1927 (with Bela Lugosi as Dracula), which set the tone and message for later versions.

Even if the playwrights and filmmakers themselves are not dedicated Christian proselytizers, they obviously expect that Stoker's Christian triumph will continue to please audiences. Hammer films are good examples. Attractive as he is, Christopher Lee's Dracula remains a superhuman Gothic villain, a demon of Satan who is destined to be defeated, again and again, by Christian virtue and faith. Hammer films abound with images and paraphernalia showing Dracula to be a perversion of Christian belief and practice—ruined chapels and Satanic rituals, for example, not to mention the wicked delight in exuberant sexuality that seems to accompany the vampire's appearances and those of his lady friends.

While many vampire movie makers may cultivate a certain superficial and temporary religious excitement, with their vampire-hunters waving around crosses and holy water, they do not seem to expect actual conversions among the audience, but rather appeal to the popular faith and the general desire to see good and happiness prevail. However, a few novelists and storywriters deliberately employ the vampire evangelistically to *preach* a Christian message. For some writers, as with Stoker, the vampire, appearing from the past to flourish in the modern world, establishes the universal truth of orthodox faith. Once we accept the vampire, we accept the whole package. This Adversary from the Dark Side becomes a witness for Christianity, standing in for Satan in the great combat myth that pervades Christian tradition.

F. Paul Wilson's story "Midnight Mass" (1990), for example, twists Richard Matheson's idea of a mass vampire takeover (which ultimately speaks against violence) into an argument that all that is needed is strong Christian faith and fortitude and a good plan to slaughter dozens of vampires *en masse* and thus to prove the superiority of Christ's religion. The story seems to prove, as well, the superiority of a true Irish Catholic priest over an evil Italian vampire one. A Jewish rabbi helps out but is ultimately sacrificed to the triumph of Christianity, although not before a sort of a miracle converts him to belief in Christ and the Catholic doctrine of transubstantiation.

In Brent Monahan's entertaining novel *The Book of Common Dread* (1993), the foppish vampire Vincent DeVilbiss is an agent of the "Dark Forces," like Stoker's Dracula, identified with Judas (145). He has made a "Faustian" (162) pact in return for doses of an elixir that, delivered regularly in the mail (!), keeps him alive and young throughout the centuries. In return, he must obey a nameless "voice" of evil that orders him to find and destroy an ancient scroll held secretly in the Princeton library. This scroll undermines the Forces of Evil by proving scientifically the existence of God. It shows that the God of the Fathers did indeed know that the world was round and knew about DNA too. DeVilbiss, in his pride, hopes to save Christianity and himself by stealing the one last copy and, in exposing it to the world, become "the new Prometheus," "warning mankind that the fear they harbored for the 'ancient foe' ever since leaving the Garden was absolutely justified" (150).

In Monahan's novel, the forces of evil are real and are manifested, unfortunately, in some non-Christians, like the foreign student rapist with "Levantine" features ("campus rape by foreigners was not uncommon") (164), and among the media who "prospered by feeding the public a diet of negative news and inciting the wicked" (152). Such forces cannot exist in light and "open air," but must "hide in dense matter" like the many gods worshipped by the likes of Easter Islanders, Hindus, and Phoenicians (230–31). In opposition to these, we have our hero, Simon Penn—who "knew in his gut that true evil was at work in Princeton" (271). The bells of the Catholic church ring throughout the story, which takes place at Christmas. The scrolls are said to be "tangible evidence of the laws of the universe—proof behind the invisible, infinite intelligence of the Creator" (285). The defeat of DeVilbiss reassures us "that God cared about mankind" (284), or at least some of them, although as is usual in such novels, God never appears. And in all the excitement, we forget to wonder why God would not get the scrolls Himself if He wanted us to know about His infinitely wise plan.

The sectarian message of S. A. Swiniarski's novel *The Flesh, the Blood, and the Fire* (1998) is even more direct. A vicious Nazi vampire, Melchior, masquerading as a German businessman, has set up operations in the corrupt city of Cleveland in the 1930s. The citizens have lost faith in God and religion, specifically Catholicism, which is the religion of the hero, Stefan Ryzard, who, in spite of his failure to go to church regularly, is one of the few honest detectives on the Cleveland police force. This corruption has opened the way for the vampire, who either is or thinks he is Satan, to take over the city, and from there, the world. His defeat depends entirely on the faith of one man, who, although he has been enslaved as one of Melchior's vampire "thralls," manages to regain his faith and take communion, thereby defeating "the blood of a devil" with "the blood of Christ" (316), even temporarily developing stigmata. He finally immolates himself, along with the vampires and many (unsuspecting) mortals, to save the world.

In Robert R. McCammon's *They Thirst* (1981), the cosmic battle emerges again. Having traveled from the Old World, the Master Vampire Conrad Vulkan attempts to take over Los Angeles for his new vampire race. The Catholic police detective Palatazin, of Hungarian origin, admires the people of the old country: " 'They know that Satan gives power and unholy life to the *vampir*, just as God gives life to all the good things of this world' " (326). At the end of the novel, the good priest Father Silvera sacrifices himself to destroy Vulkan, whose plans, in any case, have been thwarted by God, we are told, in the form of an earthquake and tidal wave that drowns the entire city and most of its inhabitants as hundreds of church bells chime.

In such works, the vampire is a visible and active Vice Adversary whose evil is not just an occasional infringement of communal values (a little blood-sucking here and there) but the defiance and disruption of the universal order as God created it and as the church teaches it, including promises of an immortal afterlife. Even worse, the vampire destroys hope by undermining faith. For it is, after all, the shared belief of others that shores up our own. The authority of institutionalized religion and its time-tested theology confirms the truth of its promises of eternal life. The vampire's scorn and defiance of this truth leaves the individual in a vacuum of despair. Thus, in these works, separation from shared faith represented by formal religion and the church is itself a kind of death. The isolated and godless self, outside the comforting communion of the church, cannot long survive.

In a rampage of stereotypes and prejudice, Tom Holland in *Lord of the Dead* (1995) affirms this point by turning Byron's (George Gordon, again) ideals of individualism and free thought against him. Such ideals can result only in a world of unmitigated gloom, death, and violence—a world inhabited by pagans, foreigners, and heretics. In the tradition of Polidori, the villainous vampire actually *is* Lord Byron, who has been discovered by a descendent, Rebecca Carville, still alive in a fantastically decorated crypt in London (21).

Byron recounts his adventures in the East, where he met Vakhel Pasha, a vampire-devil who represents everything unchristian and un-English and uncivilized. Visiting the Pasha's castle, Byron explores an underground maze, built like a mosque and decorated with desecrations of Christian icons and images of "demons and ancient gods" (94). It is a former temple built to "Hades, Lord of the Dead" (107), which covers the place "believed by the ancients" to be the entrance to the underworld. The Pasha lectures Byron: " 'Hades . . . is a greater god than Allah' " (109), or, " 'A God may exist, *milord*—but if he does, then he has no interest in us' " (111)—a point borne out by His total absence from the novel. After much conflict and disturbing unpleasantness, he turns Byron into a vampire destined to be himself "Lord of the Dead," the embodiment of Evil at least on earth. We again find ourselves in an apparently dualistic world, but one in which Evil reigns everywhere while God seems to have gone missing. Even Byron's passion for the Pasha's slave girl Haidee, all pure love and goodness, does not seem to offer any redemption although it represents his sole virtue. His former Romantic rebellion and defiance of convention (admired by so many of us) has ended only in the isolation from God and humanity that is death.

Like the old witch-hunters and like Stoker's Van Helsing, such works attempt to promote Christianity primarily by threats of doom, represented by the vampire and the horrors of damnation. A problem is that there often seems to be a little too much of horror and a little too little of God. For example, in spite of many allusions to God and Ryzard's belief that God has saved him "for a reason" (346), the power of Evil is everywhere manifest and that of God tenuously dependent on this one man alone. Ryzard's reward, apparently, is nothing more than self-satisfaction and a violent death. Tom Holland does not offer us even that. Almost all the good people in such works are shown as weak-willed and easily misled by Satan's emissaries. In contrast, the depiction of evil—for example, in Swiniarski's novel, a parade of sensational tortures and murders—is more interesting, active, and graphic than seems necessary to prove the existence of goodness, which gets much briefer notice. Nevertheless, his serious message is clear: have faith, take communion, go to confession, and if you are not a Catholic, consider becoming one. Faith alone gives us victory and immortality. Ryzard's *belief* that he is saved is his reward, for as we know, he does not defeat the Nazis.

Not all such novels are Catholic. Critic Joel Porte in his essay "In the Hands of an Angry God: Religious Terror in Gothic Fiction" (1974) charges that Gothic literature is a covert "expression of a fundamentally Protestant theological or religious disquietude" (43). Gothic fiction, says Porte, represents "a religious drama, the dark rites of sin, guilt, and damnation" suffered by Protestants because of their loss of faith: It "owes its gloomy 'Gothic' *ambiance* to a brooding sense of religious terror which is notably Protestant in its origin and meaning" (45). Perhaps taking a thematic hint from a movie of the same name (1988), William Hill's novel *Vampire's Kiss* (1994) illustrates Porte's argument. The protagonist David Matthewson's obsession that he is a vampire—and therefore evil and outcast—derives partly from his guilt for his wife's death and his consequent lack of faith in God. Unbelief is not evil here; it is simply devastating. For, whether or not he is to be taken as a vampire, his suffering grows from his refusal to accept the hope and forgiveness that Christianity offers. Ironically, his lack of faith eventually leads to his death and supposedly a true immortality in another world, where, as the (Protestant) Reverend Cooper says, " 'He will find peace in the hands of the Lord' " (474).

Some such "religious terror," as Porte suggests (or an adolescent version of it), might be partly responsible for the popularity of the Gothic writings of Stephen King. For in *Salem's Lot* (1975), Stephen King also rather unsympathetically shows what can happen to the people in a small town who have lost their sense of community and their faith. Selfish, mean spirited, and suspicious, they are easy marks for a vampire looking for ready converts to a shiftless un-life of preying on others. Even the good guys, seemingly solid emblems of social order and cohesion, the priest and the constable, for example, are easily talked out of their flimsy convictions and are, one by one, paralyzed into victimhood by the stronger will of the vampire. The result is complete collapse of the superficial civilization that masked the real nature of this hellish little town. The failure of religion to inspire true faith—in their God, in their fellow beings, or even in themselves—is demonstrated by the vampire Barlow in a showdown with the weak-minded priest (354–55).

Finally, after nearly everyone has fled or been vampirized or just killed, two people, a writer, Ben Mears, and a boy, Mark Petrie, are left, almost by chance, the sole representatives of decency and sanity, whose duty, naturally, is to return to "purify" the town by burning it to the ground and killing all the vampires who escape (their former friends and neighbors). The message is gloomy. Damnation is Jerusalem's well-deserved "Lot." King brings the cosmic battle to ordinary people in a small town familiar to his readers. Again, God's party is sadly underrepresented and, reduced to relying on small heroes and mass destruction, clearly the loser in this skirmish.

In modern vampire literature and films, defending God and righteousness often requires so much violence and cruelty that it is difficult to tell the good from the evil. Critic Gregory A. Waller, relying on Rene Girard's *Violence and the Sacred* (1972), explains why it is all right for good people to be brutal and murderous on God's behalf. He insists on the value of both *destructive violence* and *regenerative violence*, "the violence that purges and thereby restores the status quo" and "the violence that creates new bonds among the living" (348). Avoiding direct Christian references, Waller expresses the old cosmic battle of good versus evil in terms of the struggle of civilization against the forces of chaos and disorder that threaten to break down "all important distinctions (between life and death, for example)" (350). To Waller, civilization, the social order, even, apparently, the status quo, is "life." Whatever threatens this is "death."

Thus, not only in Stoker's *Dracula* but also in the Hammer vampire films and *Salem's Lot*, the pursuit of the vampire is a holy crusade against true, "unmixed malignity" that cannot be cured or reformed but only destroyed (251). Through their crusade, the vampire-hunters are "regenerated" as they "suddenly awaken to the reality of Good and Evil" (that is, to a dualistic cosmic order, without ambiguity); they "mature and assume responsibility (and often . . . discover a new father)"; they are "initiated into a new life that is in fact an old life, stripped clean of the selfishness and skepticism that render modern man vulnerable, corrupt, or corruptible" (347). To Waller, the value of vampire-hunter violence is that it discourages unpleasant deviations from the social order and disruptive independence of thought, and teaches instead "the importance of faith and tradition" (256).

Even some superficially modern, expansive, and daring science-fiction vampires soar through time and the universe to come up with the same reactionary message. For example, in a Gothicized science-fiction fantasy, *Dracula Unbound*, Brian Aldiss manages to glorify the international military/industrial complex as the epitome of righteousness and order. His skeptic protagonist Joe Bodenland (a billionaire inventor and industrialist) gradually finds himself being converted from unbelief as he and (yes) Bram Stoker travel back and forth in time on a "Christian crusade" to defeat Dracula and save the universe. Most of Aldiss's vampires are worse than animals—brainless reptilian birds or sociopathic ex-humans. They all obey Dracula, "horned and gigantic, more devil than man" (159), whose aim is to take over the world and use the humans as cattle.

The Stoker character points out that the vampires' immortality is an eternal " 'night of Earth' " compared with Christianity's " 'light of Heaven' " (171). Joe's daughter-in-law explains the reasoning that justifies the existence of horrors like Dracula: " 'with no evil in the world, good has no reason to exist. Which is why the Lord permitted sin to enter the Garden of Eden' " (180). Huge Evil allows noble heroes to have huge victories by which to prove themselves. Good triumphs, as it should, by blowing the enemy to bits with military-industrialist Joe's super "F-bomb" (and incidentally wiping out the "Cretaceous dinosaurs") (190).

Tim Powers, in *The Stress of Her Regard* (1989), also tosses together a complicated hodge-podge of science, science fiction, folklore, Gothic literature, ancient mythology, ancient prophecies, fantasy, history, and what-all into a sort of universal stew of a nineteenth-century world in which the vampires are stone—or the stones are vampires—"nephelin,"[1] who become active through little pebbles and stone statues, like that of Galatea. The vampires are the ancient " 'giants in the earth . . . descendents of Lilith,' " explains George Gordon, Lord Byron (now a good guy), " 'who sometimes laid [*sic*] with the sons and daughters of men' ": " 'They're the creatures God promised to protect us from when He hung the rainbow in the sky as a sign of his covenant' " (113). They are like the ancient Titans who must be kept locked down. Powers alludes to a number of myths that have to do with stones or statues to develop a kind of parable of the powerful, chaotic, and ancient evil of nature versus civilization, reason, and at some points, Christ and Christianity. A villainous character named Werner[2] tries to become a kind of reverse Christ to resurrect the rule of the nephelin; one blood-drinking scene is set as a perverted crucifixion (337–39). But eventually, human love wins out over the violent, selfish passions inherent in nature—and stones.

Powers's book is similar to Brian Lumley's *Necroscope* in associating vampires with the ancient chthonic underworld of nature and in setting them in a world full of various supernatural creatures and mysterious phenomena that interact causally with history and with individual lives. These fantasy/science-fiction types of vampire books draw a picture of a cosmos in which all things are related, interpenetrating, interactive—not only the supernatural and the real, but also fiction and nonfiction, past and present. Opposites intermingle and overlap. Only Good and Evil, Spirit and Nature remain clearly demarcated. Lumley's vampire is a disgusting shapeless monstrosity imprisoned under a rock while the protagonist Harry Keogh, in the middle of the story, turns into a glowing angel, all spirit, sent to save the world, or at least the West, from the Russians and the East European vampires. These vampires are part of the natural world of brutality and continual struggle, as opposed (we imagine) to an eternal heaven of high virtue and splendid euphoria. Although we are not introduced to this heaven or its God, the defeat of these vampires promises that we *can* defeat death and then time-travel for all eternity.

Dualism Breaks Down (or: Who Are the Good Guys, Anyway?)

Not all Christian vampire literature presents vampires as the epitome of evil or as viceroys of Satan and the vampire slayers as God's own knights. Many writers question or even make fun of the idea that High Virtue resides in cruel and violent conflict with a supposed Natural or Unnatural Evil. In Fred Saberhagen's *The Dracula Tape* (1975), Dracula, a reasonable vampire, wonders (as we all must have): "Will you tell me that the mere existence of a vampire creates a blot of unexampled evil upon the earth?" (128). This Dracula demonstrates in his own story that evil, for example Van Helsing's bungling, is often simply a matter of fatuous stupidity (147).

Some other works attack a privileged and institutionalized Christianity that sets up straw enemies to combat. Both the movie *John Carpenter's Vampires* (1998) and the book by John Steakley on which it is based, *Vampire$* (1990), although superficially dualistic, depict the vampire-hunting heroes as a bunch of disreputable ragtag mercenaries led by Jack Crow, covertly engaged by the Catholic Church, to attack and eliminate the (genuinely) bloodthirsty vampires that, admittedly, are already nearly defunct, but that serve to simplify the conflict of good and evil and give the witch-hunters and the self-righteous something to rail at (355). The hunters do this pointless killing in the name of the church and a fat reward. So much for dualism and God's noble knights. In the film version, the vampires are said, anyway, to have been the creation of the medieval church—in a kind of unexplained accident during a "reverse exorcism." As for the promise of eternal heaven, the bishop in charge of the vampire-hunting project sells out both the hunters and the church—in return for the earthly immortality only the vampires can give.

Nancy Collins's *Sunglasses after Dark* frankly attacks the abuses of evangelical Christianity through the protagonist Sonja Blue, who is a vampire by no fault of her own. In the course of trying to rediscover her "true" identity as a human, she becomes the victim of the human Catherine Wheele, the widow of "Zebulon 'Zeb,' Man of God, Healer of the Sick, Speaker of Prophecy, and founder of the Wheeles of God Ministry" (16)—and needless to say, a fraud. Catherine Wheele is a psychopathic killer, a monster. Many of the more dogmatic Christian writers and critics treat the vampire as the mythical embodiment of an abstract concept of Evil, but, like Stoker, they often ignore the actual suffering and cruelty in the world, especially that perpetrated by the religious and the godly. Not in this book. One of Collins's vampires refers to humans as "myopic little beasts intent on destroying their world" (139), who are prevented from doing so at least partly by the supernatural creatures living among them (140). In this book, there is no special honor or godliness in being mortal.

Quentin Tarantino's sardonic film *From Dusk Till Dawn*, like *John Carpenter's Vampires*, parodies the use of mayhem and grisly murder to preach a morally empty Christianity in a godless world. His band of "hunters" are a couple of psychopathic killers and their hostages, a demoralized, unbelieving preacher and his two children, harmless but weak. Crossing into Mexico to hide out in a sleazy strip club, they find themselves in a vampire hell, more vicious and deadly than anything even the two killers could have perpetrated.

Only two manage eventually to survive—but not because they are holier or more deserving. Tarantino takes the superficially pious clichés of both realistic and supernatural horror and gives them (guess what?) an ironic twist.

Toward the end of their frantic fight for their lives, the saner of the two killers, Seth Gecko, attempting to buck up the preacher's faith, unconvincingly asserts that great evil (even greater than his own) proves the existence of great good:

> I always said that God could kiss my ass. But I just changed my lifetime tune about thirty minutes ago. Because I know that whatever is out there trying to get in is pure evil straight from hell. And if there is a hell and those sons of bitches are from it, then there has *got* to be a heaven.

But this banal, self-serving declaration and the vampires' traditional sensitivity to crosses and "blessed" water only underscore Tarantino's implication that the religious motif in so many vampire films (and novels) is a thin gesture to justify the viewer's real interest, an evening of vicarious sex, brutality, and gore. No evidence of God or heaven appears in the movie, in spite of the impressive display of apocalyptic evil and chaos. At dawn, when the ordeal is over, the camera pulls back to give a panorama of the grisly strip club from the back, showing it to consist of the top of a Mayan temple (where pain and gore also did not produce god). In this parody, a murderous and morally weak humanity and a doubtful Christianity barely and only partly escape from the ancient pagan bats out of hell.

Lawson tells us that the Greek folkloric personification of death as, say Charos, often finds his job distasteful and apologizes to his victims (101–02). Likewise, even the traditional predatory vampires, although killers, are not always depicted as *wholly* evil, but often appear confused, rueful, and forlorn, like Varney. In J. R. Planché's Lord Ruthven in his *The Vampire; or, The Bride of the Isles: A Romantic Melodrama* (1820), based on Polidori's story, Lord Ruthven laments his appalling need to "walk the earth to slaughter and devour" and pities his prospective bride and victim Margaret (1:2). Twentieth-century *Dracula* spin-offs also soften the force of the harsh Manichaean standoff between the forces of darkness and light. For example, Gloria Holden in the film *Dracula's Daughter* (1936) desperately tries to resist her bloody urges, as does the reluctant Lon Chaney Jr. as *Son of Dracula* (1943) or Anne Rice's guilt-ridden and constantly agonizing Louis Pointe du Lac. And of course we know of the many modern vampires who do not have to *murder* people to survive, like Nicholas Knight, or Saint-Germain, or even Saberhagen's Dracula.

Yet some writers continue arbitrarily to assign the vampire to the forces of Darkness, even against the gist of their own stories. In Jeanne Kalogridis's *Covenant with the Vampire* (1994), our understanding of what constitutes evil remains unclear. The hero Arkady Dracul, has just been turned into a vampire by his uncle Vlad (yes, *that* Vlad). And even though he has permitted this attack as a personal sacrifice to save the lives of his wife and baby and eventually to destroy his uncle, he nevertheless regards himself as now belonging to Vlad's pact with the Devil, making him a being *inherently* evil. He attributes his downfall to his sinful lack of faith in God. He finally prays:

> *"God, in Whom I had put no faith, help me! I do not believe in You—did not, but if I am to accept such infinite Evil as I have become, then I pray infinite Good exists as well, and that it has mercy on what remains of my soul.*
>
> *I am the wolf. I am Dracul. The blood of innocents stains my hands, and now I wait to kill him . . ."* (351–52)

Although we cannot see in what essential way Arkady differs from before, and although he swears to " 'see even this great Evil turned to Good, for love's sake' " (352), and although he is now immortal, he is nevertheless irrevocably (and unaccountably) a soulless devil, trapped in the camp of the Evil One, but still battling for Good.

This inability of many writers and filmmakers to give up Stoker's model of the soulless, innately evil vampire continues to create confusion for their treatment of this potentially most interesting and attractive figure—so attractive sometimes that the audience finds itself rooting for evil—as with Langella's really sexy Dracula or Richard Roxburgh's Dracula in the movie *Van Helsing* (2004), who is more interesting than the title character, who looks so very bored. Even the vampires are often confused: In Stephanie Meyer's popular Twilight Saga (2005–2008; so called after the name of the first novel of the series), the sensitive and gorgeous vampire hero Edward Cullen constantly worrywarts that the folklore may be true; he may arbitrarily be evil and soulless and thus barred from eternal spiritual life. But who cares? Certainly not the heroine, who, as so often is the case, seems additionally attracted by the power and danger of his blood lust as well as his dark past and his potential damnation.

A prolonged confusion is found in Joss Whedon's Spike and Angel in the *Buffy* and *Angel* television series. For example, however witty and sexy and even nice Spike may be, as a vampire without a soul, he is a disgusting "thing" that must be destroyed. But the human mayor and high school principal (with souls, right?) are sociopathic monsters. The mere arbitrary designation of having a soul (being human) or not having a soul (vampire) seems to be all that distinguishes between the good and the bad, those who should *destroy* the others and those others who should *be destroyed*, no matter what they are doing or have done. These designations seem simple and clear-cut, but they do not work throughout the series. The failure to develop or clarify the distinction in terms of action or character creates an ongoing moral and ethical confusion in *Buffy* and *Angel* between what is said and what is done.

In both *Buffy* and *Angel*, soulless, evil beings invariably come from underground—tombs, crypts, sewers, the school basement—and like troglodytes, belong to the dark workings of nature like decay, death, and what seems to be very fertile soil. In the well-worked tradition of Stoker, Whedon associates evil with the dark, earthy, nighttime side of nature and good with the sunlit, airy, blond elements—and with "having" a soul. Like the abstract concept of evil, this intangible soul, which plays an extensive role in moving the plots, is ambiguous because it often seems to be a physical thing that can be put in and taken out like a computer chip. Being bitten by a vampire takes it out, apparently, and justifies the victim's immediate annihilation. It is very difficult to get it back: Spike has to go through all sorts of agony in Demon Hell—although he has, earlier, had an actual computer chip that seemed to work just as well. The soulful Angel rather annoyingly reverts to the vicious Angelus like a mechanical doll whenever the soul is removed (by love, of all things). The effect of this is to detract from his complexity and depth as a character. And we are still not sure what a soul might be or why it has this effect when many humans, like the partners at the law firm of Wolfram and Hart, who by definition *do* have souls, are so vile. And how is this soul related to immortality?

For, in *Buffy*, the vampires are often turned to powder before they even get out of the cemetery, and nothing is said about what *then* happens to their immortal souls. By all standards of justice and decency, efforts should be made to return their souls to them—as in folklore and Stoker's *Dracula*, for example. They are all kept under control by one little blond killer angel, whose ruthless slaughters are all right (Waller might say) because she is human and has a soul and leads a band of noble warriors engaged in a regenerative communal activity to save the world. She too never doubts the ethical rightness of annihilating these thinking, articulate beings who have not yet done any wrong because, by some formula, they have automatically been transformed into agents of pure evil—but by whom we never know. If by the devil, then, where is God? And why is He doing this?

Christian Vampires for Christ

Vampires are not, of course, Christian nor part of any Christian theology or mythology. Christianity does not really require them to be agents of Satan or monstrous adversaries of God or to exist at all. Traditionally (folklorically), they may or may not have souls. I doubt that anyone can say for sure when the first "good" vampire appeared in literature (goodness having many possible meanings). But in the twentieth century, after the two Wars (plus several smaller ones) demonstrated the *human* capacity for mass slaughter (not to mention the accomplishments of men like Stalin or Mao), most vampire predations seem relatively minor. Many writers have preferred to place their vampires (or some of them) on God's team in the Christian combat. Their power and transcendence are directly identified with God and goodness within the text.

Although vampire virtue may create ambiguity, especially if one is stuck on Stoker's absolute dualism, it has several clear advantages for the reader. First, the reader no longer has to wonder why God is doing nothing while the poor humans are fighting to the death for Him—or why an all-powerful God needs this kind of sacrifice or protection. And who is running the universe, anyway? Second, at least one active supernatural being stands with the good guys to even the odds against evil humans as well as evil vampires. Moreover, the vampires—evil and good—become more humanized and often more complex (and somewhat easier to identify with). Evil is no longer a towering figure of cosmic iniquity and power that no human could believably be expected to defeat, at least not without reliable supernatural help. But the major advantage of good vampires is that readers and viewers no longer have to condone evil and incur guilt to enjoy vicariously the vampires' immortality, good looks, and super powers. God can confer these powers as well as Satan and provide His own special superheroes. Why, vampires might even be priests—or vice versa.

Alan Ryan, in his story "Following the Way" (1982) explicitly deals with the obvious parallel between the vampire's (supposedly perverted and unchristian) drinking of blood and the Christian rite of communion by which the communicant achieves immortal life—that is, the immortal life that is Christ. Before being bitten by the very persuasive older priest, the young Catholic narrator has an "epiphany": "the realization, revelation, moment, insight, the ancient secret of the Church," which is its "power," through the priests, "of transforming ordinary wine into sacred blood, an endless supply for an endless lifetime." According to the doctrine of transubstantiation, the communion wine and wafer actually *become* the blood and body of Christ, so partaking of these can be seen as a kind of vampiric feeding on Christ's immortality (572). The drinking of blood *in itself* cannot be regarded as a perversion—nor can the fear of death and desire for immortality be regarded as sinful (or as neurotic, for that matter).

Along with good vampires and in line with more popular attitudes, many vampire stories present a much kinder, more loving, and beneficent idea of God and Christianity than the rigid Manichaeans. They tend to be freer in their approach to vampire dogma ("lore") and to give little weight to religious paraphernalia and rites, like holy water or exorcisms—or sacred violence. In Barbara Hambly's novel *Those Who Hunt the Night*, although the vampire condition is presented as "natural" in that it apparently has physical causes, the choice to live on forever, even when it means murdering others, is evil, and most of the vampires in the novel are a danger to others. A Christian position is presented through the character of the ancient monk Brother Anthony, a vampire, who, like old Mr. Swales in Stoker's *Dracula*, tells his friends that when " 'the Trumpet will blow,' " all humankind will be reassembled in their bodies. Only the vampires, he worries, " 'will continue undead, unjudged, and alone,' " will " 'never know what lies upon the other side' " (197). Ultimately, however, the human protagonist tells him, " 'It is one of the tenets of faith . . . that there is no sin, *nothing*, that God will not forgive, if the sinner is truly repentant' " (199). So finally, wearing "a look of strange serenity," the monk sacrifices his earthly existence to save the lives of others (330). Vampire salvation rather than damnation demonstrates the goodness of God.

Like many vampire works, including Stoker's *Dracula*, Hambly's novel illustrates that religious *belief* in salvation and a happy afterlife is more comforting and meaningful than any actuality set forth in the text. For Brother Anthony, the belief is all. At the same time, a temptation is offered to the reader to indulge freely in fantasies of earthly immortality by identifying with one of the not-so-bad vampires like the romantic Spaniard Don Simon Ysidro. While leaving a Christian interpretation open, such works reveal a distaste for an uncompromising dualism that justifies murder and mayhem in the name of "defending God" or for a catalogue of titillating Gothic horrors à la Montague Summers or Holland's *Lord of the Dead*. In some, the vampires themselves stand for Christianity.

Tanya Huff's vampire in *Blood Price* (1991) fights on God's side. Henry Fitzroy, the illegitimate son of Henry VIII (Why not?), is shown near the beginning of the book in a cathedral in Toronto. He is a good Catholic, after all, and part of the normal order of things—as are the demons who threaten to take over Toronto. They are supposed to stay in another dimension (as in *Buffy*), but some evil human is calling them up. Fortunately, on Easter Sunday, the day Christ rises, they are temporarily deactivated, giving Henry and his human friend Vicki an opportunity to stop them: "The Gloria almost raised the roof off the church and just for that moment the faith in life everlasting as promised by the Christian God was enough to raise a shining wall between the world and the forces of darkness" (163). Godly faith in the Christian promise of immortality defeats the rambunctious demons rather than bloody slaughter by the protagonists. In a final showdown, Henry *reasons* the Demon Lord into returning to his dimension, making a bargain that he expects the Demon to keep (268–69). Even Demon Lords are not wholly without honor.

Stories with good vampires often take the kind of rational position that we found in *Varney*, that vampires, naughty or nice, are part of the natural order created by God. In Michael Romkey's *I, Vampire* (1990), both humans and vampires engage in a worldwide conflict of evil versus good, represented on the one hand by the likes of Cesare Borgia and Hitler, " 'disciples of darkness' " (197), and on the other by Rasputin (of all people) and Mozart and many other artists and thinkers. Evil consists not of affronting the Christian God but of doing harm to other humans. In a reversal of Stoker's setup, the vampire hero David Parker is a young "squire," learning to be a "knight" so he can become one of the "*Illuminati*," a fellowship of "enlightened" vampires whose occupation it is to guide the world toward good.[3] Parker's fears that his soul will be damned are brushed off as a ridiculous superstition (201). As for God and the afterlife, his mentor, the vampire Mozart, can say only that there must be a god and that our reason for being here is " 'to strive for the infinite' " (202). Romkey's knightly vampires promote a sense of piety and faith in the possibility of a redeeming goodness that can lead to spiritual transcendence for vampires and mortals alike.

In Romkey's novels, the vampires make up a very exclusive group and even the evil ones accept only the most superior new recruits. In her series featuring Anita Blake, Vampire Hunter, Laurell K. Hamilton offers everyone a choice—to be or not to be a vampire. Surprisingly, many reject the offer. Hamilton makes little effort to account for the existence of vampires or God's intentions (if any). In contrast to the fretful dissatisfaction and doubt in the works of Anne Rice and Joss Whedon, Hamilton's interest extends to integrating vampires and other monsters convincingly into the life, expectations, and beliefs of the ordinary people who are her characters and readers. In spite of living in a modern St. Louis filled with preternatural figures, including zombies, shape-shifters, werewolves, witches, and vampires, her narrator-protagonist Anita attends church regularly and maintains a conventional, generally middle-class stance on religion. And so, oddly enough, do many of the "monsters" she deals with.

The vampires even have their own "church," the Church of Eternal Life, although it is one without God, as Anita scornfully tells us. Nevertheless, the vampires are still easily controlled and even defeated by Christian icons like the cross and holy water—if they and/or their human adversaries believe in them, which they frequently do. The vampire church, says Anita, is "the first church in history that could guarantee you eternal life, and prove it. No waiting around. No mystery. Just eternity on a silver platter" (*Guilty* 122). She sums up the attractions of this church—and of vampires in general: "They were preying on one of the most basic fears of man—death. Everyone fears death. People who don't believe in God have a hard time with death being it. Die and you cease to exist. Poof" (*Guilty* 250). But the vampire church gives you eternal life—and youth—which is all right, "As long as you don't believe the soul becomes trapped in the vampire's body and can never reach Heaven. Or worse yet, that vampires are inherently evil and you are condemned to Hell" (*Guilty* 250).

In a world that provides no evidence of the existence of God or heaven, Anita Blake relies on *belief* to sustain her, just in case: "When the world is full of vampires and bad guys, and a blessed cross may be all that stands between you and death, it puts church in a different light. So to speak" (*Guilty* 235). The "fact" that vampires avoid crosses proves to Anita the power of what the cross stands for. But Hamilton's vampires are not all bad guys, not the Old Enemy of God nor agents of Satan. They are natural beings in the universal order, some good, some bad, who, like most humans, just want to live (although sometimes a bit disreputably). Hamilton acknowledges the appeal of the vampires' immortality—and offers few caveats against accepting it, except the usual Christian threat (sensibly modified, as noted earlier) of possible punishment and eternal damnation—if you believe in it. In such works, God seems to be generally a pretty tolerant and amiable Fellow.

As He is in P. D. Cacek's satirical parody *Night Prayers* (1998), where the power of belief is forcefully tested. The "hunter" position is filled by an itinerant preacher named Mica, "chosen Preacher to the People" (9), as he has designated himself ever since Jesus made the mark of the cross on his forehead when he was thirteen. In contrast to most of our vampire slayers, even Van Helsing, Mica is in direct communication with God, who guides him in his street ministry to the lost souls of Los Angeles. There he gets a paying job as a tout for a club of strippers and exotic dancers, who also happen to be vampires. Mica is immune to their attacks (not their seductiveness) because he is a Believer. When he falls in love with Allison, one of the strippers, God tells him that his job is to "lift [her] off the street of Self-indulgence and Pride and set her firmly back on her spiritual feet" (91). With all its humor, this is a story with a serious Christian message: Mica's Christian duty is to defeat evil (which is essentially misguidedness) not with violence but with goodness, by patient exhortation of the vampires and the whores and all those " 'who have fallen by the way' " (92). When his vampire landlady attacks him; he tells her, " 'I'll fucking *bless* the sin right out of you' " (before he is unfortunately forced to stab her in self-defense with a statue of the Virgin Mary) (161). These vampires are not eternally damned, as Mica realizes when he sees the peaceful look on his dead landlady's face: "She'd been Blessed and Welcomed Back" (162).

This is one vampire book in which Evil appears weak and confused, and Good, in the person of Mica, strong and determined although somewhat inept and a bit "off." Nevertheless, Goodness is slated to win. However, the simple Mica recognizes the problem (that scholars like Russell and Waller seem to miss) that these distinctions are not always clear. Mica pleads to God, " 'I *need* things to be in black and white. I need Your narrow line to follow' " (185). But there is no narrow line. In the end, God demonstrates his "marvelous sense of humor" (34) when, in Mica's worst moments of doubt, Allison, vampire and whore, saves his soul by urging *him* to believe. Like Coleridge's Ancient Mariner, Mica asks God to bless the vampires: " 'They were tempted by the dark pools of sin and fell away from the bright light of Truth and Love. Show them You Love them, Lord—Love Thy Enemies and Bless them Lord! BLESS THEM!' " (208). At the end, having learned a new tolerance and forgiveness of each other, Mica and Allison head off to Las Vegas, where he will preach and she will strip. The line between good and evil remains fuzzy, and the meaning of a Christian life is love for all God's people, living or dead.

Dualism Under God

If God lets evil into the world, He must have a good reason. A rather odd vampire novel that sets both good and bad vampires working for God is *The Cowboy and the Vampire: A Very Unusual Romance,* by Clark Hays and Kathleen McFall (1999). Each chapter is headed with a cross and the titles of the three sections are Death, Resurrection, and Redemption. These apply to the progress of the heroine Lizzie Vaughan as she learns to deal with becoming a vampire, and more, learns that her actual father is a bad vampire named Julius. Julius argues that the vampires' evil has a beneficial purpose, intended by God, for, in this old-fashioned Manichaeism, creation was " 'a cosmic circumstance pitting good against evil' " (93). Within the vampire community, Lizzie learns that there are two parties of vampires, bad and good. The bad vampires, led by Julius, believe that their *raison d'être* is to advance evil through " 'cruelty, perversion, and exploitation of the weak' " (94). Now, he insists, vampires are ready to replace humans as the elite of the universe (95) because the God-given religions of Christianity, Judaism, and Islam have failed to move man toward a greater goodness, especially in the selfish and mean-spirited twentieth century (as usual, half the world is ignored). In their confrontations with evil, humans were expected to become more like God, to become good, but the expectation failed (97) in spite of God's gift of heavenly immortality (100).

God gave the vampires a Messiah, too, named Susej, a mirror and parallel of the other, in order to " 'restore faith among the Vampires, faith in the morality of evil.' " God also gave vampires an earthly afterlife, for vampires do die, every night, and are reborn again each day. Susej too was resurrected; his spirit was taken to Heaven, where he sits on the left hand of God, claims Julius. Julius and Lizzie are direct descendents of this Susej (101). In opposition are the good vampires led by Lazarus (175–76), who have no desire to rule the world. Their mandate, as Lazarus sees it, is only to destroy evil humans in order to maintain the balance of good and evil (188). Lazarus believes that their Susej gave vampires this purpose: " 'We must hate so that love can exist. We must be evil so that good may exist. Ours is to contain the darkness that others may contain the light' " (266). Both views restate the ancient dualistic narrative of creation in which Darkness is as necessary as Light. Hays and McFall make modern use of the old Eastern European Manichaean or Bogomil belief that Satan is God's other son, a brother of Jesus, (or sometimes, in folk belief, an equal of God). This novel takes up the modified Christian version that *all* creation—angels and demons alike—belongs to God. The vampires can testify to this truth. For Lazarus was made a vampire by Jesus himself and therefore, as one human says, " 'knew the real thing. No mystery. No faith. Historical fact. Damn, . . . the implications are astounding' " (287). Thus, the vampires themselves provide proof for the existence of a universal Providence that explains death and even evil as meaningful and necessary in terms of a Christian dualism.

Christopher Golden's vampires in *Of Saints and Shadows* bring the good news affirming the faith while attacking the dogma and institutions of the church. As in *Cowboy*, Golden's vampires are a separately ordained class of beings, whose existence threatens the power and authority of the Roman Catholic hierarchy. An ancient book kept hidden by the church, called *The Gospel of Shadows*, explains the true place of vampires in God's intended plan. For the book affirms that "there was a plan and therefore a being or beings who had devised this plan" (*Saints* 42). The corrupt human Cardinal Liam Mulkerrin intends to use this book to take over the church and then the world. The book contradicts the church's (supposed) teachings about the innate wickedness of vampires and about their silly superstitions like fear of crosses or sunlight, which only work because the vampires themselves believe them.

Peter Octavian, a rational and enlightened vampire, realizing the truth, sets himself to help misguided vampires to mend their unnaturally wicked ways and become champions of man as God intended. They must defeat the demons and other monsters controlled by the church. In both this novel and its sequel *Angel Souls and Devil Hearts* (1995), the vampires move in and out of other realities that include a hell and a heaven, the existence of which is confirmed by "The Stranger," whom we might take to be Jesus (*Angel* 382). Golden's novels are a complicated hodgepodge of motifs from the Bible to *The Divine Comedy* to *Dracula* to H. P. Lovecraft's hidden existences, assuring the reader that not only is there a God but also a vast, active, and heavily overpopulated supernatural world barely separated from this one. The vampire, existing in at least two of these worlds, coming and going, knowing the past, present, and sometimes future, promises us that death is not final.

The religious sentiments in these Christian novels ring true. However fantastic, they are not merely an effort to pander to readers' superficial religiosity but represent a sincere piety (if not literal beliefs) of the authors and their sincere desire to share their faith by means of the popular figure of the vampire. Anne Rice may be the most sincere of all, with her intensely soul-searching, anguished, and God-obsessed vampires. Her series The Vampire Chronicles begins in New Orleans in the eighteenth century with Louis Pointe du Lac pursuing his Faustian desire to *know*—if there is a God, a reason for faith, or if there is nothing at all. The vampires are bringers of death, but why do they exist? Why does death exist? And what comes after it? Throughout the series, not only Louis but also his cynical "maker" Lestat de Lioncourt and their vampire friends and relatives wallow in Gothic gloom as they try to understand themselves, their origins, and the reason for the wrongs they—and others—commit, for the death they bring, and even more important for the horror and suffering that God imposes in all forms—if there is a God. For the most part, they fail. Death, inevitable and irrevocable, dominates the entire series, always within a Christian context despite the vampires' supposed Egyptian origins (in *Queen of the Damned*).

But in *Memnoch the Devil* (1995), Rice engages in an amazing attempt to deal with these mysteries through the vampire Lestat, whose self-assertiveness and defiance of God and the Devil earn him a special respect from these powerful Beings, each trying to get him to join his party. The dualism is superficial. In spite of Louis's constant agonizing in *Interview with the Vampire* about being damned, Rice's vampires are not innately evil; they are just another of God's creations, as is the Devil Memnoch. In addition to retaining a good deal of Catholic doctrine and sensibility, Rice has obviously read a good deal about the history of Christianity before beginning this volume, which is full of details about everything from Sumerian gods to the church's persecution of the Manichaean Cathars in the thirteenth century. In Michael Riley's *Conversations with Anne Rice* (1996), she mentions Mircea Eliade and Jeffrey Burton Russell, Karen Armstrong's *A History of God*, as well as apocryphal gospels and histories of witchcraft (283). I would also have guessed Neil Forsyth's *The Old Enemy* from the way her God continually designates Memnoch as His necessary, even beloved, Adversary. Forsyth introduces his study as "The Devil's *Story*" (3, my italics), for he regards Satan as a character in a narrative myth about God's "old enemy" (13). Memnoch, God's Adversary, retells this story to Lestat, and Lestat retells it to us.

Rice somewhat revises the traditional Christian narrative in this prolonged (and somewhat tedious) discussion between Lestat, Memnoch, and sometimes God. Memnoch both tells about and shows Lestat the Other World in its various manifestations. All the universe belongs to God (although no account is given of the cosmos at large, other galaxies, for example, or black holes—the usual serious gaps in most Christian versions). God, a sort of Deist, has designed the universe to evolve itself infinitely in some direction that He has apparently planned, but refuses to specify. He seems to have done so as a kind of amusing experiment, to see if it goes there, but he cares little what happens in the meantime. He is a God of Heaven, glorying in the praise and adoration of His angels, one of which is the not-so-impressed Memnoch.

Memnoch, as one of the Watchers sent to observe God's evolving creation, is appalled at the misery and horror of human life that is alleviated neither by humanity's desperate invention of religion or God's (actual) incarnation in Christ, or by their death and translation to the other world. Tired of his criticism, God finally tosses Memnoch out of Heaven, to live only among humans on Earth or in Hell (Sheol). He agrees to admit some more humans to Heaven if they praise and glorify Him and His creation. Memnoch points out that appreciation of the magnificence of creation is easy for those who have an easy life, but that most humans justifiably hate God and curse Him on earth and later in Hell, where they wander about lost and forlorn. Most dead humans are doomed to be as miserable in the other world as in this one—in spite of what their religion tells them. To justify misery and death, all God can come up with is, " 'Memnoch, Life and Death are part of the cycle, and suffering is its by-product' " (*Memnoch* 334).

Memnoch, like Lestat, is a rebel. Once on earth, he preaches against the sanctification of " 'self-sacrifice and suffering,' " and of " 'aggression and cruelty and destruction.' " Instead, Memnoch teaches delight and love of life (374). That is, Rice takes a Blakean view in which the devil stands for joy and expansiveness as opposed to a narrow and limiting God. In Hell, Memnoch teaches the lost souls what God failed to teach them with his Crucifixion but which He requires for their souls' entrance into His Heaven: " 'awareness of Creation and the Understanding of its deliberate unfolding; an appreciation of its beauty and laws which makes possible an acceptance of suffering and seeming injustice and all forms of pain' " (327–28). They learn to say, "We did not know," and to *forgive God* for His wrong to them, even to love Him. God wants them to love Him; Memnoch wants them to love one another. But he wants more; he wants to destroy God, he tells Lestat:

> "He's created beings more conscientious and loving than Himself. And the final victory over human evil will come only when He is dethroned, once and for all, demystified, ignored, repudiated, thrown aside, and men and women seek for the good and the just and the ethical and the loving in each other and for all." (374)

He wants Lestat to die (again), to join him in this worthy work. But souls are suffering in Memnoch's Hell as well; and Lestat finally refuses: " 'You're mad, the two of you! I won't help you' " (388). However, back on earth, Lestat inadvertently promotes orthodox faith by revealing a supposed Veronica's veil, which he picked up on his visit to God's Crucifixion. (Time does not *pass*, it seems, in the Other World.) The veil causes a great religious stir, a revival of faith—but it may be a lie, as Lestat knows, who trusts neither God nor Memnoch.

Ultimately, it is what one *believes* that makes him happy or miserable, what one thinks one knows. And Lestat can testify only to *himself*: " 'I am the Vampire Lestat. This is what I saw. This is what I heard. This is what I know! This is *all* I know' " (434). Like Faust in his quest for knowledge, Lestat never really gets where he is going. Although Anne Rice may think that readers will share and find meaning (hardly consolation) in this talky, dense, and confused adventure through Lestat's existential Heaven and Hell, it is unlikely. Nevertheless, in all this gloom, she *has* taken as a given and asserted, throughout the text, the grandeur of God's creation, the existence of some sort of other world, and the immortality of the soul. Her God says that He *has* a plan—which may be cyclical or may progress in a line to a rewarding or even an apocalyptical end. The plan may or may not have a meaning. The happy people are those who believe in the veil and the goodness of it all. It is no surprise to know that Anne Rice has given up on her cynical vampires and turned to Jesus and the angels to bring, I suppose, the really good news, but one doubts that she will ever entirely convince herself.

6

The Vampire God

Nature and the Numinous

Not all modern vampires proselytize for Christianity or incite absolute Good to wreak havoc on absolute Evil (or vice versa). For many writers of vampire literature, evil and good reside, often mixed, in vampires and humans alike and can be identified in their motives and behavior. Writers like P. N. Elrod, Chelsea Quinn Yarbro, and Kim Newman, whose focus lies elsewhere, do not apologize for their failure to place the vampire in a Christian story. Nor do writers of vampire literature for young people. Whatever the religion of the author, Stephanie Meyer in her Twilight series shows more direct concern about interpersonal relations and social adjustment without obvious Christian messages or moral judgments than with theological speculations of any kind, although such works do, of course, offer the usual vampire fantasy of immortality and otherworldliness.[1]

For adult readers, the scientific revolution and freedom of religion have made many of us into skeptics, especially given the innumerable and conflicting religious sects, each claiming a different truth. Even in the apparent religious revival of the millennium, many remain unconvinced by so many questionable faiths promising heavenly rewards in return for empty formulas and mechanical rituals. But they nevertheless hope to find meaning in this life and the intimation of some sort of immortality and ultimate transcendence of the merely material. For this, much vampire literature can provide a focus for speculation and even hope. Where "good" (or even just not-bad) vampires are characters, their immortality can be taken as an enjoyable fantasy, a pleasurable "what-if" as in Saberhagen's or Yarbro's novels, without dogmatic underpinnings and without punishment. We identify with these agreeable vampires who, as in a fairy tale, "live happily ever after." Even more, we have the opportunity to participate with them imaginatively in the defeat of evil and the defense of righteousness. In some cases, as with

Simmons's or Stableford's novels, they suggest—with scientific underpinnings and without punishment—the possibilities for the actual prolongation of the human life span.

Yet, although no longer the embodiment of pure evil (if they ever were), most modern vampires retain the mystery and erotic power of the old vegetation gods from which they very likely originated. They belong to a world in which sexuality is a natural manifestation of the life force in the great cycle. Jules Zanger recognizes this, but does not like it. Dracula, for him, along with other vampires, has lost the moral force he had as an "inverted Crusader in the service of a transcendent evil" (23). Zanger points out, regretfully, that many modern vampires possess "very little of that metaphysical, anti-Christian dimension, and his or her evil acts are expressions of individual personality and condition, not of any cosmic conflict between God and Satan" (18). The vampire has become, Zanger says, very much like a pagan god of the Greeks or Hindus: "The transformations of the vampire . . . might be understood analogically as a shift from a monotheistic, moralistic structure to a pagan hegemony of power and pleasure" (21). We might say, instead, that the vampire has, for the most part, backed away from Stoker's Puritanical (Hebraic) "moral enormity" (Zanger 24) in a universe of moral absolutes, and has *reverted* to his more compromising and humanized Hellenistic and Eastern sources as a free-spirited god of the weather and the seasons and, by the way, death and rebirth. He is, like Hades or Charon, personal, whimsical, and dangerously unpredictable. He is no longer a grand cosmic abstraction, but is an active agent in the natural world order, while remaining, like Death, beyond the bounds of reason or understanding.

Not only that, he is very sexy, especially in the movies, an arousing and seductive figure in line with his origins as demon lover, Byronic Hero/Villain, or ruler of the underworld (male or female), a combination of the sinister and the erotic. Beth E. McDonald (1992), in a Jungian analysis, cheerfully praises Stoker's Dracula as an archetypal "trickster" figure, a kind of god of Death, whose malicious depredations and disruptions of established order are necessary to bring about change. That is, he is also a god of fertility and new life. In *Our Vampires, Ourselves*, Nina Auerbach too *admires* Stoker's Dracula for his "animal affinities" (95) and the "subterranean vitality" (94) that "energizes" his victims into life (95). The vampire's "erotic vitalism," earthiness, and animalism (not Satanism) as played by Bela Lugosi was responsible for the popularity of that movie. To her, the horror that Dracula arouses in his victims and among the respectable is not the fear of death, but the fear "of being alive" (94). For, Auerbach points out, "Stoker's Undead do not drain vitality; they bestow it" (96). After Lucy is bitten, for example, she "enthralls spectators because she is not stilled. After death, she continues to writhe and foam, prowl and shriek, turning not to marble, but to blood" (97).

Auerbach seems less impressed with the Hammer Draculas played by Christopher Lee, because, she believes, they have become weakened and cut off from human life and from the cosmos by their sensitivity to sunlight (not a problem in Stoker's novel or in folklore). They cannot move about freely as before and, "bounded by senses and flesh," lose the effect of godlike power (121–22), as do most movie vampires following them. It is true that too many of their descendents have become, we might say, almost wimpy, more like two-bit hit men in fancy clothes, or the tricksters of cap and bells, or mournful lovers than like grand satanic figures. One reason might be that many moviemakers and novelists have weakened them with more and more pointless rules and sensitivities (like the sunlight rule or the no sex rule). Worse, in my view, they have put them into clubs or "covens" or street gangs in slummy "hoods" with bossy leaders whom they "must" obey like a bunch of whiney adolescents (see *Underworld*, for example). Perhaps, this is why most of Whedon's Hellmouth vampires are so easily disposed of. The loner, self-sufficient vampires Angel, Spike, or Glory have a much greater staying power.

Christopher Lee's Dracula is one of the loners and the stayers, hard to defeat and easily reborn with just a little blood dropped on his ashes as in *Dracula Prince of Darkness* (1965). In fact, in these earlier films, Lee's Dracula projects a powerful chthonic godlike authority of his own, more ferocious and aggressive than Lugosi's. In spite of a regrettable susceptibility to priests and crosses, he proves impossible to destroy, except, as Auerbach points out, temporarily by the sun. That is, in my view, he is stopped, like any ancient nature god, by impingement on the territory of another perhaps stronger deity (whom, as usual, we do not meet): sun gods are sky gods, after all, whereas the vampire is a god of the storm and the underworld and the cycles of life and death. Hammer's Dracula is effectively satanic in his contempt for puny mortals and in his ability to arouse horror and panic. He calls up the passions of women and quashes their would-be defenders with a single hypnotic glance. By his very nature, he is sexual and vital and wholly without remorse or guilt, just as a god of the underworld ought to be. In contrast, Peter Cushing's vampire-hunter Van Helsing is skinny, cold, competent, and dull, a perfect foil of Enlightenment rationality and puny technology. Hammer's vampire women in films like *The Vampire Lovers* (1970) and *Countess Dracula* (1970) display a comparable sensual energy and disruptive power. After Hammer's sexy undead, vampire movies were more likely to show the victims as responsive and encouraging than earlier films. Badham's Lucy or Coppola's Mina, or Whedon's Buffy are not victims at all but warm and willing coconspirators.

The Vampire Lover

As we have noted, this arousing and seductive quality of literary vampires (as opposed to the cloddishness of most folklore vampires) is inherent in their role as a form of demon lover. Polidori's story sold, no doubt, because of a general sympathy with Byron's wicked charms (or charming wickedness). Although Stoker's Dracula does not actually make love, Stoker's ambivalent treatment of him as a powerful and passionate Byronic villain suggests that possibility. Early Dracula films like Murnau's *Nosferatu* and Browning's *Dracula*, by reducing Stoker's four Christian "heroes" to one or two helpless and ineffective young businessmen and one old man, focus our interest and sympathy on the vampire, whose energy and singleness of purpose almost overwhelm the passive and inept human protagonists. Even the dismal Nosferatu appears as a forlorn image of doomed love, as does the determined Carmilla in both Le Fanu's story and the Hammer film *The Vampire Lovers* based on it. In most modern versions of *Dracula*, the Christian significance expounded by Stoker's Van Helsing vanishes in our inability to admire the twerpy Jonathan or really to derogate either the handsome and well-groomed Bela Lugosi or the elegant and articulate Frank Langella as a "foul thing of the night." It is Dracula we are in love with or even want to be—the vampire lover who bestows immortality.

In Badham's film *Dracula* (1979), Frank Langella carries on as King of the Dark Lovers, an affront to respectable men. God and Satan are not an issue for Langella's Dracula. *His* heresy is his rejection of the dreary conventions and routines of Victorian life. He rescues the eager Lucy from the dullness and pettiness of Jonathan and her father. (The girls' names are reversed in this film.) His Byronic soul transcends their trivial conceptions of right and wrong, guilt and innocence. How can she resist? Moreover, her human protectors are so full of flaws, so weak and vain and selfish, that they can hardly be taken as knights of Christ. Nor can they assert either spiritual or intellectual authority over Dracula's passion and knowledge—or the vast *extent* of his power "over land and sea." His refusal to die even in the sunlight emphasizes his role as a kind of god of eternal return. (If you think he is dead and done for, look again.)

Francis Ford Coppola's Dracula, played by Gary Oldman, is also a lover. Although old and dried-up at home, in England he introduces himself to the ladies by bounding into their garden in the form of a wildly erotic fantasy beast. But Coppola's England is ready for him. In spite of its title, *Bram Stoker's Dracula*, Francis Ford Coppola's version seems to miss Stoker's point about the orderly, civilized England of knightly youth and virtuous maidens. Instead, it is a turbulent hothouse of raging prurience and disorderly passion before Dracula ever shows up. The young ladies snickering at pornographic pictures are hardly models of Victorian purity and repression, nor is there anything about the slovenly and raving Van Helsing that resembles an Arthurian knight defeating the dragon of Hell or even an intrepid scientist confronting the terrors of the irrational like Hammer's Peter Cushing. The film deliberately undermines the Christian dualism on which it is ostensibly based (if based on Stoker). To hold Lucy in her tomb, Van Helsing waves a cross at her, bellowing, "We are strong in the Lord and the power of His might!"—but, if this is the case, most of us (like Mina) would prefer the "soulless" Dracula with his old-fashioned self-restraint and meticulous courtesy (in human form at least).

Superficially, Coppola presents Dracula as a fierce enemy of God, who turned himself into a vampire by cursing God, attacking a cross, and drinking the blood that ran from it. But, in spite of this and of his gargoyle performance in the garden, what he really brings into England is "true love" in the sense of the modern drugstore romance. At the beginning, Dracula asks Jonathan, "Do you believe in destiny? That time can be altered by a single purpose and the luckiest man alive is the one who finds true love?" Dracula is redeemed by love in spite of all those people he stuck on posts. And, his beloved wife, damned for all eternity (for suicide), is also redeemed by being reincarnated in the devoted Mina, a good woman, after all, who will do anything for her man. In the modern world, apparently, only romantic passion can offer the ecstasy and wonder *and* redemption that used to be taken as a sign of holiness and spiritual transcendence.

At the end, back in Transylvania, Mina's love for Dracula relights the candles in Dracula's abandoned church, and Dracula begins to glow like Jesus in an old painting. Mina declares, "I understand how my love could release us all from the powers of darkness. Our love is stronger than death." After he is "saved," Dracula asks Mina to "give me peace," and to the sound of something like choirs of angels, she cuts off his head. The conclusion represents less Christianity and more a kind of sentimental or romantic New Ageism in which the power of human emotion alone can exalt the individual beyond the bounds of mortality. In such stories, love replaces religion as the way to ecstasy and immortality—not love of mankind, which seldom comes up, or God—but the romantic pairing off of the kind that landed Paolo and Francesca in the Inferno.

Love stories between a human (usually female, but not always) and a vampire (usually male, ditto) do comprise a vast portion of vampire novels. A blurb on the back cover of Maggie Shayne's *Wings in the Night* seems to sum up the religious element, the modern substitution of love for faith and piety as the way to heaven: "For centuries, loneliness has haunted them from dusk till dawn. Yet now, from out of the darkness, shines the light of eternal life . . . eternal love." The idea seems to be this: if, as Ariès says, the modern concept of heaven is a place where we meet those we love, then love will get us there. Possibly, the ecstasy of love on earth *is* heaven or will lead us straight on into an everlasting euphoria. In the popular novels by Stephanie Meyer, the irresistible vampire lover promises an earthly immortality of committed love. (This is for young people, after all.) A demon lover need not be a "monster," as his willing "victim" Bella Swan keeps reminding him—especially when he can lift her to heaven with every kiss, can indeed become her "savior" in the end.

In *Buffy the Vampire Slayer*, the vampires Angel and Spike also find salvation in love. In season 6, Spike goes so far as to get himself a soul (whatever that means), at the cost of considerable suffering, all for love of Buffy—and then, in the final episode of the series, sacrifices his life for her, positively beatified in a blaze of (apparently) heavenly light. For Angel, "true happiness" seems to lie in having really good sex with someone he really loves. In works like these, it is sometimes the vampire himself who, through love, brings redemption to the aimless and the lost, or anyway, the bored. All this might not seem like religion, but to find true love forever, for many Americans (of a certain age and life experience), *is* the meaning of life and the path to eternal joy.

Alternative Lives: *Buffy* and *Angel*

All this means that, no matter how much we hear about the victims and the hunters and their friends and families, vampire literature is *about* vampires and what they can do for us—which is to find us immortality. Vampire stories find immortality in all sorts of places in addition to English gardens, crypts, and Mayan strip joints. Many of them, as we have seen, join with science fiction in positing complex other realities or dimensions that exist alongside and interact closely with this one, as in, for example, the novels of Christopher Golden or Brian Lumley. One advantage of this approach is that, like fairyland or Shangri-La, it offers other *places* for a kind of physical immortality—or at least continuation of the self—to occur without committing the writer to a judgmental Christian Manichaeism—a cruel eternal damnation or a sappy happy heaven. Christianity need not be an issue at all (although it often is). Moreover, the vampire's ability to cross easily between or even among various dimensions suggests that we too may share in these other realities without recognizing them (yet).

The vampire shows us that immortality is, somehow, somewhere, possible. Nancy A. Collins, for example, in *Sunglasses After Dark* creates a parallel "in-between" world, usually disguised or invisible, of assorted supernatural beings, including the dead. Around and among living humans are the Pretenders, witches, ogres, succubi, vampires, revenants, even angels (59–61). They are a ragtag crowd but generally harmless to humans and often helpful. Limited humans cannot perceive all that exists around us; our inability to see the dead does not mean they are not there. Life as we understand it is a temporary condition in a universe of apparently endless possibilities. In Collins's works, it is the vampire who introduces some of these possibilities to us—as Rice's sexy vampires lure us into the convoluted streets and the dark possibilities of her Gothic mystery cities.

Joss Whedon's *Buffy* and *Angel* series present an even more convoluted universe with whole realms of other places, including some rather casually Christian ones. For example, there may be, after all, a traditional Christian Afterlife that Buffy's mother *might* briefly have come back from. The soulless Angel, slain by Buffy, goes off to suffer somewhere referred to as Hell. Later, when Buffy is brought back from the grave (it *can* be done!—by magic, of course, not God or Satan), she tells Spike that she *thought* she was in heaven because she was so happy. Walking through walls and materializing from furniture in the last season of Angel, the now truly deceased Spike demonstrates that there is indeed an Other, immaterial, or ghostly reality.

Through Buffy, Angel, and their friends, we are introduced to a world where the dead as well as other supernatural beings are all around us, walking among us, offering us a drink or passing out business cards. As in Newman's *Anno Dracula* or Collins's *Sunglasses After Dark*, the line between life and death, the living and the dead, even body and spirit is reassuringly vague, almost nonexistent (although in *Buffy* evil and good are rigidly demarked and labeled: soul versus no soul). Even more exciting alternatives to mere death exist in the myriads of other dimensions or other, parallel realities that the characters can sometimes draw on or move in and out of, like the Quor-Toth dimension in *Angel* where the spiffy demon Lance comes from and which one can reach through a portal in his karaoke club. Or, magically, the familiar world can shift into something different, as in season 3 of *Buffy* ("The Wish") when Anya conjures up a different Sunnydale without Buffy (à la *It's a Wonderful Life*). In season 5, Buffy acquires a full-grown sister who pops into the flow of time as though she had always been there.

Ordinary concepts of linear time and fixed place are continually called into question along with the trustworthiness of our perceptions—and even the concreteness of physical objects. An ordinary high school girl turns out to be a super-powered vampire slayer; the dull librarian turns out to be her trainer and "Watcher" and, later, reveals an exciting past of his own. Magic reverses the identities of a crazed cheerleader mom and her reluctant daughter. A high school teacher is revealed to be a giant bug. One young lady is turned into a rat, demons live in the computer, Giles becomes a demon, and on and on. Even Dracula shows up—but from where? In the final season, "The

First" (the Devil?) appears in the guise of Buffy's mother, of schoolmates, even of Buffy. In *Angel*, Cordelia's previsions from the Powers-That-Be (God or gods?) knock her into a different "astral plane" and eventually into a new kind of being. For even integrity of Self can suddenly be transformed, as Oz becomes a werewolf, the mayor becomes a giant demon-worm, and Wesley, Glory, and Spike show up again in *Angel*, just when we thought they were gone forever.

All these variations and transformations of time, place, and being suggest (in a kind of New Age/science fiction/California way) that life and death are, perhaps, merely facets of a complex multidimensional existence or even a dream, in which, with a little effort, we can find another life. By the time we have been through *Buffy* and *Angel*, we have traveled through a regular rabbit warren of tunnels, portals, escape holes, traps, lives and relives, deaths and revivals, ghosts and demons, dreams and fantasies, heavens and horrors that twine endlessly in and out of one another so that, when the apocalyptic end finally approaches (at the end of *Buffy* and then *Angel*), we are pretty sure our friends in California will simply find themselves in another dimension or another town. Again, it will be vampires who reveal these alternate existences to us. Without Whedon's Undead, we might never consider that death *might be* just a transferal to another plane or a metamorphosis of being.

In a book about Joss Whedon, Candace Havens reports that Whedon describes himself as a "bitter atheist" who finds meaning only in his creations:

> "I'm a scary, depressive fellow. There's no meaning to life. That's kind of depressing. There's no God. That's a bummer too. You fill your days with creating worlds that have meaning and order because ours doesn't. And so, yeah, I'd say the fact that I'm a pretty depressive fellow also has to do with my ambition, staving off the inevitable." (158)

In *Images of Fear: How Horror Stories Helped Shape Modern Culture* (1990), Martin Tropp reminds us that the "final revelation" of Gothic horror is "Death itself." Horror literature fascinates, he says, because it compels us to confront our "fear of our own mortality" (219). Through Gothic literature, we learn, not faith and transcendence, but "to accept the certainty of death, to laugh at the madmen running the universe, to find joy in the midst of despair" (218). In creating his two television series, Joss Whedon has become one of those madmen. In his world, "The First" is not a beneficent god who creates an orderly and benign universe but the ultimate destroyer, creator of chaos, whose goal is Death.

Nevertheless, this self-proclaimed atheist pursues the two religious aims we have focused on in vampire literature: (1) the search for transcendent meaning and order in the universe that might give us (2) an understanding of death. *Buffy* and *Angel* testify to his failure. For although both these series continually allude to systems, concepts, and constructs of many areas of experience—religion, literature, science, anthropology—Whedon's use of them tends to be whimsical, superficial, and disconnected from a supporting context of belief or even consistent unbelief. *Buffy* and *Angel* play with (I hesitate to say *explore*) popular religious concepts that might *seem* to *offer* meaning (or hope), not only Christian but many others—witchcraft, occultism, devil and demon worship, magic, New Age spirituality, a sort of pantheism, various paganisms, and so on. In no case do Whedon or his writers explore them deeply or appear to take them seriously. They show up more like pictures in a Time-Life world mythology volume (or scenes from a low-budget sci-fi series) than like thoughtfully considered windows onto the meaning of existence. The occasional treatment of Christianity, for example, in the form of secretive cowled monks or hypocritical fundamentalist preachers, appears superficial and casually contemptuous.

Even as god of his own world, Whedon cannot seem to come up with a satisfactory formula. Nevertheless, although not traditionally religious, Whedon's *Buffy* and *Angel* illustrate Delbanco's argument that moderns are seeking some more clearly defined life goals than mere social and economic self-promotion. In the end, however, these dramas fail to define such goals because, in their simplistic dualism, their categories of good and evil are filled with cartoonlike stereotypes—the evil, for example, with murderous monsters, all too like the giant bugs or ghouls or evil aliens of early horror films and comic books, or the icy ruthlessness of megalomaniac government and legal institutions (the secret military Initiative in *Buffy* and the law firm of Wolfram and Hart in *Angel*). With a few exceptions (Dracula, Spike, and Angel), these evildoers have no narrative of their own to justify or explain their senseless but dedicated wrongdoing—or even their existence. Good and evil are not defined by a philosophy or a thought or a need or a passion, but consist primarily of arbitrary designations.

In Sunnydale, Good equals the sunny innocence, neatness, and orderly society of this privileged, well-groomed, middle-class happy valley. As in Stoker's genteel England, ugly disruption threatens when the vampires appear. Not from foreign lands but from Sunnydale's own cemeteries and sewers come intolerable death and decay. Naturally, they must be suppressed, and Buffy and her pals are forced out of their placid lives into an urgent struggle against the forces of chaos. At first, this is accomplished with a great deal of panache and good cheer by Giles and Buffy and her trusty band of really nice kids. Sunnydale remains sunny. But a mournful darkness gathers as we move through *Buffy* and into *Angel* and gradually deepens into gloom. In the brutal slums and high finance of Angel's Los Angeles, where all that counts is money and power, darkness seems to prevail even in daytime. In both series, Evil is depicted as powerful, pervasive, active. Good is weak, intermittent, and confused, even among the slayers and their helpers. Struggle itself for some small decency and rightness becomes the meaning of life—and something more, a kind of tragic nobility in maintaining hopeful persistence in the face of the vast apocalyptical Nothing.

Through the vampires—bad and good—Buffy and friends become aware of how close their cheerful, carefree lives are to that secret, dark world that is never admitted to or discussed by the adults, at school or home. As a result, Buffy and her young friends congratulate themselves on knowing more about "reality" than the adults, whom they feel they are saving (until they find how deeply many of them—the principal and the mayor, for example—are corrupted). *Buffy* also points up the truth that, in the modern world, parents really do not know what or how much their kids know about death, for example, or even family or community "skeletons." While the parents aim to keep them innocent as long as possible, the kids battle deadly monsters whose existence is ignored or denied by the adults. For young viewers, identification with Buffy and her "Scoobies" may fulfill a yearning to feel that they are useful and knowing, not trapped in prolonged childhood ignorance and easiness, but instead, engaged in a noble and necessary battle for significant goals. Even this yearning is undercut when, in the episode "Normal Again" in season 6, we find Buffy in a mental hospital, where a kindly doctor attempts to convince her that her slayer life and world have been nothing more than a prolonged schizophrenic hallucination. Like a modern teenage Don Quixote, she chooses to return to the heroic hallucination.

Like Stoker's *Dracula* and Rice's Vampire Chronicles, *Buffy* and *Angel* are about death and the need to come to terms with it. Superficially, at the beginning of the *Buffy* series, the vampires and the demons from Hellmouth would seem to stand for, or be, Death itself. They are the "unnumbered dead" that threaten the living in ancient and present myth (*Gilgamesh*, for example, and *Night of the Living Dead*). The subject of unnatural, violent death appears in almost every episode of *Buffy* and *Angel* and is often openly discussed. In season 5, Spike tells Buffy that slayers like her are killed ultimately because they have a "death wish," are "a little bit in love with it" ("Fool for Love"). This obsession with death is another important reason for the popularity of these vampires with young viewers, who are discouraged from knowing and speculating about this taboo subject—or any unpleasantness, for that matter. They want to *know*, not about sex (which they apparently know very well), but about death and the horrors that go with it. No doubt, too, they envy the excitement and danger that Buffy enjoys. In spite of seeming to propose some sort of continued life after death, these series suggest that awareness of death—or the risk or challenge of death (even in fantasy)—is what gives life whatever meaning it has.

And not just for individuals, for in *Buffy* and *Angel*, the world is in constant danger of a final vast and sudden assault from the Hellmouth. Again, Delbanco may be right: our whole society longs for some meaningful challenge, which it expresses in contemporary millennial apocalyptic hysteria (which Whedon's two series simultaneously encourage and make fun of). *Buffy* and *Angel* have numerous parallels—and no doubt sources—in pop "documentaries" about ancient prophecies and codes that predict upcoming catastrophes (appearing even on channels that purport to be about history or science), not to mention alien infiltrations, deadly plagues, and unknown hordes of "people out there who want to hurt us." The rescue of the world from apocalyptic disaster is so often repeated in *Buffy* and *Angel* that it becomes a running joke.

Like Stoker's *Dracula*, *Buffy* and *Angel* assure us that with hope, sincerity, and know-how we can stave off our doom. But, even though the word *apocalypse* calls up Christian associations, in these modern, popular works, no one expects God to help. No one blames God either. He just is not there. Indeed, a good deal of *Buffy* is a comment on the ineffectuality of conventional religion when it comes to explaining or dealing with death and disaster. As in Stoker's *Dracula*, assorted superstitions, incantations, magical objects and rituals, ancient tomes, glowing globes, smoking incense, mysterious bones, and, of course, stakes are the keys to self-preservation, when they work. In this meaningless world where superstition and magic pass for religion, these *things* are the only recourse for our little band of knights as they struggle to stave off Armageddon for another day.

For, from the first murder of Buffy's schoolmate Jesse, to the anticipated final battle in the last season of *Angel*, in Whedon's chaotic and unstable world, only death is sure; only death has meaning. As the apocalypse approaches in season 7 ("Potential"), Buffy angrily sums it all up for the potential slayers, telling them that this is "all about death." Death is what the slayer breathes and dreams about. She tells them to stop complaining: "You're all going to die." Death is "the big dessert at the end of the meal." If she did not say this so angrily, it might sound like a joyful promise, but it is not. It is just a fact. No one is to blame, really. Life is an effort to prolong and protect one's own existence often at the expense of others; vampires, after all, are just hungry. But the vampires also teach that life is worth fighting for and hanging on to even though the best one can do is to assert one's self (or one's imagined self) in a noble Byronic gesture of defiance against the annihilating powers. And there may be, after all, another dimension to hop into at the last minute. For even without God (or logic), Whedon's television vampires and their humans and happenings do manage to transcend the tedium and humdrumness of everyday life to reveal other exciting and magical worlds.

The Gothic Numinous

Even when no reference is made to religion or the afterlife, the vampire teases us with dreams of transcendence and of defeating death on this earth. By their very nature, even the silliest or dullest vampires, so long as they have human form, lead us from our ordinary lives into the realm of the immortals. In her essay "Teaching the Vampire: *Dracula* in the Classroom" (1997), Norma Rowen says that when she asked students what they found most attractive about the vampire, they most often answered "immortality." She found that they were "very drawn to the idea of the vampire as a spiritual being," although she seems to be dismayed that they "did not see this figure as connected with any specifically religious concept of good or evil" (Christian dualism?). What did fascinate them was "the possibility of some kind of transcendence of this world," which she attributes to "the human need for transcendence." She reluctantly concludes that for some, "the vampire has assumed the space vacated by God" (235). Possibly they are being seduced by Anne Rice's glamorous vampires, who live in an "immensely exhilarating" world of "luxury and brilliance," free from human limitations and trials (242).

Tony Thorne identifies these "latest forms of vampirism"—free and exhilarating—with an "upsurge of new-age pantheism, the elevation of angel and faery archetypes over saints," even an actual "embracing of the Dark Half" in popular religion (53)—all this deriving from an ancient "shamanistic tradition." (How it derives is not clear.) And he claims: "The human individual is once again treating the inhabitants of the shadow–realm not as something unreachable and insubstantial but as entities to impersonate, as magic dramas to enact," and by doing so, to experience their power and transcendence (54). In an essay on "Carmilla" (1999), Robert F. Geary points out the irony that while it is "the lure of the supernatural" and "the chill of numinous dread" that sells Gothic fiction, these are often the very qualities that are most embarrassing to modern critics (19–20). Religion, death, and the afterlife are not acceptable topics socially or academically, and they are often retranslated by critics into more manageable psychological or sociological paradigms. Yet Geary reminds us that the function of such literature has always been to assure readers that a supernatural realm exists (22)—although, as we have seen, not always a Christian one.

Other critics agree with Geary that the intention of Gothic literature is to inspire a sense of supernatural wonder, what the Romantics called the Sublime. Some critics adopt the term *numinous* from Rudolf Otto in his book *The Idea of the Holy* (1923) to designate this aura of the mysterious or sacred. In his study *The Gothic Flame: Being a History of the Gothic Novel in England* (1957), Devendra Varma, for example, regards the Gothic as a reassertion of the numinous against the clockwork view of the universe posited by Rationalism. Gothic novels rose from "an awestruck apprehension of Divine immanence penetrating diurnal reality." The Gothic quest is not just a quest for horror and forbidden thrills but for "other-worldly gratification" (211). In this context, he says, vampires "are mute witnesses of our alliance with a greater power and make us aware of our fleshly infirmity and our higher destiny" (212).

Also drawing on Otto, S. L. Varnado (1987) discusses the Gothic search for a sense of "awe, mystery, and fascination" that leads to an awareness of a supernatural, transcendent reality (15). Varnado is critical of those who try to understand books like *Dracula* in realistic terms, say, of sexual frustration or economic competition (96), preferring instead the interpretations of critics like David Punter or Leonard Wolf, who see a "mythic quality" in the work (97). To Varnado, *Dracula* "dramatizes the cosmic struggle between the opposing forces of darkness and light, of the sacred and profane" (97–98), both elements of the "divine power," lifting us, ultimately, beyond the rational and "into a region of dread and wonder" (111).

Not everyone approves of this Gothic blurring of distinctions, however. Linda Bayer-Berenbaum deplores the fact that Gothic literature is essentially religious in its desire for transcendence yet ignores institutionalized religion or, worse, denigrates it. In the first place, she accuses the Gothic of being fascinated with death for "the absence of limitation it implies, for its absolute finality, for the mystery of its void, and for its primeval chaos." This is the other side of the Gothic "need to prove life forces, to test them" (31). The Gothic is indeed a search for the numinous. But instead of accepting the given religious projection of the supernatural into a remote and heavenly realm, she says, the Gothic supernatural "permeates the world around us, looming, fantastic and immediate" (32). Gothic literature involves not only "the materialization of the spiritual" but also the "spiritualization of the material" (33). Opposites are fused; limits are broken down between the living and dead, the sacred and the profane, the natural and supernatural, mundane and holy (33–35): "The devil can be worshipped as well as God" (35).

The vampire is a good example: "A spirit incarnate in life," the vampire is a "perverted Christ figure who offers the damnation of eternal life in this world rather than the salvation of eternal life in the next" (35). Moreover, the vampire is bloodthirsty, oversexed, and incestuous—but all of this with echoes of Christian belief and ritual, such as the communion blood of Christ (36). She speculates that the Gothic represents a sort of "religious depravity" by providing "a cathartic outlet for the sense of guilt that accompanies the decline of a strong religion." It is "a decadent religion that continues to express the existence of the spiritual in the absence of belief in a benevolent God" (37).

Harold Bloom addresses this modern search for the spiritual in a book called *Omens of Millennium: The Gnosis of Angels, Dreams, and Resurrection* (1996). He discusses the American obsession with angels, near-death experiences, and astrology as symptoms of (at the time) premillennial anxiety. These are debased versions of an ancient Gnosticism, he argues, promises of some sort of personal immortality (depending on our religious beliefs). The popular imagination of a "guardian angel" (227) for each of us can be equated with the humanized popular version of Jesus, who loves us, who promises that God loves us, and who absorbs all our anxieties. Focusing on the desire for spiritual transcendence through ecstatic experiences, Bloom—in a reversal of Delbanco—intentionally ignores the great popularity of books, movies, and television specials about Satan and so-called Satanism, ghosts, vampires, serial killers, and other representations of the dark side.

Yet one cannot help believing that, in some way, these macabre imaginings belong to the same obsession, the same need to confront, understand, and gain control over evil and death as do the angels. They are not themselves signs of defiance or a death wish or the love of evil, but a crude recognition, perhaps, of God's other son, lord of the material not-so-perfect world. They may well be signs that conventional religion does not adequately respond to doubts concerning the meaning of a life that is so short and so easily and pointlessly ended. Many books about vampires and other dark mysteries, for example, no doubt represent the same kind of shallowness and commercialization that corrupts popular books of religious inspiration. But with a difference: they both cater to a desire for mystery and transcendence, but unlike angels, vampire stories seldom promise easy comfort or facile solutions. Even humorous vampire literature retains a kind of melancholy arising (so to speak) from awareness of the Dark Side, of death and the unknown, brought home in the figure of the vampire.

The Vampire God

For, villain or hero, the dual nature of the vampire, human and supernatural, living and dead, makes him unique even in Gothic literature and makes it possible for him to appear as a powerful god—or goddess—offering more than mere fantasy. As a living human, he resembles the "Dark Romantic" figure that G. R. Thompson discusses in the introduction to his *Gothic Imagination: Essays in Dark Romanticism* (1974)—akin to the suffering, conflicted, uncompromising Byronic Hero. Yet, such figures, says Thompson, are "emblems of supernatural power external to the human mind" and at the same time, emblems "of the agony within the human mind and spirit" (7). Thus, Thompson speculates that "the major Gothic works contain within them mythic sources that account for their hidden power. The Gothic thrusts us forward into an existential void as it simultaneously recalls us to the Age of Faith" (10). Writers of vampire literature in the Gothic mode, like Rice and Whedon, positing and then undermining issues of religion, philosophy, or ethics at every turn, would almost seem to be deliberately illustrating Thompson's discussion, especially Whedon as he seeks for meaning and hopes for an immortality that he cannot believe in, even for vampires.

The modern vampire also crosses boundaries to combine the mystery of the undead with the romance (and nice clothes) of the Gothic villain or the Byronic Hero—or the ambition and arrogance of Faust, or the grand, self-sacrificial suffering of Prometheus, or even more, the healing power of Jesus. To enhance the vampire's awesomeness, many writers portray him as a superhero or super-villain of the night, wearing his own classy uniform (even Angel has that coat), and surrounded by the gloomily impressive trappings of Gothic literature and old horror films. And everywhere they fill the works with assorted Christian icons, imagery, and references, not to mention some very unchristian images of the underworld, ghosts, demons, witchcraft, and powerful pagan death gods—to arouse a sense of Gothic wonder and otherworldliness. Even the rather unexciting Varney produces some horrifying moments lurking over his intended victims or skulking around in charnel houses and ruins. And funny vampires like Elvira in *Elvira, Mistress of the Dark* (1988) or Sesame Street's Count von Count or George Hamilton's flashy Dracula in *Love at First Bite* or the un-neighborly vampires of *Fright Night* (1985) or child vampires of *The Lost Boys*, because they are undead, carry a bit of the sense of wonder and fear that goes with death itself—even more so with death rising back to life.

Even the most matter-of-fact, humanized vampire crosses the impassable divide and radiates with the glow of the numinous even as he horrifies with the decay of the tomb. For the vampire—both human and god, profane and sacred—represents all humanity and their mystifying plight, caught between their eager hopes of immortality and their devastating awareness of the finality of death. Also, because the vampire wields supernatural powers, including some control over nature, it retains the aura of the sacred that it must have had in its original role as a deity of death and storm and dark as well as of vegetation and fertility. David J. Skal believes that, even in funny toys or silly movies, the vampire, particularly Dracula, "provides secular society with a quasi-religious engagement/exorcism of the demon Death" because it is "equated literally with power, resurrection, and beneficial energy" (*Monster* 347).

The modern vampire has reclaimed his position as at least a minor deity. He has become a significant figure in an imaginative pantheon of gods, heroes, angels, witches, devils, and alien visitors that make up our modern folklore. On the occult shelves in our bookstores, books about vampires and demons are set side by side with books about angels and fairies. This array suggests the revival or persistence of age-old traditions of superstition, magic, and religion among the modern folk who patronize the bookstores. That Whedon, for example, draws on all of these indiscriminately indicates that his many viewers are at least superficially familiar with them and many accept them as fascinating and wonderful. Here too we find J. Gordon Melton's *Vampire Book: The Encyclopedia of the Undead* (1999), a most compendious and useful general reference book on vampires. Even under the label of Christianity, books about God and Jesus sit next to books about Satan and his minions—at various levels of scholarship, superstition, and orthodoxy. For the literary vampire is a well-known symbol of cosmic forces, powerful, immortal, and knowledgeable, a kind of dark divinity, who has become an American icon.

On the other hand, as Zanger noticed, as his popularity has increased, the vampire has become increasingly humanized, increasingly one of us. A writer about modern religion, Stephen Prothero, in his book *American Jesus: How the Son of God Became a National Icon* (2003), may offer a clue to the reason. Like Bloom, he comments on the American tendency to adopt a simplified and optimistic view of things, in this case, of the figure of Jesus. In an interesting parallel with the vampire, Prothero describes how Americans have gradually adopted and Americanized Jesus, making him over in their "own image" (7), while at the same time relegating the harsh God of the Puritans to a background or nonexistent role. In the process, Jesus has been transformed, Prothero says, "from a distant god in a complex theological system into a near-and-dear person, fully embodied, with virtues they could imitate, a mind they could understand, and qualities they could love" (13). Gradually, too, Jesus has become liberated from scripture and, in some cases, even from Christianity itself by Hindus, Buddhists, and even Jews, who could feel "free to embrace whichever Jesus fulfilled their wishes" (14). Over the years, Jesus has come to be viewed, not only as the Son of God, but as a sympathetic and loving friend, a father or brother, a comfort and a guide, sometimes a revolutionary, a hero, a celebrity, and a role model.

The vampire, too, since Stoker, has become more human, and like Prothero's cheerful Jesus, in his own way also reflects American optimism about all things, even death. For while the vampire still retains his iconic significance as a god of the dark side, as Prothero says of Jesus, "his popularity only seems to have increased as he has become more human" (300). Like the folk, we moderns need supernatural beings we can identify with, not vague images of vast incomprehensible abstractions. And so we respond to the foppish vampires of Anne Rice's New Orleans or the annoying adolescents of *The Lost Boys* or the brutal killers of *Near Dark* (1987). But the vampire survives because he is not simplified, mindless destruction like a giant bug or an alien "Thing" or even a vast amorphous Satan so often overcharged with whatever we fear or hate. Even as a good guy with human flaws, like Newman's Kate Reed (*Anno Dracula*) or television's Nicholas Knight, he is more like us than the sinless Jesus ever could be. For he is a complex personality in conflict with his own divided condition and his place in a confusing cosmos.

Sometimes, the vampire is a kind of dark angel, a help to humankind, a hero or a savior in his own right, like Yarbro's Saint-Germain, who survives from age to age to right wrongs and rescue deserving ladies, or Nicholas Knight or Angel, who are atoning for their evil deeds in a previous time, or Christopher Golden's first vampire, the Stranger, with "an angel's soul and a devil's heart" (*Angel* 383), who defines the modern vampire's mixed nature. He may be almost a kind of Jesus himself, as in Patrick Whalen's *Night Thirst*, where the persecuted vampire-hero Braille develops the power of healing the sick. (Like Jesus, Braille too becomes the victim of a vast government machine.) The vampire is still also often a killer and destroyer, but also, like each of us, a loner, an outcast, an existential self locked in his own being and circumstances.

Thus vampires, even at their happiest, offer only a melancholy hope in face of the existence of evil, the limitations of mortality, and the inevitability of death. These themes pervade even such cheery vampire comedies as *Love at First Bite* or *My Best Friend Is a Vampire* or *Innocent Blood* in which Communists take over, peasants attack, our placid lives are suddenly reversed, friends must say goodbye, and vampires too can die. The more humanized vampires are, the more they are bound by earthly concerns, and the more they humanize the "dark side," denying a rigid dualism, qualifying its supposed malevolence or demonstrating its complexity and ambiguity. Even an unequivocally satanic vampire like Stephen King's Barlow, although not himself wracked by doubts and ethical conflicts, is not so much a demon from outside who brings evil into an innocent and unsuspecting community as the emblem and fulfillment of the very human envy, greed, and lust of its ordinary inhabitants.

Yet, no matter how wicked or how reformed, how earthly or how remote, the vampire remains active and vital in this world, to which he has such an intense attachment. In ancient and modern literature, an irresistible demon or vampire lover often serves as a personification of death. Yet we might recall Frazer's identification of the gods and goddesses of death with those of fertility and vegetation and the cycles of life. The objection might be raised that many modern (male) vampires are deprived, by their creators, of normal sexual potency (often under a mistaken belief that this is the folklore tradition) and thus can hardly be said to represent fertility. In spite of this, some critics regard vampires as strongly sexual—and many writers strive hard to fulfill this expectation: even impotent vampires give very erotic bites. Female vampires (excepting, of course, the "good girls," as in Yarbro's novels) are almost always blatantly erotic, from Goethe's "Bride of Corinth" to Le Fanu's Carmilla to Selene in the recent movie *Underworld.*

Anyway, even without sex, vampires *do* make other vampires. Most of them, like Dracula, *do* at least manage to rise from death over and over again (often at Halloween) in an eternal cycle—like gods of the corn and the seasons. More important, their impotence (or sterility—sometimes it is not clear) may actually serve to enhance the effect of their godlike nature. (We don't see Jesus producing any offspring, do we? Even God only had one.) In any case, many vampires, male and female, express their earthy vitality through brief and indiscriminant pairings, just like those frivolous Greek deities. A lot of little vampire offspring would certainly undercut their godlike status and authority, not to mention threatening the food supply. Moreover, dhampirs, the ungrateful children of vampires and humans, are notorious in folklore for destroying their undead parents. And in any case, how could they be "our" vampires, as Auerbach calls them, if they have a big family to look after?

The failure of vampires to produce offspring can also be seen as a modern adaptation that responds to timely issues of potential overpopulation—or at least relieves the writer from having to address this problem. Even more important, it relieves vampires of the concerns and responsibilities of parenthood, which invariably detract from sexual desirability as well as undercutting the image of independence and power (and evil). (Whedon almost destroyed Angel with that ridiculous baby in the third season.) Freedom from family entanglements keeps the free and feral vampire, well, free and feral. It allows the vampire embrace, the death bite, so to speak, to become in itself the ecstatic union with the god of life and death that John Cuthbert Lawson argues was the meaning of the ancient mystery cults of the vegetation gods and goddesses. It offers the imagination of mystical transcendence of the kind that Bloom says Americans long for and find in near-death experiences. Vampire offspring would certainly complicate the moment.

Moreover, for all their freedom, it is surprising how little sex the ancient gods and goddesses of death and fertility actually indulge in. *They* die, and *they* return, and with them all nature. Byron, in his fragment of a story, refers to both Diana, the *virgin* goddess of the moon *and* fertility deity, and the corn goddess Demeter, a rather no-nonsense but not very prolific mother. The vampire's occasional desire for intimacy—and nourishment—is human; his detachment from the everyday human lot, his aloof self-sufficiency is godlike. Nature lives off nature, and much vampire literature specifically equates the vampire with at least a minor god or goddess of nature and/or the underworld. Holland's Byron is supposedly *Lord of the Dead* (although not a very convincing one since he spends most of his time sulking in a crypt). In Michael Cecilione's *Thirst*, the vampire Julian recalls his decision to become a vampire: " 'I would become a god, not the pale half-god formulated by the Jewish monotheists, but God as He was feared and venerated before He was cleaved in two. I would be a force of nature, impersonal and powerful, a dispenser of both life and death' " (272).

Anne Rice's novels abound with references to the vampire's godlike powers, particularly in the matter of distributing death to humanity. In *Interview with the Vampire*, Lestat urges Louis to accept his power:

> "God kills, and so shall we; indiscriminately He takes the richest and the poorest, and so shall we; for no creatures under God are as we are, none so like Him as ourselves, dark angels not confined to the stinking limits of hell but wandering His earth and all its kingdoms." (89)

He praises to Louis the vampires' godlike detachment from the lives they watch and influence: " 'The ability to see a human life in its entirety, not with any mawkish sorrow but with a thrilling satisfaction in being the end of that life, in having a hand in the divine plan' " (*Interview* 83). *The Vampire Lestat* (1985) and *The Queen of the Damned* speculate that vampires are descended from ancient gods, and in *Memnoch*, God calls Lestat, " 'my brave bringer of death to so many' " (340). Lestat may not be God or even Satan, but, in Rice's novels, he is the agent of God. And he and most other literary vampires have at least the powers of a middle-level Greek or Roman deity along with their immortality. Like Hades, Osiris, Persephone, they are gods of the dead, or like Charon, at the very least, conductors to another world. Like Hermes, the trickster and fertility god, or like "Godfather Death," the vampire, even though he conducts souls to the underworld, also has the capability to heal and to bring prosperity.

Like folklore vampires, most literary vampires are not Satan or opponents of the Christian God. Rather, they have become minor gods of the cycle of life and death in a modern folklore pantheon, often but not always explicitly subordinated to the Christian God. Thus, the vampire stands for both the power of death and the triumph of life. We often forget that, from folklore to the present, the vampire's real crime is his excessive love of life on this earth, his refusal to give it up for some vague promise of bodiless immortality. It is not only the demonic and the dark of the vampire that appeals to us; it is the energy and vitality—and humanity—set against a religion that, at its very best, offers self-denying contemplation and a remote, unattainable, incomprehensible mystery. The vampire has the enviable choice to die or not, to take an action in the matter rather than to wait passively for it to happen. For us, death is an inevitable finality, but the vampire offers an image of death as an active life force that entails an action on the part of the dying—whether it is one of acceptance or resistance. The vampire is the "distinguished thing" that Henry James is supposed to have thought of when he believed he was in the process of dying. If nothing else, the vampire makes death fascinating, exciting, sexy.

One might complain that too much vampire literature fades into mere shallow emotionalism, sentimental romance, and/or disgusting violence and cruelty that obviates any genuine sense of wonder or spiritual transcendence. Evil is still simplistically reduced to sex, brutality, and sadism, ultimately the mindless nastiness of the serial killer. Too much vampire literature fails to find any meaningful vision. But at its best, the vampire, as a numinous figure, gives death a significance and a grandeur that it seems to have lost in the twentieth and twenty-first centuries when it is so often hidden, ignored, or reasoned out of existence. The powerful figure of the vampire justifies our innate awe and fear of death in a world that brushes off such emotions as irrational and childish—or, worst of all, unproductive—or buries them in unconvincing promises of a misty eternity of saccharine sweetness. Moreover, the vampire as a personification of death assumes the role of an immortal god, of Hermes or even Hades. He is not just an accident of nature, but a vast personality, who takes a personal interest in each of his victims. From Polidori's Lord Ruthven to most of the Draculas to Anne Rice's Lestat, vampires carefully select, follow, and watch their victims. Indeed, most vampires choose their prey carefully, understand them, and even absorb their minds and experiences. Death does not just happen; it makes choices—to leave, to take, or to transform—that are often contingent upon the victim's circumstances and character.

The vampire's defeat may be misrepresented as a defeat of death, as in Stoker or the Hammer films. But we know he is really undefeatable; he will always come back. Good or evil, Christian or pagan, the vampire is immortal and promises immortality, one way or the other, in this world or the next. For the whole concept of the vampire, from its beginnings in folklore to present-day fiction, is based on the idea of the immortal soul.

Notes

Introduction

1. Some good *examples* of them appear in *Dracula: The Vampire and the Critics* (1988), edited by Margaret L. Carter; *The Blood Is the Life: Vampires in Literature* (1999), edited by Leonard G. Heldreth and Mary Pharr; *Blood Read: The Vampire as Metaphor in Contemporary Culture*, edited by Joan Gordon and Veronica Hollinger (1997); and Carol Margaret Davison's (ed.) *Bram Stoker's Dracula: Sucking Through the Century, 1897–1997* (1997).

2. The authorship of this serialized novel has frequently been debated or even split up between two known writers of popular "penny dreadfuls": Thomas Peckett Prest or James Malcolm Rymer. I am going to accept E. F. Bleiler's convincing attribution of the work to Rymer in his "Note on Authorship" in the Dover reprint of 1972 (even though he contradicts the great "authority" Montague Summers—of whom more in the text).

3. See, for example, Richard Wasson, "The Politics of Dracula"; Carol A. Senf, "Dracula: The Unseen Face in the Mirror"; and Burton Hatlen, "The Return of the Repressed/Oppressed in Bram Stoker's Dracula"—all three reprinted in Margaret Carter's excellent collection *Dracula: The Vampire and the Critics* (1988).

4. A good example of our society's refusal to discuss death openly is illustrated by how many critics reject the opportunity to do so offered by Dracula and other vampire literature, and instead prefer reexamining the livelier, life-affirming topic of sex.

5. This includes such folktales as those in Jan L. Perkowski's *Vampires of the Slavs* (1976) from the Ukraine and Serbia (235–247) or almost any other collection of Slavic folklore; good examples are tales by Alexis Tolstoy, collected in *Vampires: Stories of the Supernatural* (1969), written from the end of the 1830s to the beginning of the 1840s, according to the translator Fedor Nikanov. The story of Goethe's "Bride of Corinth" apparently originated in an ancient Greek folktale and reappears occasionally in collections of Greek or Slavic folklore (see note 1 to chapter 3).

6. Van Helsing's whole speech goes as follows:

> [To Audience.] Just a moment, Ladies and Gentlemen! Just a word before you go. We hope the memories of Dracula and Renfield won't give you bad dreams, so just a word of reassurance. When you get

> home tonight and the lights have been turned out and you are afraid to look behind the curtains and you dread to see a face appear at the window . . . why, just pull yourself together and remember that after all *there are such things*.

I have spoken to people who saw the play when they were young and who claim that they were thoroughly spooked by this dreadful warning.

Chapter 1. Vampires and Science

1. What Calmet finally said was that, given the paucity of evidence and scarcity of actual eyewitnesses, he did not feel justified making a final and absolute decision, especially one that would seem to limit the abilities of God:

> What has principally prevented me from giving rules and prescribing a method for discerning true and false apparitions is, that I am quite persuaded that the way in which they occur is absolutely unknown to us: that it contains insurmountable difficulties; and that consulting only the rules of philosophy, I should be more disposed to believe them impossible than to affirm their truth and possibility. But I am restrained by respect for the Holy Scriptures, by the testimony of all antiquity, and by the tradition of the Church. (2:361–62)

This can hardly be taken as an endorsement.

2. According to Philip Jenkins, Saint-Germain was the model for the magus in Edward Bulwer-Lytton novel *Zanoni* (1842), and figured in a prominent role as a model and master for various occultists including Madame Blavatsky and the Theosophists (72). Colin Wilson in *The Occult* treats him as a charming adventurer and con man (314–17). For an example of Saint-Germain's alchemical teachings, see, for example, *Saint Germain on Alchemy: Formulas for Self-Transformation*, recorded (we are told) by Mark L. Prophet and Elizabeth Clare Prophet (Corwin, MT: Summit University Press, 1993).

3. In trying to find a scientific reason for the vampire superstition, some writers and critics have associated the fictional vampire "disease" with actual illnesses, particularly with porphyria. According to R. S. Day in an article in *New Scientist* (1984), such efforts, whether motivated by a genuine scientific interest or the desire to create a sensation in the press, are completely inaccurate in their understanding of the causes and symptoms of porphyria. But worse, they have thoughtlessly created embarrassing problems for those people who actually have the disease but because of this kind of unfounded association feel compelled to conceal it from their credulous neighbors and even to risk their lives by avoiding treatment. In fact, there is no similarity between the symptoms of porphyria and the characteristics of vampires except for sensitivity to sunlight, a problem for many of us.

4. I feel compelled to make it clear that I do not believe that there can be a "science" of vampires (a scientific study of vampires), as some enthusiasts suggest, any more than there can be a science of fairies or elves. Those who study people who think they are vampires should be the same as those who study people who think they are Cleopatra or Jesus—that is, psychologists or psychiatrists. There *can*, of course, be a science of fairy tales and folklore.

5. This is the title character in a story by M. R. James, "Count Magnus," published in *Ghost Stories of an Antiquary* (1904). The name was possibly taken from Count Gabriel De la Gardie (1622–1686), a Swedish statesman. The manor house may have been based on De la Gardie's ancestral home. No doubt he also provides the name of Lestat's "sire" in the Anne Rice novel. Wilson cites the whole name and develops the background on pages 87 and 96–98.

Chapter 2. Vampires and Society

1. Here are a few short passages from sample laments recorded by Kligman during her research in Romania. These laments are spoken by the mourners.
In this, a dead godmother says farewell to her family:

> "May you remain in good health.
> Stay well, I say to you all,
> Godsons and goddaughters,
> For those that I have wronged,
> Please forgive at the end.
> You friends and neighbors,
> I wish everyone well;
> Until the second coming
> For eternity remembered." (294)

To a young girl in a death wedding that Kligman witnessed:

> "Little beauty and bride,
> Young you leave home,
> Get up, beauty, around the house
> And we'll ready you as a bride
> Oh, we'll ready you as a bride
> And then go to swear
> Like everyone does.
> Oh beauty, dearest girl,
> You are well married;
> You will never come to us,
> We'll live with sorrow,
> Oh, little beauty and bride,
> Oh, your husband won't fight with you,
> But we'll be upset." (302)

Danforth records similar laments from Greek villagers:

> "Uncle, we are all here. What can we do for you? You used to gather us around like your children. We all would have come—husbands and grandchildren too—if the taxi driver had let us. Wake up and talk to us for the last time, uncle. You won't be here for the wedding of Vassiliki [his ten-year-old granddaughter].
>
> Uncle, uncle, we'll shout for you for three days if you want. Wake up, uncle. Wake up and hear the songs. This is the last time we'll see you. Uncle, what can we give you to take to Anna [their dead sister]?" (128)

2. Vampires provide an irresistible vehicle for moral lessons and social and political satire. Frayling cites an article from the *London Gentleman's Magazine* (May 1732) that suggests these reports from the East are concealed political attacks in an "*Allegorical Style*" in which vampires that "torment and kill the *Living by sucking out all their Blood*" represent corrupt government ministers, for "Private Persons may be *Vampyres*, or *Blood-Suckers*, i.e. *Sharpers, Usuers, and Stockjobbers, unjust Stewards* and the *dry Nurses of the Great Estates*; but nothing less than the Power of a *Treasury* can raise up a compleat *Vampyre*" (rpt. in Frayling 27). Voltaire in the supplement to his *Dictionnaire Philosophique*, compares "speculators, tax officials and businessmen" to "bloodsuckers" although, in his mind, the "true vampires are the churchmen who eat at the expense of both the king *and* the people" (qtd. in Frayling 31).

Today, too, the indestructible bloodsucking vampire is perfect for satirizing the ruthless sociopathic greed of modern business practices. In Floyd Kemske's novel *Human Resources* (1995), the vampire Pierce becomes the chief financial officer of an American company, Biomethods, Inc. where his job is to be hatchet man and thin out the ranks of employees. Fritz Leiber's "Girl with the Hungry Eyes" (1949) is an advertiser's dream, "the quintessence of the horror behind the bright billboard":

> She's the smile that tricks you into throwing away your money and your life. She's the eyes that lead you on and on, and then show you death. . . . She's the lure. She's the bait. She's the Girl.
>
> Like modern merchandizing, she says, " 'Feed me, baby, feed me' " (347–48).

In Brian Aldiss's *Dracula Unbound*, Dracula comments, without humor, on human iniquity in general:

> "Your kind regards my kind as evil. I have been forced to observe your kind over the centuries, since you huddled in caves against the ice. Has ever a day gone by, or a night, in all those centuries, when you have not put someone to death? Women subjected to all kinds of injury, children abused, babies flung over cliffs, slaves beaten, preachers stoned, witches drowned, villages burned, wars fought over nothing . . . a litany

> of murder in more various forms than we of the Un-Dead could ever command. Your sins are endless and committed willfully. What we do we cannot help." (166)

His argument is strengthened by the fact that his listener, the protagonist Joe Bodenland, has invented a super "F-bomb" capable of far greater destruction than any previous weapon as well as a "Time Train" with which he intends to dump nuclear waste somewhere else in time without a thought for the consequences. A popular subtheme of many modern vampire stories is the innocuousness of a few vampires versus the vastness of human viciousness.

3. Men of the fifties and sixties also seem to have been liberated from the naïve belief that the "good girls" played by Debbie Reynolds and Doris Day were really what they wanted. Hammer Films' buxom, forward, and frankly sensual females—vampires and otherwise—surely shook a few young men into the sexual revolution of the sixties and seventies—and suggested there might be more thrills to life than a steady income and a rose-covered cottage.

Chapter 3. Vampires and Psychology: Body, Soul, and Self

1. The poem is based on a story that first appears in the Book of Marvels compiled by Phlegon of Tralles who served under the Emperor Hadrian (117–138 CE). But it has frequently been retold since then, and Goethe probably got it from a German translation. Goethe added a Christian/pagan religious complication and set it in Corinth. It pops up now and then, with modifications, in books of Greek or Slavic folktales. See Phlegon of Tralles's *Book of Marvels*, translated and with an introduction by William Hansen (Exeter, UK: U of Exeter P, 1996).

2. In his book *The Living Dead: A Study of the Vampire in Romantic Literature* (1981), James B. Twitchell finds the popularity of the Dracula figure in this very selfishness and self-assertiveness:

> Dracula is terrifically alluring; he has everything we want: he has money and power without responsibilities; he parties all night with the best people, yet he doesn't need friends; he can be violent and aggressive without guilt or punishment; he has life without death; but most attractive of all, he has sex without confusion. . . . It's all take, no give. If only he didn't have those appetites! (134)

Moreover, he is "articulate, shrewd, decidedly upper-class, intelligent, and sexually potent" (134).

3. In his introduction to *Immortal Engines: Life Extension and Immortality in Science Fiction and Fantasy* (1996), Eric S. Rabkin quotes Woody Allen: "I don't want to achieve immortality through my work, I want to achieve it through not dying" (xi)—that is, by continuing in his breathing, sentient, conscious *self.* But some writers in this volume, including Rabkin, are concerned with the contradictions involved

in *wishing* for personal immortality of any kind. Rabkin entitles his introduction "Immortality: The *Self*-Defeating Fantasy" (ix). For even the Christian promise of "a perfect immortality" in eternal obedience to God falls short when we consider how "dependent is our happiness on notions of individual freedom and of desire" (x).

Chapter 4. The Religious Vampire: Reason, Romantics, and Victorians

1. The Society for Psychical Research, founded in England in 1882, was the most respected and respectable of the various organizations dedicated to spiritual and psychic phenomena, first, because of its insistence on strict adherence to scientific procedures and methods in its research, and second, because of its highly educated and prominent membership. Members included men like Henry Sidgwick, professor of Moral Philosophy at Cambridge (first president of the SPR); Frederick William Myers, classical scholar and philosopher; Alfred Russell Wallace, biologist; William James, American psychologist and philosopher; Arthur Balfour, prime minister 1902–1905; Andrew Lang, anthropologist; Henri Bergson; Gilbert Murray, and on and on. The American Society for Psychical Research was founded in 1884, by men with equally impressive credentials. Both organizations remain active today.

2. Most people who enjoy these imaginative works know that they are fantasies. But in their book *The Gothic World of Stephen King: Landscape of Nightmare* (1987), Gary Hoppenstand and Ray B. Browne see horror literature as providing a modern "cultural context," a "belief system," that operates very much like religion and superstition (9). Leonard Heldreth and Mary Pharr believe that many moderns consciously and sanely inhabit fantasy worlds at least part of the time:

> Among the ironies of contemporary Western culture is a dependence on admitted artifice, a tendency not to believe but rather to savor pretense itself as if it were a belief. Fantastic universes are constructed almost by committee mandate and are treated as though they had an independent existence. (4)

Examples include the fictional Narnia or Buffy's Sunnydale or life on the *Enterprise* and especially in the landscapes of popular role-playing games. In these worlds, groups of (usually young) individuals share a "pretend" alternative existence that runs concurrently with this world—like the games published by White Wolf, *Vampire: The Dark Ages* or *The Masquerade*, with elaborate rules for Gothic vampire fantasies.

3. A look at these earlier beliefs and practices may help make some sense of the oddities associated with folklore vampires, particularly some of the seemingly arbitrary and often rather silly means of dealing with them. The methods of killing Death or the old year, for example, are similar to those used to kill vampires, involving fastening the effigy to a tree or an obvious substitute, like a wooden pole. (Vlad Tepesh was not the first impaler.) The effigy is usually burned or drowned, but may also be stabbed or staked—often by a specific type of wood that has particular

magical significance—decapitated, or torn to shreds, all of these ways of immobilizing or destroying the "body."

Thus the various means of containing or destroying vampires can be related to more ancient practices or beliefs related to their vegetative role. Covering the vampire's grave with seeds or grain or nets on which to count the knots (a common method of thwarting vampires) might be suggestive of some former god's function as a vegetation deity (especially if we remember that gods of the sea were also often associated with the underworld as well). Frazer indicates that the killing of the old vegetation was also often the occasion for saving or planting of new seeds (1:252). (We might think of the scattering of Osiris's "seed" after his dismemberment and rebirth.) This explanation of the seeds or net certainly makes more sense than the folklore "explanation" that vampires are so very slow in counting that they never get around to going out. Instead, they are being "pacified" with offerings.

Barber indicates that in Romania and Hungary a sickle was often buried with a corpse to keep it from coming back as a vampire—possibly because of its sharpness (50), like a weapon perhaps—but a sickle is not a weapon; it is the tool of the reaper, the scythe of the old year. Frazer discusses the sacredness of certain kinds of plants, such as fern, mistletoe, or oak, as in the myth of Balder, who could be slain only by mistletoe. These sacred associations suggest to us why specific kinds of plants or wood are regarded as inimical to vampires. Certain animals, too, like wolves or horses, also commonly associated with vampires, may have been identified with various vegetation deities (Barber 94). (Garlic seems to be identifiable with almost everything.)

4. I have photographs of at least two such urns, labeled as Roman, taken in the Metropolitan Museum of Art. Harrison's discussion appears in a section entitled "The Hero as Snake," for the snake might be honored as an incarnation of an ancestor's ghost or an ancient local hero (Harrison 326–27).

5. Roxana Stuart, in *Stage Blood: Vampires of the 19th-Century Stage* (1994), gives a thorough account of the many popular plays based on this story, beginning in Paris with Charles Nodier's melodrama *Le Vampire* in 1820 (see pages 45ff.), followed by six parodies of it within a few weeks (55). Also, in 1820, another successful adaptation appeared on the London stage, *The Vampire; or The Bride of the Isles*, by James Robinson Planché. Stuart lists twenty-nine vampire plays from the nineteenth century as examples of the vampire craze that also expressed itself in stories—and even an opera—in France and America as well as in England.

6. Mario Praz, in his book *The Romantic Agony* (1933), offers the Byronic Hero as an example (along with Shakespeare's villains and Milton's Satan) of the British public's "innate Manichaeism" (60). Indeed, as G. R. Thompson says, Gothic literature originates in the English inability to ignore the Dark Side both in man and the cosmos, as well as in the Romantic fascination with the "duality of the Middle Ages" (3).

7. In her biography of Bram Stoker, Barbara Belford points out how much Stoker was drawn to occult ideas popular with so many of his friends and acquaintances. For example, in Dracula's seduction of Lucy and Mina, Stoker makes use of the ideas of mesmerism and hypnotic trances. In *Dracula*, he refers to the psychologist Jean-Martin Charcot (*Dracula* 235), who popularized hypnosis as a treatment for

hysteria, and he attended at least one meeting of the Society for Psychical Research, at which F. W. H. Meyers spoke about Freud's experiments with hypnosis (Belford 212). A number of good friends belonged to the Hermetic Order of the Golden Dawn, such as Pamela Colman Smith, a clairvoyant, who illustrated the first edition of Stoker's novel *The Lair of the White Worm* (213). Other friends were Constance Wilde, who became a devotee of Madame Blavatsky, and Hall Caine, who shared Stoker's interest in spiritualism (Belford 216, 218). Although there is apparently no evidence of Stoker's direct participation in such groups, he was clearly acquainted with their theories about the nature of spirit and the soul.

8. Van Helsing is one of the "Experts in the Identification of Evil," who are the subject of chapter 3 in David Frankfurter's study *Evil Incarnate: Rumors of Demonic Conspiracy and Satanic Abuse in History* (2006). He is the one "who articulates the uniform, coordinated threat posed by demons and the Devil—a threat corresponding to the power he himself brings against it." In doing so, he articulates a general anxiety or worry in concrete terms that can be dealt with and becomes himself "a heroic, solitary warrior against evil" as he "lays out the nomenclature and intentions of the demonic" (32) and then shows how this evil can be identified and purged by "embracing the prophet's ideology and submitting to his rituals of healing and purification" (33).

Van Helsing fits this description so fully and consistently throughout the novel that one wonders—what one has not wondered before—if this is not what Stoker intended: an oblique attack on those who stir up fear of ghoulies and ghosties and other supernatural horrors for their own amusement or to gain control of others, like an old nursemaid scaring the little children.

Chapter 5. The Religious Vampire: The Twentieth Century

1. According to *Webster's*, nepheline is a crystalline silicate of sodium, potassium, and aluminum common in igneous rocks.

2. Abraham Gottlieb Werner was the name of an important seventeenth- and eighteenth-century geologist, a professor of mining and mineralogy. His significant contributions had to do with the formation of rocks and his pioneer work in the classification of rocks and minerals. Some consider him to be the father of modern geology. (Why are we demonizing stones? Is this a joke?)

3. Romkey's location of Illuminati meetings in Bavaria links them with an actual secret society founded there in 1776 by Adam Weishaupt, based on Enlightenment ideas and opposed by the church. Thus, like Varney, Romkey's vampires hold rationalist principles and believe in a benign and rational God.

Chapter 6. The Vampire God: Nature and the Numinous

1. See Deborah Wilson Overstreet, *Not Your Mother's Vampire: Vampirism in Young Adult Fiction* (2006) for a survey of some recent vampire literature written for adolescents.

Works Consulted

Ackroyd, Peter. *Albion: The Origins of the English Imagination.* New York: Nan A. Talese-Doubleday, 2002.

The Addams Family. By Charles Addams (characters), Caroline Thompson, and Larry Wilson. Dir. Barry Sonnenfeld. Perf. Anjelica Huston, Raul Julia, Christopher Lloyd, Elizabeth Wilson, Christina Ricci, Judith Malina. Paramount Pictures, 1991.

Aldiss, Brian W. *Dracula Unbound.* New York: HarperCollins, 1991.

Alexiou, Margaret. *The Ritual Lament in Greek Tradition.* London: Cambridge UP, 1974.

Anderson, Richard. "*Dracula,* Monsters, and the Apprehensions of Modernity." *Bram Stoker's Dracula: Sucking Through the Century, 1897–1997.* Ed. Carol Margaret Davison, with Paul Simpson-Housley. Toronto: Dundurn Press, 1997. 321–29.

Andersson, C. Dean. *I Am Dracula.* New York: Zebra Books-Kensington, 1993.

Angel. By David Greenwalt, Joss Whedon, Tim Minear et al. Dir. James A. Conner, David Greenwalt, Tim Minear, Joss Whedon, Bill L. Norton, Terrence O'Hara. Perf. David Boreanaz, Alexis Denisof, J. August Richards, Charisma Carpenter, Andy Hallett, Amy Acker. Prod. Mutant Enemy, Kuzai Enterprises, Sandollar Television, 20th Century Fox Television, David Greenwalt Productions. WB Television Network, 1999–2004.

Ariès, Philippe. *The Hour of Our Death.* Trans. Helen Weaver. New York: Oxford UP, 1981.

Auerbach, Nina. *Our Vampires, Ourselves.* Chicago and London: U of Chicago P, 1995.

Baker, Nancy. *Kiss of the Vampire.* (Formerly titled *The Night Inside*). New York: Fawcett Gold Medal-Ballantine, 1993.

Baker, Scott. *Ancestral Hungers.* New York: Tor-Tom Doherty, 1995.

Barber, Paul. *Vampires, Burial, and Death: Folklore and Reality.* New Haven: Yale UP, 1988.

Bayer-Berenbaum, Linda. *The Gothic Imagination: Expansion in Gothic Literature and Art.* Rutherford, NJ: Fairleigh Dickinson UP, 1982.

Becker, Ernest. *The Denial of Death.* New York: Free Press-Macmillan, 1971.

Belford, Barbara. *Bram Stoker: A Biography of the Author of Dracula.* New York: Alfred A. Knopf, 1996.

Bell, Michael E. *Food for the Dead: On the Trail of New England's Vampires.* New York: Carroll & Graf, 2001.

Bergstrom, Elaine. *Mina.* New York: Berkley Books, 1994.

Bierce, Ambrose. "The Death of Halpin Frayser." 1893. *The Undead.* Ed. James Dickie. London: Pan Books, 1971. 145–61.

Blackwood, Algernon. "The Transfer." 1912. *The Penguin Book of Vampire Stories.* Ed. Alan Ryan. London: Penguin Books, 1987. 203–12.

Black Sunday. 1960. [La Maschera del Demonio]. By Nicoli Gogol (story), Ennio De Concini, and Mario Serandrei. Dir. Mario Bava. Perf. Barbara Steele, John Richardson, Andrea Checchi, Ivo Garrani, Arturo Dominici, Enrico Olivieri. Prod. Alta Vista Productions. American International Pictures, 1961.

Blackula. By Raymond Koenig and Joan Torres. Dir. William Crain. Perf. William Marshall, Vonetta McGee, Thalmus Rasulala, Denise Nicholas, Vonetta McGee. Prod. Power Productions, American International Pictures (A.I.P.), 1972.

Blade. By David S. Goyer. Dir. Stephen Norrington. Perf. Wesley Snipes, Stephen Dorff, Kris Kristofferson, N'Bushe Wright, Donal Logue, Udo Kier. New Line Cinema, 1998.

Bleiler, E. F. Introduction. *Varney the Vampyre or The Feast of Blood.* By James Malcolm Rymer. London: E. Lloyd, 1847. 2 vols. New York: Dover, 1972. v–xv.

Blood and Roses. [Et mourir de plaisir.] By Sheridan Le Fanu (based on Le Fanu's "Carmilla"), Claude Brulé. Dir. Roger Vadim. Perf. Mel Ferrer, Elsa Martinelli, Annette Vadim, Marc Allegret, Rene-Jean Chauffard, Marc Allegret. Paramount, 1960.

Blood Ties. By Richard Shapiro. Dir. Jim McBride. Perf. Harley Venton, Patrick Bauchau, Kim Johnston Ulrich, Michelle Johnson, Jason London, Bo Hopkins. Prod. Richard and Esther Shapiro Productions. Fox Network, New Horizon Pictures, 1991.

Bloom, Harold. *Omens of Millennium: The Gnosis of Angels, Dreams, and Resurrection.* New York: Riverhead Books, 1996.

Blum, Richard, and Eva Blum. *The Dangerous Hour: The Lore of Crisis and Mystery in Rural Greece.* New York: Charles Scribner's Sons, 1970.

Bram Stoker's Dracula. By Bram Stoker (novel), James V. Hart. Dir. Francis Ford Coppola. Perf. Gary Oldman, Sadie Frost, Winona Ryder, Anthony Hopkins, Keanu Reeves, Richard E. Grant. Prod. American Zoetrope, Osiris Films. Columbia Pictures, 1992.

The Breed. By Christos N. Gage and Ruth Fletcher. Dir. Michael Oblowitz. Perf. Adrian Paul, Bokeen Woodbine, Ling Bai, Péter Halász, James Booth, Lo Ming. Prod. Motion Picture Corporation of America (MPCA). Columbia, TriStar Home Video, 2001.

Brownell, M. R. "Pope and the Vampires in Germany." *Eighteenth Century Life* 2 (1976): 96–97.

Bruce, Steve. *Religion in the Modern World: From Cathedrals to Cults.* Oxford: Oxford UP, 1996.

Buffy the Vampire Slayer. By Joss Whedon et al. Dir. Joss Whedon et al. Perf. Sarah Michelle Gellar, Nicholas Brendan, Alyson Hannigan, Anthony Head, James Marsters, Emma Caulfield, Michelle Trachtenberg, Kristine Sutherland, Charisma Carpenter, David Boreanaz. Prod. 20th Century Fox Television, Mutant Enemy, Kuzui Enterprises, Sandollar Television. Twentieth Century Fox Film Corporation, 1997–2003.

Burger, Gottfried August. "Leonora." 1773. Trans. Alfred Ayres. *The Vampire in Verse: An Anthology*. Ed. Stephen Moore. New York: Dracula Press, 1985. 13–20.

Byron, George Gordon. "Fragment of a Novel." 1816. *The Penguin Book of Vampire Stories*. Ed. Alan Ryan. London: Penguin, 1987. 1–6.

———. *The Giaour*. 1813. *Byron's Poetry: Authoritative Texts, Letters and Journals, Criticism, Images of Byron*. Ed. Frank D. McConnell. New York: Norton, 1978. 84–114.

———. *Manfred*. 1817. *Byron's Poetry: Authoritative Texts, Letters and Journals, Criticism, Images of Byron*. Ed. Frank D. McConnell. New York: Norton, 1978. 124–59.

Cacek, P. D. *Night Prayers: A Vampire Novel*. Darien, IL: Design Image, 1998.

Čajkanović, Veselin. "The Killing of a Vampire." Trans. Marilyn Sjoberg. *Folklore Forum* 7.4 (1974): 260–71.

Calmet, Augustine. *The Phantom World or, The Philosophy of Spirits, Apparitions*. 1746. With an introduction and notes by Reverend Henry Christmas. 2 vols. London: Richard Bentley, 1850. (Originally published as: Dissertations sur des Anges des Demons et des Esprits, et sur les revenants, et Vampires de Ningrie, de Boheme, de Moravie, et de Silesie. Paris, 1746.)

Campbell, Ramsey. "The Brood." 1980. *The Mammoth Book of Vampires*. Ed. Stephen Jones. New York: Carroll & Graf, 1992. 94–105.

Carter, Margaret L., ed. *Dracula: The Vampire and the Critics*. Ann Arbor: UMI Research Press, 1988.

———. *Specter or Delusion? The Supernatural in Gothic Fiction*. Ann Arbor: UMI Research Press, 1987.

———, ed. *The Vampire in Literature: A Critical Bibliography*. Ann Arbor: UMI Research Press, 1989.

Cave, Hugh B. "Murgunstruum." 1933. *A Taste for Blood: Fifteen Great Vampire Novellas*. Ed. Martin H. Greenberg. New York: Dorset, 1992.

Cecilione, Michael. *Thirst*. New York: Zebra Books-Kensington, 1996.

Chandler, Alice. *A Dream of Order: The Medieval Ideal in Nineteenth-Century English Literature*. Lincoln: U of Nebraska P, 1970.

Charmaz, Kathy. "Conceptual Approaches to the Study of Death." *Death and Identity*. Ed. Robert Fulton and Robert Bendiksen. 3rd ed. Philadelphia: Charles Press, 1994. 28–59.

Charnas, Suzy McKee. *The Unicorn Tapestry*. Albuquerque, NM: Living Batch Press, 1980.

Children of the Night. By Nicolas Falacci et al. Dir. Tony Randel. Perf. Karen Black, Peter DeLuise, Ami Dolenz, Maya McLaughlin, Evan MacKenzie, David Sawyer. Prod. Columbia Pictures, Fangoria Films, 1991.

Collins, Nancy A. Midnight Blue series: Midnight Blue: The Sonja Blue Collection, consisting of *Sunglasses After Dark*, *In the Blood*, and *Paint It Black*. Ed. Susan Barrows, Robert Hatch, and Liz Tornabene. Stone Mountain, GA: White Wolf, 1999.

———. *Sunglasses After Dark*. New York: Onyx-Penguin, 1989.

Countess Dracula. By Alexander Paul et al. Dir. Peter Sasdy. Perf. Ingrid Pitt, Nigel Green, Sandor Elès, Maurice Denham, Patience Collier, Peter Jeffrey. Prod. Hammer Film Productions. J. Arthur Rank Film Distributors, 1971

Craft, Christopher. " 'Kiss Me with Those Red Lips': Gender and Inversion in Bram Stoker's *Dracula*." *Representations* 8 (1984): 107–33. Rpt. in *Dracula: The Vampire and the Critics*, ed. Margaret L. Carter. Ann Arbor: UMI Press, 1988. 167–94.

Crawford, Anne. "A Mystery of the Campagna." 1887. *Dracula's Brood*. Ed. Richard Dalby. New York: Dorset, 1991. 64–91.

Crossing Over with John Edwards (talk show). Dir. Dana Calderwood. Perf. John Edwards and guests. The Sci-Fi Channel, Studios USA Television, 1999–2004.

Crusie, Jennifer. "Dating Death." *Seven Seasons of Buffy: Science Fiction and Fantasy Writers Discuss Their Favorite Television Show*. Ed. Glenn Yeffeth. Dallas, TX: BenBella Books, 2003. 85–96.

Danforth, Loring M. *The Death Rituals of Rural Greece*. Princeton: Princeton UP, 1982.

Dark Shadows. By Dan Curtis et al. Dir. Lela Swift et al. Perf. Jonathan Frid, Alexandra Isles, Joan Bennett, Louis Edmonds, Grayson Hall, Nancy Barrett. Prod. Dan Curtis Productions. American Broadcasting Company (ABC), 1966–1971.

Darnton, Robert. *Mesmerism and the End of the Enlightenment in France*. Cambridge: Harvard UP, 1968.

Davenport-Hines, Richard. *Gothic: Four Hundred Years of Excess, Horror, Evil and Ruin*. New York: North Point Press-Farrar, Straus and Giroux, 1998.

Davison, Carol Margaret (with Paul Simpson-Housley), ed. *Bram Stoker's Dracula: Sucking Through the Century, 1897–1997*. Toronto: Dundurn Press, 1997.

Day, R. S. "Bloodlust, Madness, Murder and the Press." *New Scientist* 13 (September 1984): 52–53.

Deane, Hamilton, and John L. Balderston. *Dracula [1927]: The Ultimate, Illustrated Edition of the World-Famous Vampire Play*. Edited and Annotated by David J. Skal. New York: St. Martin's Press, 1993.

Delbanco, Andrew. *The Death of Satan: How Americans Have Lost the Sense of Evil*. New York: Farrar, Straus and Giroux, 1995.

Les Deus orphelines vampires (The Two Orphan Vampires). By Jean Rollin. Dir. Jean Rollin. Perf. Alexandra Pic, Isabelle Teboul, Bernard Charnacé, Nathalie Perrey, Anne Duguel. Prod. Les Films ABC, Avia Films, 1996.

Dömötör, Tekla. *Hungarian Folk Beliefs*. Bloomington: Indiana UP, 1981.

Doty, William G. *Mythography: The Study of Myths and Rituals*. 2nd ed. Tuscaloosa: U of Alabama P, 2000.

Dracula. By Bram Stoker (novel), Hamilton Deane, John L. Balderston, Garrett Fort. Dir. Tod Browning. Perf. Bela Lugosi, Helen Chandler, David Manners, Dwight Frye, Edward Van Sloan. Universal Pictures, 1931.

Dracula (aka *Horror of Dracula*). By Bram Stoker (novel), Jimmy Sangster (screenplay). Dir. Terence Fisher. Perf. Peter Cushing, Christopher Lee, Michael Gough,

Melissa Stribling, Carol Marsh, Olga Dickie. Prod. Hammer Film Productions. Universal Pictures, J. Arthur Rank Distributors, 1958.

Dracula. By Bram Stoker (novel), Richard Matheson. Dir. Dan Curtis. Perf. Jack Palance, Simon Ward, Fiona Lewis, Nigel Davenport, Penelope Horner, Pamela Brown. Prod. Dan Curtis Productions. CBS Television, 1973.

Dracula. By Bram Stoker (novel), Hamilton Deane, John L. Balderston, W. D. Richter. Dir. John Badham. Perf. Frank Langella, Laurence Olivier, Kate Nelligan, Donald Pleasence, Trevor Eve, Jan Francis. Universal Pictures, 1979.

Dracula A.D. 1972. By Don Houghton. Dir. Alan Gibson. Perf. Christopher Lee, Peter Cushing, Christopher Neame, Stephanie Beacham, Michael Coles, Caroline Munro. Prod. Hammer Film Productions. Warner Brothers Pictures, 1972.

Dracula: Dead and Loving It. By Bram Stoker (novel), Rudy De Luca, Steve Haberman, Mel Brooks. Dir. Mel Brooks. Perf. Leslie Nielsen, Peter MacNicol, Steven Weber, Amy Yasbeck, Mel Brooks, Lysette Anthony. Prod. Brooks Films, Castle Rock Entertainment. Columbia Pictures, 1995.

Dracula: Prince of Darkness. By Anthony Hinds, Jimmy Sangster. Dir. Terence Fisher. Perf. Christopher Lee, Barbara Shelley, Andrew Keit, Francis Matthews, Suzan Farmer, Charles Tingwell, Thorley Walters, Philip Latham, Walter Brown. Prod. Hammer Film Productions, Seven Arts Productions. Twentieth Century Fox, 1965.

Dracula's Daughter. By Bram Stoker (novel), David O. Selznick et al. Dir. Lambert Hillyer. Perf. Otto Kruger, Gloria Holden, Marguerite Churchill, Edward Van Sloan, Gilbert Emery, Irving Pichel. Universal Pictures, 1936.

Dracula 2000. By Joel Soisson, Patrick Lussier. Dir. Patrick Lussier. Perf. Gerard Butler, Christopher Plummer, Jonny Lee Miller, Justine Waddell, Colleen Fitzpatrick, Jennifer Esposito. Prod. Carfax Productions, Dimension Films, Neo Art & Logic, Wes Craven Films. Dimension Films, Miramax, New Films International, 2000.

Dragomanov, M. P. *Notes on the Slavic Religio-Ethical Legends: The Dualistic Creation of the World.* Trans. Earl W. Count. Russian and East European Series 23. Bloomington: Indiana University Publications, 1961.

Dresser, Norine. *American Vampires: Fans, Victims, Practitioners.* New York: Vintage-Random House, 1989.

du Boulay, Juliet. "The Greek Vampire: A Study of Cyclic Symbolism in Marriage and Death." *MAN* (Journal of the Royal Anthropological Association) 17.2 (1982): 219–38.

Elrod, P. N. *Blood List.* The Vampire Files, Book 1. New York: Ace Books, 1990.

Elrod, P. N., and Martin H. Greenberg, eds. *The Time of the Vampires.* New York: Daw Books, 1996.

Elvira, Mistress of the Dark. By Sam Egan, John Paragon, Cassandra Peterson. Dir. James Signorelli. Perf. Cassandra Peterson, William Morgan Shepherd, Daniel Greene, Susan Kellerman, Jeff Conaway, Edie McClurg. Prod. NBC Productions, New World Pictures, 1988.

The Fearless Vampire Killers (aka *Dance of the Vampires*). By Gérard Brach, Roman Polanski. Dir. Roman Polanski. Perf. Jack MacGowran, Roman Polanski, Alfie

Bass, Jessie Robbins, Sharon Tate, Ferdinand Mayne, Iain Quarrier. Prod. Cadre Films, Filmways Pictures. Metro-Goldwyn-Mayer, 1967.

Fischer, John Martin, and Ruth Curl. "Philosophical Models of Immortality in Science Fiction." *Immortal Engines: Life Extension and Immortality in Science Fiction and Fantasy*, Ed. George Slusser, Gary Westfahl, and Eric S. Rabkin. Athens, GA: U of Georgia P, 1996. 3–12.

Florescu, Radu R., and Raymond T. McNally. *Dracula, Prince of Many Faces: His Life and His Times*. Boston: Little, Brown, 1989.

Forever Knight. By James D. Parriot et al. Dir. Clay Boris. Perf. Geraint Wyn Davies, Catherine Disher, Nigel Bennet, John Kapelos, Deborah Duchene, Natsuko Ohama. Prod. Paragon Entertainment Corporation, TeleMünchen, USA Network. Columbia TriStar Domestic Television, 1989–1996.

Forsyth, Neil. *The Old Enemy: Satan and the Combat Myth*. Princeton, NJ: Princeton UP, 1987.

Frankfurter, David. *Evil Incarnate: Rumors of Demonic Conspiracy and Satanic Abuse in History*. Princeton: Princeton UP, 2006.

Frayling, Christopher. "Lord Byron to Count Dracula." *Vampyres: Lord Byron to Count Dracula*. Ed. Christopher Frayling. London: Faber and Faber, 1991. 3–84.

Frazer, James G. *The Golden Bough: The Roots of Religion and Folklore*. 1890. New York: Avenel Books, 1981. 2 volumes in one. [Orig. published in two volumes as *The Golden Bough: A Study in Comparative Religions*. London: Macmillan.]

Fright Night. By Tom Holland. Dir. Tom Holland. Perf. Chris Sarandon, William Ragsdale, Amanda Bearse, Roddy McDowall, Stephen Geoffreys, Jonathan Stark. Prod. Delphi IV Productions, Vistar Films. Columbia Pictures, 1985.

From Dusk Till Dawn. By Robert Kurtzman, Quentin Tarantino. Dir. Robert Rodriguez. Perf. Harvey Keitel, George Clooney, Quentin Tarantino, Juliette Lewis, Ernest Liu, Salma Hayek, Cheech Marin. Dimension Films, 1996.

Fulton, Robert, and Robert Bendiksen. Introduction. *Death and Identity*. Ed. Robert Fulton and Robert Bendiksen. 3rd ed. Philadelphia: The Charles Press, 1994. 3–11.

Gautier, Theophile. "Clarimonde." 1844. Trans. Lafcadio Hearn. *The Vampire in Verse: An Anthology*. Ed. Steven Moore. New York: Dracula Press, 1985. 87–88.

Geary, Robert F. " 'Carmilla' and the Gothic Legacy: Victorian Transformations of Supernatural Horror." *The Blood Is the Life: Vampires in Literature*. Ed. Leonard G. Heldreth and Mary Pharr. Bowling Green, OH: Bowling Green State University Popular Press, 1999. 19–29.

Gelder, Ken. *Reading the Vampire*. London: Routledge, 1994.

Gerard, Emily. *The Land Beyond the Forest: Facts, Figures, and Fancies from Transylvania*. 1885. New York: Harper and Brothers, 1888.

Gilbert, William. "The Last Lords of Gardonal." 1867. *Dracula's Brood: Neglected Vampire Classics by Sir Arthur Conan Doyle, Algernon Blackwood, M. R. James and Others*. Ed. Richard Dalby. New York: Dorset Press, 1987. 13–42.

Girard, Rene. *Violence and the Sacred*. 1972. Trans. Patrick Gregory. Baltimore: Johns Hopkins UP, 1977.

Girouard, Mark. *The Return to Camelot: Chivalry and the English Gentleman*. New Haven, CT: Yale UP, 1981.

Goethe, Johann Wolfgang von. "The Bride of Corinth." 1797. Trans. Christopher Middleton, W. E. Aytoun, and Theodore Martin. *The Vampire in Verse: An Anthology*. Ed. Steven Moore. New York: Dracula Press, 1985. 21–26.

Golden, Christopher. *Angel Souls and Devil Hearts*. New York: Berkley Books, 1995.

———. *Of Saints and Shadows*. New York: Jove Books, 1994.

Gomez, Jewelle. *The Gilda Stories; Bones & Ash*. New York: Quality Paperback Book Club, 2001.

Gordon, Joan, and Veronica Hollinger. "Introduction: The Shape of Vampires." *Blood Read: The Vampire as Metaphor in Contemporary Culture*. Ed. Joan Gordon and Veronica Hollinger. Philadelphia: U of Pennsylvania P, 1997. 1–7.

Gorer, Geoffrey. *Death, Grief, and Mourning*. Garden City, NY: Anchor Books-Doubleday, 1967.

Gottlieb, Sherry. *Love Bite*. New York: Warner Books, 1994.

Griffin, Gail B. " 'Your Girls That You All Love Are Mine': Dracula and the Victorian Male Sexual Imagination." *International Journal of Women's Studies* 3 (1980): 454–65. Rpt. *Dracula: The Vampire and the Critics*. Ed. Margaret L. Carter. Ann Arbor: Research Press, 1988. 137–48.

Grixti, Joseph. *The Terrors of Uncertainty: The Cultural Contexts of Horror Fiction*. London: Routledge, 1989.

Gunn, James. "From the Sublime to the Ridiculous: Immortality and *The Immortal*." *Immortal Engines: Life Extension and Immortality in Science Fiction and Fantasy*. Ed. George Slusser, Gary Westfahl, and Eric S. Rabkin. Athens, GA: U of Georgia P, 1996. 13–23.

Hall, Stephen S. *Merchants of Immortality: Chasing the Dream of Human Life Extension*. Boston: Houghton Mifflin, 2003.

Hambly, Barbara. *Those Who Hunt the Night*. New York: Dell Rey-Ballantine, 1988.

Hamilton, Laurell K. *Guilty Pleasures*. New York: Berkley Books, 1993.

———. *The Lunatic Café*. New York: Ace Books,1996.

Harris, Stephen B. "The Immortality Myth and Technology." *Immortal Engines: Life Extension and Immortality in Science Fiction and Fantasy*. Ed. George Slusser, Gary Westfahl, and Eric S. Rabkin. Athens, GA: U of Georgia P, 1996. 45–67.

Harrison, Jane Ellen. *Prolegomena to the Study of Greek Religion*. 1903. 3rd ed. Cambridge UP, 1922. 3rd ed. Princeton, NJ: Princeton UP, 1991.

Hathorn, Richmond Y. *Greek Mythology*. Beirut: American U of Beirut P, 1977.

Hatlen, Burton. "The Return of the Repressed/Oppressed in Bram Stoker's *Dracula*." 1980. *Dracula: The Vampire and the Critics*. Ann Arbor: UMI Research Press, 1988. 117–35.

Havens, Candace. *Joss Whedon: The Genius Behind Buffy*. Dallas, TX: BenBella Books, 2003.

Hays, Clark, and Kathleen McFall. *The Cowboy and the Vampire: A Very Unusual Romance*. St. Paul, MN: Llewellyn Publications, 1999.

Heldreth, Leonard G., and Mary Pharr. Introduction. *The Blood Is the Life: Vampires in Literature*. Ed. Leonard G. Heldreth and Mary Pharr. Bowling Green, OH: Bowling Green State U Popular P, 1999. 1–6.

Heller, Terry. *The Delights of Terror: An Aesthetics of the Tale of Terror.* Urbana, IL: U of Illinois P, 1987.

Hennelly, Mark M., Jr. "Dracula: The Gnostic Quest and Victorian Wasteland." 1977. *Literature of the Occult: A Collection of Critical Essays.* Ed. Peter B. Messent. Englewood Cliffs, NJ: Prentice-Hall, 1981. 139–55.

———. "The Victorian Book of the Dead: *Dracula.*" *Journal of Evolutionary Psychology* 13.3–4 (1992): 204–11.

Hill, William. *Vampire's Kiss.* New York: Pinnacle Books-Windsor, 1994.

Holland, Tom. *Lord of the Dead: A Novel.* New York: Pocket Books-Simon & Schuster, 1995.

Hoppenstand, Gary, and Ray B. Browne. *The Gothic World of Stephen King: Landscape of Nightmare.* Bowling Green, OH: Bowling Green State U Popular P, 1987.

Howard, Robert E. "The Hills of the Dead." 1930. *A Taste of Blood: Fifteen Great Vampire Novellas.* Ed. Martin H. Greenberg. New York: Dorset Press, 1992. 153–71.

Huff, Tanya. *Blood Price.* New York: Daw Books, 1991.

The Incredible Hulk. Dir. Reza Badiyi, Chuck Bowman. Perf. Lou Ferrigno, Bill Bixby, Jack Colvin, Frank Orsatti, Reza Badiyi, John McPherson. CBS Television, 1978–1982.

Innocent Blood. By Michael Wolk. Dir. John Landis. Perf. Anne Parillaud, David Proval, Rocco Sisto, Chazz Palminteri, Anthony LaPaglia, Robert Loggia. Warner Brothers Pictures, 1992.

Interview with the Vampire: The Vampire Chronicles. By Anne Rice. Dir. Neil Jordan. Perf. Tom Cruise, Brad Pitt, Kirsten Dunst, Stephen Rea, Antonio Banderas, Christian Slater. Warner Brothers Pictures, Geffen Pictures, 1994.

James, M. R. (Montague Rhodes). "An Episode of Cathedral History." 1919. *The Penguin Book of Vampire Stories.* Ed. Alan Ryan. London: Penguin, 1987. 225–40.

Jameson, Fredric. "Longevity as Class Struggle." *Immortal Engines: Life Extension and Immortality in Science Fiction and Fantasy.* Ed. George Slusser, Gary Westfahl, and Eric S. Rabkin. Athens, GA: U of Georgia P, 1996. 24–42.

Jenkins, Philip. *Mystics and Messiahs: Cults and New Religions in American History.* New York: Oxford UP, 2000.

John Carpenter's Vampires (aka *Vampires*, *Vampire$*). By John Steakley (novel), Don Jakoby (screenplay). Dir. John Carpenter. Perf. James Woods, Daniel Baldwin, Sheryl Lee, Thomas Ian Griffith, Maximilian Schell, Tim Guinee. Film Office et al. Columbia Pictures, 1998.

Jones, Ernest. *On the Nightmare.* 1931. New York: Liveright, 1971.

Kalogridis, Jeanne. *Covenant with the Vampire.* New York: Dell, 1994.

Kemske, Floyd. *Human Resources.* North Haven, CT: Catbird Press, 1995.

Kendrick, Walter. *The Thrill of Fear: 250 Years of Scary Entertainment.* New York: Grove Weidenfeld, 1991.

Kerr, Howard. *Mediums, and Spirit-Rappers, and Roaring Radicals: Spiritualism in American Literature, 1850–1900.* Urbana, IL: U of Illinois P, 1972.

Kerr, Howard, John W. Crowley, and Charles L Crow, eds. *The Haunted Dusk: American Supernatural Fiction, 1820–1920.* Athens, GA: U of Georgia P, 1983.

King, Stephen. *Salem's Lot*. New York: Signet-Penguin, 1975.

Kligman, Gail. *The Wedding of the Dead: Ritual, Poetics, and Popular Culture in Transylvania*. Berkeley: U of California P, 1988.

Kornbluth, C. M. "The Mindworm." 1950. *The Penguin Book of Vampire Stories*. Ed. Alan Ryan. London: Penguin, 1987. 349–61.

Kostova, Elizabeth. *The Historian: A Novel*. New York: Little, Brown and Company, 2005.

Kramer, Heinrich, and James Sprenger. *The Malleus Maleficarum*. 1487. Trans. Montague Summers. 1928. New York: Dover, 1971.

Kübler-Ross, Elisabeth. *On Death and Dying: What the Dying Have to Teach Doctors, Nurses, Clergy, and Their Own Families*. 1969. New York: Touchstone-Simon and Schuster, 1997.

Kuttner, Henry. "I, The Vampire." 1937. *The Vampire Omnibus*. Ed. Peter Haining. Chartwell Books-Book Sales, 1995. 178–95.

Laderman, Gary. *Rest in Peace: A Cultural History of Death and the Funeral Home in Twentieth-Century America*. New York: Oxford UP, 2003.

Lamb, Lady Caroline. *Glenarvon*. London: Colburn, 1816.

The Last Man on Earth. By Richard Matheson (novel), William Leicester, Furio M. Monetti, Ubaldo Ragona. Dir. Ubaldo Ragona. Perf. Vincent Price, Franca Bettoia, Emma Danieli, Giacomo Rossi-Stuart, Umberto Raho, Christi Courtland. Prod: Associated Producers, Produzioni La Regina. American International Pictures (AIP), 1964.

Lawson, John Cuthbert. 1909. *Modern Greek Folklore and Ancient Greek Religion: A Study in Survivals*. New Hyde Park, NY: University Books, 1964.

Leatherdale, Clive. *Dracula: The Novel and the Legend: A Study of Bram Stoker's Gothic Masterpiece*. Wellingborough, Northamptonshire: Aquarian Press, 1985.

Lee, Tanith. *Personal Darkness. Second in the Blood Opera Sequence*. New York: Dell, 1993.

Lee, Vernon. "Marsyas in Flanders." *Dracula's Brood*. Ed. Richard Dalby. New York: Dorset, 1987. 226–37.

Le Fanu, J. Sheridan. "Carmilla." 1872. *The Penguin Book of Vampire Stories*. Ed. Alan Ryan. London: Penguin, 1987. 71–137.

Leiber, Fritz. "The Girl with the Hungry Eyes." 1949. *The Penguin Book of Vampire Stories*. Ed. Alan Ryan. London: Penguin Books, 1987. 334–48.

Loos, Milan. *Dualist Heresy in the Middle Ages*. Trans. Iris Lewitova. Prague: Academia (Publishing House of the Czechoslovak Academy of Sciences), The Hague: Martinus Nijhoff, 1974.

Loring, F. G. "The Tomb of Sarah." 1900. *The Undead*. Ed. James Dickie. London: Pan Books, 1973. 92–105.

Lorrah, Jean. *Blood Will Tell*. Dallas, TX: BenBella, 2001.

The Lost Boys. By Jamie Fischer, James Jeremias, Jeffrey Boam. Dir. Joel Schumacher. Perf. Jason Patric, Corey Haim, Dianne Wiest, Barnard Hughes, Edward Herrmann, Kiefer Sutherland. Warner Brothers Pictures, 1987.

Love at First Bite. By Robert Kaufman. Dir. Stan Dragoti. Perf. George Hamilton, Susan Saint James, Richard Benjamin, Dick Shawn, Arte Johnson, Sherman Hemsley. Melvin Simon Productions. American International Pictures (AIP), 1979.

Lumley, Brian. Necroscope. New York: Tor-Tom Doherty Associates, 1986.

MacAndrew, Elizabeth. *The Gothic Tradition in Fiction*. New York: Columbia UP, 1979.

Macdonald, David Lorne. *Poor Polidori: A Critical Biography of the Author of* The Vampyre. Toronto: U of Toronto P, 1991.

McCammon, Robert R. *They Thirst*. New York: Avon Books, 1981.

McDonald, Beth E. "The Vampire as Trickster Figure in Bram Stoker's Dracula." *Extrapolation* 33:2 (1992): 128–44.

McGrath, Patrick. "Preface: Bram Stoker and His Vampire." *Bram Stoker's Dracula: Sucking Through the Century, 1897–1997*. Ed. Carol Margaret Davison, with Paul Simpson-Housley. Toronto: Dundurn Press, 1997. 41–48.

McNally, Raymond T., and Radu Florescu. *In Search of Dracula: A True History of Dracula and Vampire Legends*. New York: Galahad Books, 1972.

Máchal, Jan. "Slavic Mythology." Trans. F. Krupička. *Vampires of the Slavs*. Ed. Jan Perkowski. Cambridge, MA: Slavica, 1976. 19—75.

Matheson, Richard. *I Am Legend*. 1954. New York: Tom Doherty Associates, 1995.

Melton, J. Gordon. *The Vampire Book: The Encyclopedia of the Undead*. 2nd ed. Detroit: Visible Ink, 1999

Messent, Peter B., ed. *Literature of the Occult: A Collection of Critical Essays*. Englewood Cliffs, NJ: Prentice-Hall, 1981.

Metcalfe, John. "The Feasting Dead." 1954. *A Taste for Blood: Fifteen Great Vampire Novellas*. Ed. Martin Greenberg. New York: Dorset, 1992. 234–95.

Meyer, Stephanie. *Breaking Dawn*. New York: Little, Brown, 2008.

———. *Eclipse*. New York: Little, Brown, 2007.

———. *New Moon*. New York: Little, Brown, 2006.

———. *Twilight*. New York: Little, Brown, 2005.

Mitford, Jessica. *The American Way of Death Revisited*. 1963. New York: Vintage-Random House, 1998.

Monahan, Brent. *The Book of Common Dread*. New York: SMP-St. Martin's Paperbacks, 1993.

Moore, Catherine L. "Shambleau." 1933. *The Penguin Book of Vampire Stories*. Ed. Alan Ryan. 1987. 255–81.

Moore, Steven, ed. *The Vampire in Verse: An Anthology*. New York: Dracula Press, 1985.

Morley, John. *Death, Heaven and the Victorians*. Pittsburgh: U of Pittsburgh P, 1971.

Murgoci, Agnes. "The Vampire in Romania." *Folklore* 27.5 (1926): 320–49.

My Best Friend Is a Vampire. By Tab Murphy. Dir. Jimmy Huston. Perf. Robert Sean Leonard, Lee Ann Locken, Cheryl Pollak, Fannie Flagg, Kenneth Kimmins, Evan Mirand. Kings Road Entertainment, 1988.

"The Mysterious Stranger." 1860. *The Penguin Book of Vampire Stories*. Ed. Alan Ryan. London: Penguin, 1988. 36–70.

Near Dark. By Kathryn Bigelow and Eric Red. Dir. Kathryn Bigelow. Perf. Adrian Pasdar, Jenny Wright, Lance Henriksen, Bill Paxton, Jenette Goldstein, Tim Thomerson, Joshua Miller. Prod. F/M, Near Dark Joint Venture. Cinema Classics, De Laurentiis Entertainment Group (DEG), 1987.

Newman, Kim. *Anno Dracula*. New York: Carroll & Graf, 1992.

———. *The Bloody Red Baron*. New York: Avon Books, 1995.

———. *Judgment of Tears: Anno Dracula 1959*. New York: Avon Books, 1998.

Night of the Living Dead. By John A. Russo, George A. Romero. Dir. George A. Romero. Perf. Duane Jones, Judith O'Dea, Karl Hardman, Marilyn Eastman, Keith Wayne, Judith Riley. Prod. Image Ten et al. Walter Reade Organization, Continental Distributing, 1968.

Night of the Living Dead. By John A. Russo, George A. Romero. Dir. Tom Savini. Perf. Tony Todd, Patricia Tallman, Tom Towles, McKee Anderson, William Butler, Katie Finneran, Bill Moseley. 21st Century Film Corporation, Columbia Film Corporation, 1990.

Nikanov, Fedo. *Preface. Vampires: Stories of the Supernatural*. By Alexis Tolstoy. New York: Hawthorne Books, 1969. 1–8.

Norris, Frank. "Grettir at Thorhall-Stead." 1903. *The Vampire Omnibus*. Ed. Peter Haining. Edison, NJ: Chartwell Books, 1995. 126–38.

Nosferatu: eine Symphonie des Grauens. By Bram Stoker (novel), Henrik Galeen. Dir. F. W. Murnau. Perf. Max Schreck, Gustav von Wangenheim, Greta Schroeder, Alexander Granach, George H. Schnell. Film Arts Guild, 1922.

Nosferatu the Vampire. By Bram Stoker (novel), Werner Herzog, Dan Van Husen. Dir. Werner Herzog. Perf. Klaus Kinski, Isabelle Adjani, Bruno Ganz, Roland Topor, Walter Ladengast, Ruth Landshoff. Prod. Werner Herzog Filmproduction et al. Twentieth Century Fox Film Corporation, 1979.

Obolensky, Dmitri. 1948. *The Bogomils: A Study in Balkan Manichaeism*. Twickenham, UK: Anthony C. Hall, 1972.

Oinas, Felix J. "East European Vampires." *Journal of Popular Culture* 96.1 (1982): 108–16.

———. *Essays on Russian Folklore and Mythology*. Columbus, OH: Slavica, 1984.

Oppenheim, Janet. *The Other World: Spiritualism and Psychical Research in England, 1850–1914*. Cambridge: Cambridge UP, 1985.

Ossenfelder, Heinrich August. "The Vampire." 1748. Trans. Aloysius Gibson. *The Vampire in Verse: An Anthology*. Ed. Stephen Moore. New York: Dracula Press, 1985. 12.

The Others. By Alejandro Amenabar. Dir. Alejandro Amenabar. Perf. Nicole Kidman, Fionnula Flanagan, Christopher Eccleston, Alakina Mann, James Bentley, Eric Sykes. Prod. Cruise/Wagner Productions. Dimension Films, 2001.

Otto, Rudolf. *The Idea of the Holy: An Inquiry into the Non-rational Factor in the Idea of the Divine and Its Relation to the Rational*. 1923. Trans. John W. Harvey. 2nd ed. London: Oxford UP, 1950.

Overstreet, Deborah Wilson. *Not Your Mother's Vampire: Vampirism in Young Adult Fiction*. Lanham, MD: Scarecrow Press, 2006.

Paglia, Camille. *Sexual Personae: Art and Decadence from Nefertiti to Emily Dickinson*. New York: Vintage Books-Random House, 1990.

Pale Blood. By V. V. Dachin Hsu, Takashi Matsuoka. Dir. V. V. Dachin Hsu, Michael W. Leighton. Perf. George Chakiris, Wings Hauser, Pamela Ludwig, Diana Frank, Darcey Demoss, Earl Garnes. Noble Entertainment, 1990.

Pater, Walter. *The Renaissance: Studies in Art and Poetry*. 1893. Ed. Donald L. Hill. Berkeley: U of California P, 1980.

Perkowski, Jan L. *The Darkling: A Treatise on Slavic Vampirism*. Columbus, OH: Slavica, 1989.

———, ed. *Vampires of the Slavs.* Cambridge, MA: Slavica, 1976.
Planché, James Robinson. *The Vampire; or, The Bride of the Isles: A Romantic Melodrama.* 1820. *The Hour of One: Six Gothic Melodramas.* Ed. Stephen Wischhusen. London: Gordon Fraser, 1975. [Facsimile rpt. from London: John Cumberland, n.d., printed from the acting copy.]
Planet of the Vampires. [Terrore nello spazio.] By Mario Bava et al. Dir. Mario Bava. Perf. Barry Sullivan, Norma Bengell, Angel Aranda, Evi Marandi, Stelio Candelli, Franco Andrei. Prod. American International Pictures, 1965.
Poe, Edgar Allan. "The Facts in the Case of M. Valdemar." 1845. *The Complete Tales and Poems of Edgar Allan Poe.* Edison, NJ: Castle Books, 2001. 99–105.
———. "The Fall of the House of Usher." 1839. *The Complete Tales and Poems of Edgar Allan Poe.* Edison, NJ: Castle Books, 2001. 171–83.
———. "Ligeia." 1838. *The Complete Tales and Poems of Edgar Allan Poe.* Edison, NJ: Castle Books, 2001. 569–79.
———. "Morella." 1835. *The Complete Tales and Poems of Edgar Allan Poe.* Edison, NJ: Castle Books, 2001. 587–90.
Polidori, John. "The Vampyre." 1819. *The Penguin Book of Vampire Stories.* Ed. Alan Ryan. London: Penguin, 1988. 7–24.
Porte, Joel. "In the Hands of an Angry God: Religious Terror in Gothic Fiction." *The Gothic Imagination: Essays in Dark Romanticism.* Ed. G. R. Thompson. Pullman, WA: Washington State UP, 1974. 42–64.
Powers, Tim. *The Stress of Her Regard.* New York: Ace Books, 1989.
Praz, Mario. *The Romantic Agony.* 1933. Trans. Angus Davidson. 2nd ed. Oxford: Oxford UP, 1951.
Prothero, Stephen. *American Jesus: How the Son of God Became a National Icon.* New York: Farrar, Straus and Giroux, 2003.
Punter, David. *The Literature of Terror: A History of Gothic Fictions from 1765 to the Present Day, Vol. I: The Gothic Tradition.* 2nd ed. London: Longman, 1996. 2 vols.
———. *The Literature of Terror: A History of Gothic Fictions from 1765 to the Present Day, Vol. II: The Modern Gothic.* 2nd ed. London: Longman, 1996. 2 vols.
Rabkin, Eric S. "Introduction: Immortality: The Self-Defeating Fantasy." *Immortal Engines: Life Extension and Immortality in Science Fiction and Fantasy.* Ed. George Slusser, Gary Westfahl, and Eric S. Rabkin. Athens, GA: U of Georgia P, 1996. ix–xvii.
Reed, John R. "The Occult in Later Victorian Literature." *Literature of the Occult: A Collection of Critical Essays.* Ed. Peter B. Messent. Englewood Cliffs, NJ: Prentice-Hall, 1981. 89–104.
Rice, Anne. *Interview with the Vampire.* Book I of The Vampire Chronicles. New York: Ballantine Books, 1976.
———. *Memnoch the Devil.* Book V of The Vampire Chronicles. New York: Ballantine Books, 1995.
———. *The Queen of the Damned.* Book III of the Vampire Chronicles. New York: Ballantine Books, 1988.
———. *The Tale of the Body Thief.* Book IV of The Vampire Chronicles. New York: Ballantine Books, 1992.

———. *The Vampire Lestat*. Book II of the Vampire Chronicles. New York: Ballantine Books, 1985.

Richardson, Maurice. "The Psychoanalysis of Ghost Stories." *Twentieth Century* 166 (1959): 419–31.

Riley, Michael. *Conversations with Anne Rice*. New York: Ballantine Books, 1996.

The Rocky Horror Picture Show. By Richard O'Brien (play), Jim Sharman. Dir. Jim Sharman. Perf. Tim Curry, Susan Sarandon, Barry Bostwick, Richard O'Brian, Patricia Quinn, Nell Campbell. Twentieth Century Fox Film Corporation, 1975.

Romkey, Michael. *I, Vampire*. New York: Fawcett Gold Medal-Ballantine, 1990.

———. *The Vampire Virus*. New York: Fawcett Gold Medal-Ballantine, 1997.

Roth, Phyllis A. *Bram Stoker*. Twayne's English Authors Series. Boston: Twayne, 1982.

———. "Suddenly Sexual Women in Bram Stoker's *Dracula*." *Literature and Psychology* 27 (1977): 113–21.

Rowen, Norma. "Teaching the Vampire: Dracula in the Classroom." *Bram Stoker's Dracula: Sucking Through the Century, 1897–1997*. Ed. Carol Margaret Davison. Toronto: Dundurn Press, 1997. 231–45.

Russell, Jeffrey Burton. *The Devil: Perceptions of Evil from Antiquity to Primitive Christianity*. Ithaca, NY: Cornell UP, 1977.

———. *Lucifer: The Devil in the Middle Ages*. Ithaca, NY: Cornell UP, 1984.

———. *Mephistopheles: The Devil in the Modern World*. Ithaca, NY: Cornell UP, 1986.

———. *The Prince of Darkness: Radical Evil and the Power of Good in Human History*. Ithaca, NY: Cornell UP, 1988.

———. *Satan: The Early Christian Tradition*. Ithaca, NY: Cornell UP, 1981.

Ryan, Alan. "Following the Way." 1982. *The Penguin Book of Vampire Stories*. Ed. Alan Ryan. London: Penguin Books, 1987. 562–73.

Rymer, James Malcolm (and/or Thomas Peckett Prest). *Varney the Vampyre or The Feast of Blood*. London: F. Lloyd, 1847. 2 vols. New York: Dover, 1972.

Saberhagen, Fred. *The Dracula Tape*. 1975. Riverdale, NY: Baen, 1999.

———. *The Holmes-Dracula File*. 1978. New York: Tor-Tom Doherty Associates, 1989.

St. Armand, Barton Levi. "The 'Mysteries' of Edgar Poe: The Quest for a Monomyth in Gothic Literature." *The Gothic Imagination: Essays in Dark Romanticism*. Ed. G. R. Thompson. Pullman. WA: Washington State UP, 1974. 65–93.

Salem's Lot. By Stephen King (novel), Paul Monash (screenplay). Dir. Tobe Hooper. Perf. David Soul, James Mason, Lance Kerwin, Bonnie Bedelia, Lew Ayres, Julie Cobb. Prod. Warner Brothers Television. CBS Televison, 1979.

The Satanic Rites of Dracula. By Don Houghton. Dir. Alan Gibson. Perf. Christopher Lee, Peter Cushing, Michael Coles, William Franklyn, Freddie Jones, Joanna Lumley. Prod. Hammer Film Productions, Warner Brothers Pictures. Columbia-Warner Distributors, 1974.

Schierup, Carl-Ulrik. "Why Are Vampires Still Alive?: Wallachian Immigrants in Scandinavia," *Ethnos* 51.3–4 (1986): 173–98.

Schneider, Kirk J. *Horror and the Holy: Wisdom-Teachings of the Monster Tale*. Chicago: Open Court, 1993.

Schopp, Andrew. "Cruising the Alternatives: Homoeroticism and the Contemporary Vampire." *Journal of Popular Culture* 34. 4 (1997): 231–43.

Senf, Carol A. "Dracula: The Unseen Face in the Mirror." *Journal of Narrative Technique* 9 (1979): 160–70. Rpt. *Dracula: The Vampire and the Critics*. Ed. Margaret L. Carter. Ann Arbor: UMI Research Press, 1988. 93–103.

———. "*Dracula, The Jewel of the Seven Stars*, and Stoker's 'Burden of the Past.'" *Bram Stoker's Dracula: Sucking Through the Century, 1897–1997*. Ed. Carol Margaret Davison, with Paul Simpson-Housley. Toronto: Dundurn Press, 1997. 77–94.

———. *The Vampire in Nineteenth-Century English Literature*. Bowling Green, OH: Bowling Green State University Popular Press, 1988.

Senn, Harry A. *Were-Wolf and Vampire in Romania*. East European Monographs. New York: Columbia UP, 1982.

Shelley, Mary. "Introduction to Frankenstein, 3rd Edition." 1831. *Mary Shelley: Frankenstein: The 1818 Text, Contexts, Nineteenth-Century Responses, Modern Criticism*. Ed. J. Paul Hunter. A Norton Critical Edition. New York: W. W. Norton, 1996. 169–73.

Siciliano, Sam. *Darkness*. New York: Pinnacle Books-Kensington, 2001.

Simmons, Dan. *Children of the Night*. New York: Warner Books, 1992.

Six Feet Under. By Alan Ball et al. Dir. Alan Ball et al. Perf. Peter Krause, Michael C. Hall, Frances Conroy, Lauren Ambrose, Freddy Rodriguez, Mathew St. Patrick. Home Box Office, 2001–2005.

The Sixth Sense. By M. Night Shyamalan. Dir. M. Night Shyamalan. Per. Bruce Willis, Haley Joel Osment, Toni Collette, Olivia Williams, Donnie Wahlberg Peter Anthony Tambakis. Barry Mendel Productions, Buena Vista Pictures, 1999.

Skal, David J. *Hollywood Gothic: The Tangled Web of Dracula from Novel to Stage to Screen*. Rev. ed. New York: Faber and Faber-Farrar, Straus and Giroux, 2004.

———. *The Monster Show: A Cultural History of Horror*. New York: W.W. Norton, 1993.

Slusser, George, Gary Westfahl, and Eric S. Rabkin, eds. *Immortal Engines: Life Extension and Immortality in Science Fiction and Fantasy*. Athens, GA: U of Georgia P, 1996.

Somtow, S. P. [Somtow Sucharitkul] *Vampire Junction*. New York: Tor-Tom Doherty, 1984.

Son of Dracula. By Curt Siodmak, Eric Taylor. Dir. Robert Siodmak. Perf. Lon Chaney Jr., Robert Paige, Louise Allbritton, Evelyn Ankers, Frank Craven, J. Edward Bromberg. Universal Pictures, 1943.

Sosnowski, David. *Vamped*. New York: Downtown Press-Pocket Books, 2004.

Southey, Robert. *Thalaba the Destroyer*. 2 vols. London: T. N. Longmans and O. Rees, 1801.

Stableford, Brian. *The Empire of Fear*. New York: Carroll & Graf, 1988.

———. "*Sang* for Supper: Notes on the Metaphorical Use of Vampires in *The Empire of Fear and Young Blood*." *Blood Read: The Vampire as Metaphor in Contemporary Culture*. Ed. Joan Gordon and Veronica Hollinger. Philadelphia: U of Pennsylvania P, 1997. 69–84.

Steakley, John. *Vampire$*. New York: Roc-Penguin, 1990.

Stephens, Walter. *Demon Lovers: Witchcraft, Sex, and the Crisis of Belief.* Chicago: U of Chicago P, 2002.

Stetson, George R. "The Animistic Vampire in New England." *American Anthropologist* 9.1 (1896). 1–18.

Stoker, Bram. *Dracula.* 1897. *The Essential Dracula.* 1975. Ed. Leonard Wolf. New York: Byron Preiss-Plume, 1993.

Strieber, Whitley. *The Hunger.* New York: Avon Books, 1981.

Stuart, Roxana. *Stage Blood: Vampires of the 19th-Century Stage.* Bowling Green, OH: Bowling Green State U Popular P, 1994.

The Subspecies Series (*Subspecies*; *Bloodstone: Subspecies II*; *Bloodlust: Subspecies III*; *Subspecies IV: Bloodstorm*). By Ted Nicolaou. Dir. Ted Nicolaou. Perf. Angus Scrimm, Anders Hove, Irina Movila, Kevin Spirtis, Melanie Shatner, Laura Tate, Michelle McBride, Ivan J. Rado, Denice Duff. Prod. Castel Film Romania, Full Moon Entertainment, 1991–1998.

Summers, Montague. *The Vampire.* London: Senate, 1995. (Formerly *The Vampire: His Kith and Kin.* London: Kegan Paul, Trench, Trubner & Co., 1928).

———. *The Vampire in Europe.* 1929. New York: Gramercy Books-Random House, 1996.

Swiniarski, S. A. *The Flesh, the Blood, and the Fire.* New York: Daw Books, 1998.

Thompson, Gary Richard. "Introduction: Romanticism and the Gothic Tradition." *The Gothic Imagination: Essays in Dark Romanticism.* Ed. G. R. Thompson. Pullman, WA: Washington State UP, 1974. 1–10.

Thompson, James M. *Dark Blood.* New York: Pinnacle Books-Kensington, 2002.

Thorne, Tony. *Children of the Night: Of Vampires and Vampirism.* 1999. London: Indigo-Orion, 2000.

Thorslev, Peter L., Jr. *The Byronic Hero: Types and Prototypes.* Minneapolis: U of Minnesota P, 1962.

Tieck, Johann Ludwig. "Wake Not the Dead." *Popular Tales and Romances of the Northern Nations.* Vol. I. London: Simpkin, Marshall, 1823. Rpt. *Vampyres: Lord Byron to Count Dracula.* Ed. Christopher Frayling. London: Faber and Faber, 1991. 165–89.

Tolstoy, Alexis. *The Vampire* (*Oupyr*). 1841. *Vampires: Stories of the Supernatural.* By Alexis Tolstoy. Ed. Linda Kuehl. Trans. Fedor Nikanov. New York: Hawthorn Books, 1969. 9–91.

Trigg, Elwood B. *Gypsy Demons and Divinities: The Magic and Religion of the Gypsies.* Secaucus, NJ: 1973.

Tropp, Martin. *Images of Fear: How Horror Stories Helped Shape Modern Culture (1818–1918).* Jefferson, NC: McFarland Classics, 1990.

Twitchell, James B. *The Living Dead: A Study of the Vampire in Romantic Literature.* Durham, NC: Duke UP, 1981.

Underworld. By Kevin Grevioux, Len Wiseman, Danny McBride. Dir. Len Wiseman. Perf. Kate Beckinsale, Scott Speedman, Michael Sheen, Shane Brolly, Bill Nighy, Erwin Leder. Screen Gems, Lakeshore International, 2003.

The Vampire Lovers. By Sheridan Le Fanu (story), Harry Fine, Tudor Gates, Michael Style. Dir. Roy Ward Baker. Perf. Ingrid Pitt, George Cole, Kate O'Mara, Peter Cushing, Ferdy Mayne, Douglas Wilmer. Prod. American International

Pictures, Hammer Film Productions, MGM-EMI. American International Pictures, 1970.

Van Helsing. By Stephen Sommers. Dir. Stephen Sommers. Perf. Hugh Jackman, Kate Beckinsale, Richard Roxburgh, David Wenham, Shuler Hensley, Elena Anaya. Universal Pictures, 2004.

Varma, Devendra. *The Gothic Flame: Being a History of the Gothic Novel in England: Its Origins, Efflorescence, Disintegration, and Residuary Influences*. 1957. Metuchen, NJ: Scarecrow Press, 1987.

———. "The Vampire in Legend, Lore, and Literature." Introduction. *Varney the Vampyre*, by James Malcolm Rymer or Thomas Peckett Prest. Ed. Devendra Varma. New York: Arno-McGrath, 1970. xiii–xxx.

Varnado, S. L. *Haunted Presence: The Numinous in Gothic Fiction*. Tuscaloosa: U of Alabama P, 1987.

Wagner, Karl Edward. "Beyond Any Measure." 1982. *A Taste for Blood: Fifteen Great Vampire Novellas*. Ed. Martin H. Greenberg. New York: Dorset Press, 1992. 331–79.

Waller, Gregory A. *The Living and the Undead: From Stoker's Dracula to Romero's Dawn of the Dead*. Urbana, IL: U of Illinois P, 1986.

Wasson, Richard. "The Politics of Dracula." 1959. *Dracula: The Vampire and the Critics*. Ed. Margaret L. Carter. Ann Arbor, MI: UMI Research Press, 1988. 19–24.

Watson, Robert N. *The Rest Is Silence: Death as Annihilation in the English Renaissance*. Berkeley, U of California P, 1994.

Weissman, Judith. "Women and Vampires: Dracula as a Victorian Novel." *Midwest Quarterly* 18.4 (1977): 392–405.

Whalen, Patrick. *Night Thirst*. New York: Pocket Books-Simon & Schuster, 1991.

Williamson, Milly. *The Lure of the Vampire: Gender, Fiction and Fandom from Bram Stoker to Buffy*. London: Wallflower Press, 2005.

Wilson, Colin. *The Occult: A History*. New York: Barnes and Noble, 1971.

———. *The Space Vampires*. New York: Random House, 1976.

Wilson, F. Paul. "Midnight Mass." 1990. *A Taste for Blood: Fifteen Great Vampire Novellas*. Ed. Martin H. Greenberg. New York: Dorset, 1992. 502–53.

Yarbro, Chelsea Quinn. "Cabin 33." 1980. *The Penguin Book of Vampire Stories*. Ed. Alan Ryan. London: Penguin, 1987. 451–504.

———. *A Flame in Byzantium*. New York: Tor-Tom Doherty, 1987.

———. *Hotel Transylvania: A Novel of Forbidden Love*. New York: St. Martin's, 1978.

———. *Out of the House of Life*. New York: Orb-Tom Doherty, 1999.

Zanger, Jules. "Metaphor into Metonymy: The Vampire Next Door." *Blood Read: The Vampire as Metaphor in Contemporary Culture*. Ed. Joan Gordon and Veronica Hollinger. Philadelphia: U of Pennsylvania P, 1997. 17–26.

Index